Re-Investing Authenticity

TOURISM AND CULTURAL CHANGE
Series Editors: Professor Mike Robinson, *Centre for Tourism and Cultural Change, Leeds Metropolitan University, Leeds, UK* and Dr Alison Phipps, *University of Glasgow, Scotland, UK*

Understanding tourism's relationships with culture(s) and vice versa is of ever-increasing significance in a globalising world. This series will critically examine the dynamic inter-relationships between tourism and culture(s). Theoretical explorations, research-informed analyses, and detailed historical reviews from a variety of disciplinary perspectives are invited to consider such relationships.

Full details of all the books in this series and of all our other publications can be found on http://www.channelviewpublications.com, or by writing to Channel View Publications, St Nicholas House, 31–34 High Street, Bristol BS1 2AW, UK.

TOURISM AND CULTURAL CHANGE
Series Editors: Professor Mike Robinson, *Centre for Tourism and Cultural Change, Leeds Metropolitan University, Leeds, UK* and Dr Alison Phipps, *University of Glasgow, Scotland, UK*

Re-Investing Authenticity
Tourism, Place and Emotions

Edited by
Britta Timm Knudsen and
Anne Marit Waade

CHANNEL VIEW PUBLICATIONS
Bristol • Buffalo • Toronto

Library of Congress Cataloging in Publication Data
A catalog record for this book is available from the Library of Congress.
Tourism, Place and Emotions/Edited by Britta Timm Knudsen and Anne Marit Waade.
Tourism and Cultural Change.
Includes bibliographical references and index.
1. Tourism–Psychological aspects. 2. Geographical perception. 3. Authenticity
(Philosophy) I. Timm Knudsen, Britta. II. Waade, Anne Marit. III. Title. IV. Series.
G155.A1T592432 2010
338.4'791-dc22 2009033599

British Library Cataloguing in Publication Data
A catalogue entry for this book is available from the British Library.

ISBN-13: 978-1-84541-128-2 (hbk)
ISBN-13: 978-1-84541-127-5 (pbk)

Channel View Publications
UK: St Nicholas House, 31–34 High Street, Bristol BS1 2AW, UK.
USA: UTP, 2250 Military Road, Tonawanda, NY 14150, USA.
Canada: UTP, 5201 Dufferin Street, North York, Ontario M3H 5T8, Canada.

The policy of Multilingual Matters/Channel View Publications is to use papers
that are natural, renewable and recyclable products, made from wood grown in
sustainable forests. In the manufacturing process of our books, and to further
support our policy, preference is given to printers that have FSC and PEFC Chain
of Custody certification. The FSC and/or PEFC logos will appear on those books
where full certification has been granted to the printer concerned.

Typeset by The Charlesworth Group
Printed and bound in Great Britain by Short Run Press Ltd.

Contents

Acknowledgements

This book is the result of a comprehensive and collaborative process of researchers gathering in different contexts and dealing with meaning and production of places. The book is also part of an ongoing interdisciplinary and international research work and network process. Many researchers, guest speakers and colleagues have been involved, and many people as well as institutions appropriate to thank.

The Scandinavian Research Network on Emotional Geography includes institutions and enthusiastic people playing an important role in relation to this book. Different guest lectures, seminars and research workshops have been arranged, and we would like to thank John Urry, David Crouch and Nigel Thrift for inspiring and valuable meetings. We also wish to thank colleagues at the University of Lund: Thomas O'Dell, Erika Andersson Cederholm, Richard Ek, Johan Hultman, Jan-Henrik Nilsson and Orvar Löfgren, as well as Troels Degn Johansson in Copenhagen and colleagues at Roskilde University: Ole Jørgen Bærenholdt, Kirsten Simonsen, Jonas Larsen and Michael Haldrup for their engagement. We thank Anne Marie Pahuus, Anke Tonnaer and Mads Daubjerg from Aarhus University for their input to our seminars, too; and we are indebted towards colleagues from Aarhus University for taking part in organising seminars, networks and discussions: Louise Fabian, Nina Schriver, Sine Agergaard, Jonas Fritsch and Bodil Marie Thomsen.

We would equally like to thank colleagues and research fellows at our places of work, respectively Scandinavian Studies and Media Studies at Aarhus University, especially Kirsten Frandsen, leader of the National Research Project on Television Entertainment, as well as Gunhild Agger, leader of the National Research Project on Crime Fiction and Crime Journalism in Scandinavia. We would not be able to do this work without their input and acceptance. The conference on Emotional Geography at Queens University, Kingston, Ontario in Canada 2006 has also been of importance to this book, and we would like to thank the organisers as well as the inspiring people we met there, especially Kay Milton and Claire Daméry. We are additionally grateful to organisers and members of the Research Priority Area Globalisation at Aarhus University for both financial support and opportunities to meet, exchange and present ongoing research work. A special thank you goes to members of the Interdisciplinary Network on Travelogues as Global Stories and the cooperation with the Scandinavian Conference on Travelogues in Relation to Old and New Media.

The Aarhus University Research Foundation has offered financial support to the project of publishing *Re-investing Authenticity*.

Last but not least we would like to say thank you to Mike Robinson and Alison Phipps for their exceptionally valuable, kind and professional cooperation to get where we are now with the publication. A special and warm thank you, too, goes to the unknown referees who have done a great job and without whom we would not be able to present the book as it appears today.

Britta Timm Knudsen and Anne Marit Waade
Aarhus/Loughborough
May 2009

Contributors

Sine Agergaard, PhD, is Associate Professor at the Department of Exercise and Sports Sciences, University of Copenhagen. Agergaard's research area is sport, integration and migration. She has focused on the spatial dimensions of enhancing the integration of social and ethnic groups, and more recently on the integration of the talents of migrants and ethnic minorities into the Danish sports system. Recent publications include: 'From engine shed to sports centre', *Stadion: Internationale Zeitschrift für Geschichte des Sports* XXXII, 173–190; 'Dualities of Space in Danish Sports', *Sport in History* 27 (2), 260–275; and 'Elite athletes as migrants in Danish women's handball', *International Review of the Sociology of Sport* 43 (1), 5–19. Email: sine@idraet.au.dk

Dorthe Refslund Christensen, PhD, is Associate Professor of Cultural Analysis, Event Culture and Experience Economy in the Scandinavian Department at Aarhus University, Denmark. She currently researches questions of performative ritualisations and eventmaking strategies in everyday life. Recent works include 'Scientology & self narrativity: Theology and soteriology as ressource and strategy', in Jim Lewis (ed.), *Scientology* (Oxford University Press, 2009); and 'Sharing death: On the performativity of grief', with Kjetil Sandvik (in press). Email: nordrc@hum.au.dk

Anne-Britt Gran, PhD, is Professor at the Department of Communication, Culture and Languages, at the Norwegian School of Management, Oslo. She currently researches questions about art and marketing, art sponsorship, and the tendencies of hybridisation in the art world. Recent publications include 'The fall of theatricality in the Age of Modernity', *SubStance* 98/99 31 (2&3); *Vår teatrale tid* (Dynamo, 2004); and *Kultursponsing* (with Sophie Hofplass), Gyldendal akademisk (2007). Email: anne-britt.gran@bi.no

Szilvia Gyimóthy, PhD is Associate Professor at the Department of History, International & Social Studies, Aalborg University, Denmark. Her research entails applying narrative and phenomenological approaches to the service-marketing and management field. Her current work focuses on ludic aspects of tourism and leisure consumption. Apart from a number of journal articles, she has co-authored *The Kro Brand: Brand Mythologies of Danish Inns* (Varemærket Kro: Danske Kroers Brand Mytologi, 2003); and (with R. Mykletun), 'Play in adventure tourism: The case of Svalbard', *Annals of Tourism Research* 31 (4), 855878. Email: gyimothy@mail.dk

Soren Buhl Hornskov, PhD in Communication and MA in Philosophy and Sociology, works as a project manager in a public organisation in Herlev, Denmark. Soren specialises in strategies for the development of commercial, political and cultural identities and in building regional professional networks. Publications include: 'On the management of authenticity: Culture in the place branding of Øresund', *Journal of Place Branding and Public Diplomacy* 3(4); and (with Ek *et al.*), 'A dynamic framework of tourist experiences: Space – time and performances in the experience economy', *Scandinavian Journal of Hospitality and Tourism* 8 (2), 122–140. Email: soren.buhl@gmail.com

André Jansson, PhD, is a Professor in Media and Communication Studies at Karstad University, Sweden. He is the co-editor of *Strange Spaces: Explorations into Mediated Obscurity* (Ashgate, 2009, with Amanda Lagerkvist) and *Geographies of Communication: The Spatial Turn in Media Studies* (Nordicom, 2006, with Jesper Falkheimer), and has published articles in journals such as *Space and Culture, Journal of Visual Culture, Urban Studies*, and *Tourist Studies*. He currently leads two research projects: Secure Spaces: Media, Consumption and Social Surveillance and Rural Networking/Networking the Rural. Email: andre.jansson@kau.se

Jakob Linaa Jensen, PhD, and MA in Political Science, is Associate Professor at the Department of Information and Media Studies, Aarhus University. His main research interests include democratic and social uses of the internet; online social networking; transformations of the public sphere in the digital age; and media and tourism. Among his recent publications are *Medier og turisme* (in Danish) written together with Anne Marit Waade; and 'Virtual tourist: Knowledge communication in an online travel community', *International Journal of Web Based Communities* 4 (4). Email: jakoblinaa@gmail.com

Britta Timm Knudsen, PhD, is Associate Professor of Culture and Media, Event Culture and Experience Economy in the Scandinavian Department at Aarhus University, Denmark. She currently researches questions about tourism and difficult heritage as bodily experience. Recent publications include 'It's live: Performativity and role-playing', in A. Jerslev and R. Gade (eds.): *Performative Realism* (2005); 'Emotional geography, authenticity, embodiment and cultural heritage', *Ethnologia Europaea* 36 (2); 'The nation as media event', in I. Salovaara and A. Roosvall: *Communicating the Nation* (2009). Email: norbtk@hum.au.dk

Hanne Pico Larsen, PhD, is Adjunct Professor of Scandinavian Folklore in the Department of Germanic Languages and Literature Columbia University, New York. Hanne is currently project leader for the joint research project: Nordic Spaces in the North and North America: Heritage Preservation in Real and Imagined Nordic Places. Her own research focuses on Danish cultural heritage on display in various foreign settings as well as themed heritage and tourism. Related publications include: 'Nordic spaces in the North and North America: Heritage preservation in real and imagined Nordic places' (Editorial: forthcoming with Lizette Gradén), and 'Danish maids and visual matters: Celebrating heritage in Solvang, California', both in *Arv, Nordic Yearbook of Folklore* 64 (Uppsala: Royal Gustavus Adolphus Academy). Email: hpl2103@columbia.edu

Maria Månsson is a PhD candidate in Service Studies at Lund University, Sweden. Her main research interest is tourism in relation to media and space with emphasis on tourist performances. She is currently working on her doctoral thesis entitled 'Mediatised tourism: The convergence of tourism and media consumption'. A recent publication is 'The role of media products on consumer behaviour in tourism', in M. Kozak and A. Decrop (eds) *Handbook of Tourist Behaviour: Theory and Practice* (2009). Email: Maria.Mansson@msm.lu.se

Niels Kayser Nielsen, PhD, is Associate Professor at the Institute of History and Area Studies, Aarhus. Fields of research include: Nordic History 1750-2000, use of history, cultural history, nationalism, body culture, food sociology, landscape and history. Selected publications include: 'Knowledge by doing: Home and identity in a bodily perspective', in David Crouch (ed.): *Leisure/Tourism Geographies: Practice and Geographical Knowledge* (1999, pp. 277–289); *Steder i Europa: Omstridte byer, grænser og regioner* (Aarhus Universitetsforlag, 2005). Email: hisnkn@hum.au.dk.

Jesper Oestergaard, PhD and MA, is a Fellow and at the Department of the Study of Religion, Aarhus University. His current research focuses on the semantic production and cognitive use of the religious landscape around a pilgrimage site in Nepal. His work emphasises the situated-ness of human cognition in a geographical setting. He connects theories from cognitive science with a focus on the concrete landscape, i.e. the 'topographic turn', to analyse how landscape is integrated as cognitive scaffolding in the pilgrim's cognitive process, thereby arguing for the human mind as a 'topographic mind'. Email: joe@teo.au.dk

Can-Seng Ooi, PhD, is Associate Professor at the Department of International Economics and Management, Copenhagen Business School. His research centres on place branding, art worlds and tourism strategies. Recent publications include 'Reimagining Singapore as a creative nation: The politics of place branding', *Place Branding and Public Diplomacy* 4, 287–302, and 'The creative industries and tourism in Singapore', in G. Richards and J. Wilson, J.: *Tourism, Creativity and Development* (Routledge, pp. 240–251). Email: ooi@cbs.dk

Karen Klitgaard Povlsen, PhD, is Associate Professor in Media Studies at the Department of Information and Media Studies, University of Aarhus, Denmark. Her current research is mainly on food in the media, crime fiction and cross-media internet studies. She has written books on magazines, media aesthetics and television soaps and has edited six anthologies, most recent of which is *Northbound: Encounters, Travels and Constructions of the North 1700–1830* (2008). Email: karenklitgaard@hum.au.dk

Dan Ringgaard, PhD, is Associate Professor at the Scandinavian Department, University of Aarhus. His fields of interest include: world literature, postnational literary history, cartography and literature. He has published books on poetry and Danish poets and is currently finishing a book on places as seen through literature together with an anthology of place theory. He is co-editor of the four-volume literary history *Nordic Literary Cultures*, published through the International Comparative Literature Association. Email: nordr@hum.au.dk

Mette Sandbye, PhD, is Associate Professor at the Department of Arts and Cultural Studies, University of Copenhagen. Her main research area is the history, theory and practice of photography. She currently researches the relationship between amateur photography and collective history since the 1950s. She was the editor of the first Danish history of photography (*Dansk Fotografihistorie*, 2004). Other publications include: 'Performing the everyday: Two Danish photo-pooks from the '70s', in Tune Gade and Anne Jerslev (eds) *Performative Realism* (Museum Tusculanum Press, 2005); 'Making visible: Thoughts on the first Danish history of photography', *Konsthistorisk Tidsskrift* 74 (2) (Routledge, 2005). Email: sandbye@hum.ku.dk.

Kjetil Sandvik, MA and PhD, is Associate Professor at the Department of Media, Cognition and Communication, University of Copenhagen. His fields of research and teaching are digital aesthetics, storytelling as format in strategic communication, new media and experience-economy, cross-media communication and computer games. Recent publications include: 'Professor Nukem: communicating research in the age of the experience economy', in Ulla Carlsson (ed.): *Nordicom Review* (issue on NordMedia '07 (2008)); and 'Mobile-based tourism as spatial augmentation. When tourists use the mobile internet to navigate physical space', in *Proceedings from 'Internet Research 9.0: Rethinking Communities, Rethinking Place'* (2009). Email: sandvik@hum.ku.dk

Torunn Selberg, PhD, is Professor at the Department of Archaeology, History, Cultural and Religious Studies, University of Bergen, Norway. Her research interests include: heritage, place and narratives and popular religiosity. Recent publications include: *Kulturelle landskap. Sted, fortelling og materiell kultur;* as editor (with Nils Gilje), 'Our Lord's Miracle', *Talking about Working Wonders;* In Kaivola-Bregenhøj, Anniki, Barbro Klein & Ulf Palmenfelt (eds): 'Narrating, doing, experiencing', *Nordic Folkloristic Perspectives/Studia Fennica Folkloristica* (2006). Email: torunn.selberg@ikk.uib.no

Carina Sjöholm, PhD in Ethnology, is Associate Professor at the Department for Service Management at Campus Helsingborg, Lund University, Sweden. Among her areas of research are media practices, arenas of popular culture, and the connections to the conditions of the tourist industry. Recent publications include: *Tankar om träd. En etnologisk studie av människors berättelser om träds betydelser*, 2007 (with Charlotte Hagström); 'Smalfilm som semesterminne' in E. Hedling and M. Jönsson (eds): *Välfärdsbilder: svensk film utanför biografen, Statens Ljud- och bildarkiv* (Stockholm, 2008). Email: Carina.Sjoholm@msm.lu.se

Birgit Stöber, PhD, is Associate Professor of Cultural Geography in the Department of Intercultural Communication and Management at Copenhagen Business School (CBS). She currently participates in the CBS research project The socio-economic Organization of Creative Industries, with special focus on place, art and culture. Recent publications include: 'Place branding: How the private creates the public', in: H.K. Hansen and D. Salskov-Iversen (2008): *Critical Perspectives on Private Authority in Global Politics* (Palgrave Macmillan, pp. 169–187); and in B. Lanvvg, A. Kalandides, B. Stöber and H.A. Mieg (2008): 'Berlin's creative industries: governing creativity?', *Industry & Innovation* 15 (5), 531–548. Email: bst.ikl@cbs.dk

Anne Marit Waade, PhD, is Associate Professor at the Institute for Information and Media Studies, Aarhus University, Denmark. She currently researches questions about the mediatisation of tourism and places. Recent publications include articles such as 'Imagine Paradis in Ads,' in the journal *Nordicom Review*, forthcoming; and 'Armchair travelling with Pilot Guides' (Falkheimer & Jansson: *Geographies of Communication*, 2006), and together with Jakob Linaa Jensen: *Medier og turisme* (Academica, 2009). Email: amwaade@imv.au.dk

Preface

In the early 1970s Dean MacCannell for the first time introduced the concept of staged authenticity in tourism. In 2007 Pine and Gilmore published the book *Authenticity: What Consumers Really Want*. Pine and Gilmore are not only thinking of tourism, but of consumer culture in general. In this period of nearly 40 years, the discussion of what authenticity really means has been going on in many different academic fields, from questions about realism, representation and reality in aesthetics and media studies, to 'authenticity as idea' related to national identity and cultural heritage, as well as 'authenticity as strategy' in marketing and place branding. Our ambition has been to view the question of authenticity as a cultural concept in tourism and consumer culture from different analytical views, and relate the discussions of authenticity in tourism studies to other theoretical and academic fields.

Researching authenticity regarding spatial experience, emotional and embodied geography has regained new interest. Many recent phenomena within the cultural economy (Ray & Sayer, 1999; Gay & Pryke, 2002) such as tourism, leisure time experiences, individual and collective identity- and history management, branding and marketing utilise authenticity strategies as important components in their design in order to appeal to certain emotional modes amongst the receivers/users. Emotional geography is a growing field of interdisciplinary research in which the second stage of globalisation and its localisation strategies is reflected, together with the effect of the experience economical paradigmatic shift (Pine & Gilmore, 1999; Gilles Lipovetsky, 2006), the increasing 'culturalisation' of the market as well as the 'marketisation' of culture (Ray & Sayer, 1999; Gay & Pryke, 2002) and the new economy in the cultural field (Löfgren & Willem, 2005).

The 21 contributors to this volume have been part of the Scandinavian Network on Globalisation and Emotional Geography, and the researchers represent a considerable range of disciplines such as literary studies; media and communication studies; cultural studies; geography of media; studies of religion; ethnography; sports science; service management; creative industries research; history and area studies; and business administration. Since 2005 the network has organised several conferences, for example

Places of Memory (Aarhus, Denmark 2005); Fantastic Places: Staging and Experiencing Provinces in Scandinavian Tourism (Aarhus, Denmark 2006); the Tourist Gaze, and the Question of Authenticity (Aarhus, Denmark 2007); and Emotional Geography, Emotions, Materiality and Mythologies (Helsingborg, Sweden 2008). The people and authors behind this book are taking part in an ongoing international interdisciplinary engagement with fruitful exchange and development, and we are happy to present the ideas and work that the authors have been dealing with to a broad and international audience.

The book includes empirical as well as theoretical reflections upon the several levels and expressions of authenticity and presents a range of suggestive studies of cases and places both inside and outside the Scandinavian context. The book is meant for students, teachers and researchers in the fields of cultural studies, Scandinavian studies, geography, media, experience economy, arts management and tourism, as well as place branding and city planning.

Chapter 1

Performative Authenticity in Tourism and Spatial Experience: Rethinking the Relations Between Travel, Place and Emotion

BRITTA TIMM KNUDSEN AND ANNE MARIT WAADE

Introduction

As the concept of authenticity continues to haunt consumers and cultures, Pine and Gilmore (2007: xii) argue: 'Now more than ever, the authentic is what consumers really want.' For Pine and Gilmore the craving for authenticity is a reaction to a strong technologically mediatised, commercialised and socially constructed reality. One could think of this 'craving' as a 'longing' for the immediate, non-commercialised, brute natural world, characterised by the *real* authentic.

In this chapter we suggest that the reaction to, or the longing for, something other than a mediatised, commercialised and socially con-structed reality is neither a 'thing' you can possess nor a 'state of mind', but something which people can *do* and a feeling which is *experienced*. In this sense, authenticity is performed, and through the term performative authenticity we aim at bridging the two positions that have emerged in tourism studies with respect to the concept of authenticity, namely: object-related (authenticity synonymous to original and trace) and subject-related modes of authenticity (existential authenticity covering bodily feelings, emotional ties, identity construction and narration related to place). Through the notion of performative authenticity we wish to point to the transitional and transformative processes inherent in the action of authentication in addition to the contradictory position existing between phenomenological and social constructivist perspectives in which mean-ings and feelings of self and place are both constructed and lived through the sensuous body.

1

Authentication is taking place in between two entities and expresses the interrelatedness of different entities. Whether one is a performing body or a city/region/country, it is possible to 'authenticate' sites, sights, places and to enhance the tourist's/traveller's understanding and their sense of intimacy, self-reflection and feelings toward their surroundings. The media play an important role in the concept of performative authenticity on several levels. Novels, film, television series and documentaries provide representations of place which can stimulate a 'desire' to visit a destination. Various other forms of *in-situ* media such as DVD narrations and audio guides, along with personal guides, act to ocument and enhance experience on site. The media in various forms also play a significant role in the communicative afterlife of a site visit. Performative authenticity is related to a striving towards indexical authenticity – a view of the place as the real thing – and it is the relation between these two actions/strivings that we develop further throughout this chapter.

In rethinking the relationships between travel, place and emotion we want to bring tourist-specific discussions into broader interdisciplinary and theoretical perspectives, in which representation, spatial practice and emotions are reflected. This book includes empirical as well as theoretical reflections regarding several levels and expressions of authenticity and presents a range of suggestive studies of cases and places both inside and outside the Scandinavian context.

Several topics are raised by the authors in their chapters, regarding authenticity and place. There are five main perspectives represented:

(1)   developing new theoretical concepts;
(2)   mediatised places;
(3)   place performances and rituals;
(4)   emotionalised places; and
(5)   branded places.

Some of the authors, such as Gran and Jansson, suggest new elements of theory on issues concerning investing in places economically, corporeally, emotionally and symbolically. Regarding the mediatisation of places and how media influence emotions and spatial experience, case studies cover writing about pervasive gaming in Stockholm (Sandvik); travelogues from the Far East (Ringgaard); personal photo narratives from Greenland (Sandbye); and online travelling and Google Earth communities (Linaa Jensen). Even though all of the chapters include, in one way or another, place performances, some of the authors deal with the concept in specific ways, such as Månsson's work on literary tourism to Scotland; Gyimóthy's work on sport tourism in Western Norway; Sjöholm's work on 'murder walks' in the Swedish of Ystad; and Kayser Nielsen's work on the small village Keurru in Finland. Contributors emphasising the emotionalising of places through myths and sacredness include Selberg, who looks at sacred geography in Norway; Klitgaard Povlsen, who examines the myths surrounding the place of Kullaberg in Sweden; and Refslund Christensen and Østergaard, who look at pilgrimage to Santiago de Compostela. Perspectives on place branding are represented in this volume through analyses of: urban design in Copenhagen (Buhl Hornskov); the branding of major cities such as Berlin and Singapore (Ooi and Stöber); the hybridity of Scandinavian place Solvang in California (Pico Larsen); and the project of Global City in Aarhus Denmark (Aagaard). In total the volume represents a comprehensive interdisciplinary approach to the study of authenticity and place experience as cultural production from both inside and outside of the Scandinavian context.

In this introductory chapter we examine the claim for 're-investing' authenticity in the light of the broader cultural frameworks of the new economy and discuss the various conceptualisations of authenticity under the following headings before introducing our own term of performative authenticity:

- *From sign to intensity* – whereby we consider the shift from a sign economy to an affective and intensive economy;
- *Emotional geography* – where we discuss this term as it is used to characterise experiences of places within the context of globalisation;
- *Hunger for reality and the indexical authenticity* – where we establish an understanding of the re-investing authenticity claim through a striving for the real;
- *Augmented feeling of authenticity* – where we position the concept in a more philosophical context.
- *Authenticity as a key issue in tourism studies* – which presents important conceptualisations of authenticity in tourism studies. We suggest two aspects of performative authenticity, either relating empathetically to the other or connecting affectively to the world.

We believe the re-investment of authenticity expresses a general discursive frame that includes different agents at different levels. Both individuals, institutions and organizations, e.g. cities, travel agencies, local authorities, agents in cultural and artistic industries, event-managers are taking part in this process.

From Sign to Intensity: Re-investing Authenticity

The symbolic economy is a sign-economy. Within such an economy the value of exchange is measured according to the kind of non-economic capital accumulated and how this produces meaning and feeds identity: what Bourdieu (1979) refers to as symbolic, cultural and social capital. The word economy is used because we recognise the affiliation with the idea of symbolic economies as defined in French cultural theory and sociology (Bataille, 1949; Baudrillard, 1976; and Bourdieu, 1979), and in British cultural and consumer studies that sees culture as economy (Lash & Lury, 2007; Lury, 2003). The term economy within these theoretical realms is used synonymously with the word exchange and the study of symbolic exchange has, since Marcel Mauss (1997), become the study of how exchange (of gifts, goods, communication, between individuals, groups, localities, nationally, globally) and value are connected. From the point of view of businesses and organisations, an increasing interest in cultural value is easily detectable (Pine & Gilmore, 1999, 2007). Associated with an intermingling between the cultural and the economic sphere theorised from the perspective of cultural theory (Gay & Pryke, 2002; Ray & Sayer, 1999), we see that the concept of value has regained interest as a sign of a growing interest in cultural relations, identity-production, emotional investment, ecology and global responsibility from the perspective of the market (Paine, 2003; Kotler & Lee, 2005).

The so-called 'New Economy' (O'Dell & Billing, 2005; Löfgren & Willim, 2005) is the label that Swedish cultural theorists have used to qualify the intermingling spheres between culture and economy. Notions of the new economy and the affective economy (Clough, 2007) present a step beyond an economy of signs. These economies are presented as being based on investment and exchange, not primarily of meaning and signs as in the symbolic economy but of involvement, energy and the capacity for the user to be affected. As Clough (2007: 25) states: 'In an affect economy, value is sought in the expansion or contraction of affective capacity.' The new economy presents a kind of post-Fordist production beyond material goods and services, which signifies a 'focus on acceleration, [but also on] intensity or 'an emotional or passionate economy', which also means highlighting aestheticisation and perform-ative qualities' (2007: 2). In line with the words of Gilles Lipovetsky, *homo consumericus* in the new economy is, within consumer studies, no longer considered to be a woman trying to compensate her inner void, but a person who wishes to be reborn via intensifying the present moment (Lipovetsky, 2006).

On both the individual and the organisational level, the new affective economy implies a comprehensive 're-investing' in authenticity. The consumer (e.g. tourist, traveller) is re-investing in authenticity as a way of intensifying experience, while the local tourist managers and authorities are re-investing in authenticity to brand their city or region. Value depends on the amount of energy invested and the qualitative 'depth' of investment: how intense was the experience? With the sign-economies replaced by intensive and affective economies we see a shift from meaning as hermeneutics to meaning as doing and its emotional impact (Thrift, 2004a; Lash & Lury, 2007). Within the new cultural economy re-investing authenticity is seen in terms of the global strivings of individuals, places, cities, organisations and communities to create experiences, places and culture and to re-intensify the general experience of already existent (insignificant) places. What forms authenticity in contemporary culture will be explored below.

Emotional Geography: Combining Constructivism and Phenomenology

We claim that authentication – the production of authenticity – has become a strategy to appropriate sites/places and a strategy to invest emotionally in places. Emotional geography is a relatively new term in geographical and cultural studies, representing an interdisciplinary field of research in which the affective aspects of places are in focus (Thrift 2004a, 2008; Davidson *et al.*, 2005). Nigel Thrift points to a very important shift from looking upon the affective as a lack of cognitive skills, to the affective as a kind of thinking, connecting bodies and connecting bodies to the world. As in the phenomenology of perception (Merleau-Ponty, 1945), sensations and affects are ways of understanding and thinking, 'often indirect and non-reflective, but thinking all the same' (Thrift, 2004a: 60).

If authenticity is no longer to be seen as objective qualities in objects or places, but rather something experienced through the body, through performance, management and media, authenticity becomes a feeling you can achieve. In tourism authenticity is a feeling you can experience in relation to place. From this perspective, we want to see constructivism and phenomenology (traditionally contrary philosophical and theoretical perspectives) as somehow linked in order to develop an understanding of how emotions and places are related.

Partly due to complex changes in the relationship between market, culture and politics, and partly due to the knock-on effect of the processes of globalisation, places have greater possibilities to become visible and valuable at the global scale (Tomlinson, 1999; Löfgren, 2003). At the same time, because of globalisation, greater value is attributed to the differences between places. Places are branded and becoming objects of consumption; both symbolically as objects for hungry tourists and concretely as they are reconstructed as consumption sites. In addition, they play the role of a cultural context for consumption (Urry, 1990, 2002). From a constructivist point of view, places are constructed, produced, staged and told, and something like an 'authentic place' is not possible.

To critical geographers such as Massey (1998) and Soja (1999) places are mobile, open, hybrid, socially produced and products of power-generated 'battles' between different social agents. Thus places are contested and objects of struggle between different social agents. We argue that it is possible to empower and to re-empower marginal territories, insignificant places, minorities and popular practices through new medias and performative strategies.

Besides the critical geographical approach, we have the phenomeno-logical and existential approaches to places as put forward by Merleau-Ponty (1945), Heidegger (1951), Bachelard (1957), Tuan (1977), Casey (1997), Crouch and Lübbren (2003), Baerenholdt et al. (2004), Davidson et al. (2005), Reisinger and Steiner (2005; 2006). The phenomenological approaches all explore the 'being-in-the world' perspective as a relational, dynamic and spatial experience of the world. In the words of Merleau-Ponty (1945: XI–XII, author's translation): 'The world is not what I think, but what I live; I am open towards the world, I communicate indubitably with it, but I do not possess it; it is inexhaustible.' A bodily phenom-enological view, such as the one Merleau-Ponty represents, permits us to work with the dynamic intermingling between inner and outer perspectives. Even if screens, images and technologies mediate between place and body, the body appropriates and lives the place sensuously, through the mediations anyway (Thrift, 2004b). Our claim is that the explicitly mediated character of places (tourism designs, sport devices, site-specific art etc. increases the feeling of authenticity within the tourist and traveler.

The articles in this volume by Månsson, Sjöholm, Linaa Jensen and Sandvik all deal with tourist designs on places that are directly inspired by mediated representations. The articles show how, and in what ways, places are enhanced by media-representations and also how this enhance-ment actually changes the status of the place – from being peripheral to being the centre of interest.

Hunger for Reality and Indexical Authenticity

/ The experience of a place happens through different ways of relating to the place. If we use a semiotic vocabulary from Charles Sanders Peirce upon the sign, a vocabulary that tourist scholars already make use of, we see different degrees of authenticity in play: symbolic authenticity, 'implying that the authenticity of a tourist destination may be defined in terms of how well it meets the customer's own ideas of what the particular destination is about' (Jansson, 2002: 439); iconic authenticity referring to 'how well the event or object resembles the real thing or accurately copies the original or real thing' (Ray *et al.*, 2006: 442) and indexical authenticity being the authentic mode in play when something 'is thought not to be a copy or an imitation' or that it is 'the original' or 'the real thing' (Grayson & Martinec, 2004, cited in Ray *et al.*, 2006: 442). A real experience of a place touches upon its effect upon the tourist and its ability to affect, touch and transform him/her. /

We will propose to look upon indexicality not as quality inherent in objects but as a possible outcome of a relation. In aesthetics it is especially Roland Barthes (1980) who in his essay on photography, 'Camera Lucida', pointed to the relation between the documentary photo-graphy and its viewer as a sensuous and affective relation mediating between the viewers now and the referential having been-there. The relation between viewer and the referential object is mediated through the photograph indicating absence and presence while being able to produce immediate affective responses, designated by Barthes as the *'punctum'* effect.

Barthes's essay has had strong impact on the theory of photography, on art and cultural theory in general, moving the center of interest from the image itself to the relation between the viewer and the image. This relation, according to Barthes, is a relation of primary emotional, affective and sensuous impact. But throughout the 1990s the relation between viewer and medium took a slightly different direction. The hunger for reality and going real tendency has, since the 1980s, been framed in different contexts by philosophers, cultural theorists and art critics (see for instance: Baudrillard, 1981; Deleuze, 1980; Foster, 1996; Knudsen & Thomsen, 2002; Zizek, 2002; Zizek *et al.*, 2006). Lash and Lury (2007) reflect the movement from the symbolic to the real as an effect of globalisation. The shift from the representational realm to a more presentational logic – an indexical authenticity – can be thought of in many ways. It can represent a general inhuman, or trans-human, framework through which bodies are connected to each other and to the world. Connecting affectively to the world through the media represents possibilities of facilitating the pursuit of people's emotional involvement and investment, and therefore producing global solidarity, cultural change and political awareness. On the other hand it can also represent an over-acute will to change and transform what is. The result can therefore be a racist, ethnic, religious or political vision of realising the dream and as a consequence 'destroy all who do not share their version of the really real' (Lindholm, 2008: 145), not to mention the possibilities of manipulation entailed by a focus on affects.

Indexical authenticity is, in our view, an alternative both to the objective authenticity criticised by Ning Wang (1999) and to the relativist attitude that could easily be the result of a light reading of Wang (see below). The quality of indexical authenticity that permits us to transcend the opposition between the objectivity of the place and the subjectivity of the guest is exactly its relational and phenomenological character. Indexical authenticity turns our attention to the inner of the tourist in relation to the place (the intensity of the feeling, the degree of affectedness) and to the referential character of the place, such as the proximity of the site to the real event.

The thrill, joy and excitement and kinaesthetic sensing, that the tourists experience at Voss, Norway in Gyimóthy's Chapter 18 is clearly the expression of an indexical authenticity because the experience of the place is a bodily performance of the landscape and the thrill is the effect on the body due to the bodily performance through the landscape. Black spot tourism (Rojek, 1993), thanatourism (Seaton, 1996), or dark tourism (Lennon & Foley, 2000) represent significant expressions of indexical authenticity, because the encounters with mass-death, disaster and destruction are real encounters of the dark past 'on the spot'. The indexicality in this case is the body being near or 'right on the spot' where horrible things and catastrophes have taken place (such as the Killing Fields in Cambodia, Auschwitz–Birkenau in Poland, Phuket in Thailand). 'Travel and Testimony: The Rhetoric of Authenticity' by Dan Ringgaard (Chapter 8) explores the quest for authenticity on historically significant places and how acts of witnessing in contemporary Danish travel writing translate the authentication experience.

Augmented Feelings of Authenticity

According to the *Oxford Dictionary of English Etymology* (1996) 'authentic can be defined as authoritative; entitled to acceptance or belief as being reliable; and actual, not imaginary, genuine, not counterfeit'. Among these definitions three important perspectives can shed light on some important aspects of the word. Authentic can mean credible, reliable (i.e. something is true and not a lie); it can have material existence (it is materially real and not imaginary); and it can in itself be an original (it is genuine and not a copy). Truth, material existence and originality seem to be inherent qualities when it comes to an essentialist understanding of the concept of authenticity. But, because of this rather heavy etymological baggage, one can find it very difficult to stick to the concept.

In a philosophical context, Theodor Adorno (1973) even argues that one should get rid of the concept, while Martin Jay (2006) in a semi-deconstructive gesture tries to read Adorno against himself, and shows how the concept survives in his thoughts in different ways. Adorno fought against totalitarian, essentialist and fundamentalist uses of the concept and this critique also appears in the later works of for instance, Castells (1997) and Lindholm (2008). Jay, on the other hand, finds two defensible notions that permit the concept to live. He argues that something can be authentic if it keeps fidelity to historical moments and modern life's historical disasters; what he terms 'the scars of damage and disruption' (Jay, 2006: 29). And something can be judged authentic if it is true to the mimetic or inauthentic nature of the self. The first of the above significations of authenticity on the side of the indexicality described above while the second is similar to Walter Benjamin's (1936) notion of the mimetic aura of copies, which he introduced in his famous essay 'The Work of Art in the Age of Mechanical Reproduction'. Jay's solution strengthens our will to re-invest in the concept of authenticity.

We will suggest that the re-investing in authenticity becomes relevant due to strategies of performances on places and due to mediations. We argue that the phenomenological relation between body and place is intensified, vitalised and re-vitalised through performative practices and through different kinds of mediations on, and of, places. Re-investing in authenticity is therefore a result of intensity-production strategies that strengthen the phenomenological relation to the world through devices that involve the body as flesh and senses. What is at stake is a body and flesh investment beyond words.

Authenticity as a Key Issue in Tourism Studies

Since Boorstin (1961) and MacCannell (1976), authenticity has become one of the central concepts in tourism studies and tourism research, and a comprehensive amount of books and articles have generated considerable debate and argument on this contested concept. MacCannell stated that tourism and sightseeing had become the preferred activity for satisfying the desire for authenticity in modernity. Authenticity expressed the desire for insight in the intimate back-stage life of others, the past or the exotic cultural otherness. The concept of staged authenticity in tourism caused a committed debate in tourism parallel to the discussion of representation in the humanities in general. The discussion of authenticity has had epistemological as well as ontological aims. By following the historical readings of the concept of authenticity in tourism studies, two main views have arisen: object-related and subject-related authenticity (Wang, 1999; Reisinger & Steiner, 2005, 2006; Yu Wang, 2007; Cohen, 2008).

(1) Object-related authenticity and the question of essentialism

Ning Wang (1999) distinguishes between two types of object-related authenticity in tourism experiences: objective authenticity and constructive authenticity. The former refers to the authenticity of origins. Correspondingly, authentic experiences in tourism are equated to an epistemological experience (i.e. cognition) of the authenticity of origins. The latter refers to the authenticity projected onto toured objects by tourists or tourism producers in terms of their imagery, expectations, preferences, beliefs, powers, etc. In this sense, the authenticity of toured object is in fact 'symbolic authenticity' (Wang, 1999).

Reisinger and Steiner (2005) suggest that the notion of authenticity should be replaced be more explicit, less pretentious terms like e.g. genuine, actual, accurate, real, and true when referring to judgements that tourists and scholars make about the nature and origins of artefacts and tourism activities (Reisinger & Steiner, 2005: 66). In their paper they suggest to use the philosophy of Heideggerian phenomenology to explain an alternative way of understanding objective authenticity:

> In contrast to constructivists and postmodernists, Heidegger as a phenomenologist advocates appreciating what appears (the phenomenon) as a gift of being, learning from it, using it, working with it, rather than obsessing over what is withheld (the postmodernist problem) of what is different each time (the constructivist problem). If Heidegger used a term like authentic to apply to things, whatever appears would be authentic. What is cannot be other than it is. What is given is always genuine, real, reliable and true, even if it is incomplete. (Reisinger & Steiner, 2005: 78)

What emerges from the world has objective existence according to the phenomenology of Heidegger. Instead of discussing whether the emergence includes staged events or not, we would point to the fact that objective authenticity matters without falling into the trap of essentialism. The concept of performative authenticity is put forward as a way of developing the phenomenological viewpoint both as a criticism of essentialism and as a criticism of relativism (see below).

(2) Subjective authenticity and the question of existentialism

Ning Wang (1999) introduced the concept of existential authenticity in order to change the perspective from the predominant object-related authenticity used in tourism research towards a focus on the personal investment of the tourist. The shift from object-related authenticity to existential authenticity represents an important step away from an essentialist viewpoint to one of placing the existential personal quests of the tourist to the centre of interest. Wang disconnects the existential state of being and the objective surroundings:

> Existential authenticity refers to a potential existential state of Being that is to be activated by tourist activities. Correspondingly, authentic experiences in tourism are to achieve this activated existential state of Being with the liminal process of tourism. Existential authenticity can have nothing to do with the authenticity of toured objects. (Wang, 1999: 352)

Wang divides existential authenticity into two types: intra-personal authenticity, that is the sensuous and symbolic bodily display of personal identity, and inter-personal authenticity that ties together small and well known communities (such as the family), as well as larger communities. Other researchers have followed and developed Wang's concepts. Mary Conran (2006), for example, explores the intimacy and the desire for reciprocal interaction in the touristic encounter in Thailand. Yu Wang (2007) is for his part focusing on the customising of home as parts of existential authenticity for both hosts and guests in Lijang, China. Yu Wang sees existential authenticity as an important aspect of identity, with the familiar and the unfamiliar as navigations poles. Stroma Cole follows up such ideas, and her argument is that it is not only the host and the guest that are playing roles in the production of identity and authenticity in tourism, villagers and the government are equally supporting the process (Cole, 2007). Cole is demonstrating how cultural commodification and the production of authenticity in tourism may give ethnic groups positive identity and empower them:

The cultural commodification of their differences has led to a recognisable 'ethnic group' identity. This process of commodification of the villagers identity is bringing them pride and self-conscious awareness of their traditional culture, which has become a resource that they manipulate to economic and political ends. (Cole, 2007: 955)

This perspective supplies the idea that existentialism is not only an individual and personal attribute, but that it can have a political and a democratic value.

(3) Performative authenticity

For the past decades tourist studies have been focusing on the visual culture of tourism and the tourist gaze. Inspired by Urry's theories, André Jansson presents, as mentioned before, his concept of symbolic authenticity (Jansson, 2002: 439). For Jansson, the tourist experiences symbolic authenticity when sites and sights live up to, or confirm, the images from the imaginary reservoir of collective images. The hyper-tourist gaze (Jansson, 2002: 439) is an image-driven reflective meta-gaze that tourists perform in order to conform to or to critique traditional tourism (such as going on nostalgic package-trips to the tourist-sights of the 1970s such as Mallorca and the Costa del Sol), or going to 'non-sights' such as nuclear power plants or industrial areas (Jansson, 2002: 440). It has been shown that tourists consume media images and mediated representations of places in order to connect to, and to enhance emotion-ally, the experience of the place (Jansson, 2002; Crouch & Lübbren, 2003; Crouch *et al.*, 2005). Because of this traffic the boundaries between imaginary, symbolic and material spaces are dissolving (Falkenheimer & Jansson, 2006). The theoretical replacement of the mirror room of images characterising a general cultural experience in (post)modernity (Baudrillard, 1981), and the tourist experience in particular is challenged from a more anthropological–phenomenological-inspired viewpoint: tourists do not only gaze but are also bodies performing at specific sights. Cultural geographers and sociologists have already for some years pointed to that fact (Crouch, 2001, 2003; Baerenholdt *et al.*, 2004).

Regarding performative authenticity, the gaze, the place and the imagined audience play an important role, but the concept of performativity covers more than visual signs, gaze and imaginations. Performativity also includes a tactile body, movements, actions and emotions. This represents a move away from a hermeneutical perspective towards a more corporeal and inter-related perspective. Our point is here that performative authen-ticity not only signifies that we do and perform places by our actions and behaviours, but that places are something we authenticate through our emotional/affective/sensuous relatedness to them.

Performative authenticity is both transcending the essentialist trap of object-related authenticity as well as the relativist trap of existential authenticity formulated by Wang ('what I hold as authentic is authentic'). Our claim is that authenticity can be considered as a relational quality attributed to something out of an encounter. Performative authenticity is dependent on proximity and in between-ness. In that sense, its relational quality appears to be highly phenomenological. It signifies a shift towards sincerity as a negotiated value between local and tourist (Taylor, 2001: 24). The power to create presence and intensity is not entirely related to subjects or objects but also has to do with what happens in between these two instances. The in-between is the locus for all sorts of mediation which are detectable both in the immateriality of place-mediations (ideas, images inside the heads of people) and in materialised or discursive place-designs. Examples of place-designs are material recycling (as in the experiential use of industrial heritage in the Emscher Park, Ruhr Germany), human guidance and witnessing on sights of difficult and undesirable heritage (tourism to former slave plantations in the Southern States of US, or tourism to the Former Nazi Party Rally Grounds in Nürnberg), and theatrical and technological devices on places (live re-enactment concepts and DVD tours). More culturally customised expressions are the case when it comes to the very competitive branding of places (as in the chapters by Gran, Buhl Hornskov, Ooi and Stöber), and in explicit mediated forms such as presented in the chapter which deals with Wallander's Ystad in Sweden and in similar cases in which the locality itself has been the referential object of popular media-representations: movies, television series, narrative commercials and novels.

Performative authenticity is related to the place and the location in a corporeal and affective way, recalling the claim Thrift made of *affectedness* as a way of thinking. Olsen (2002), Reisinger and Steiner (2005) and MacCannell (1976; 2008) are touching the idea of performance, role plays and rituals as cultural and social performances in relation to respectively object-related and existential authenticity. We suggest that the term performative authenticity is not so much about the performance and the plays as such, but rather that the performative as a theoretical concept in which presentational realism and reflexivity is related to one another (Butler, 1999; Gade & Jerslev, 2005).

Reisinger and Steiner (2005: 80) state that 'if Heidegger is right, everything that the tourists experience, what they see, touch, hear, smell and taste, is real and authentic in itself'. We would prefer to say that everything that the tourists experience, what they see, touch, hear, smell and taste, may be performed and produced as real and authentic. Performativity can thus take place in standard forms, or as a more negotiated, creative, ironic and opposed activity. As Edensor (2001: 63) so beautifully articulates: 'Tourist performance is socially and spatially regulated to varying extents [...] the organisation, materiality and aesthetic and sensual qualities of tourist space influence – but not determine – the kinds of performances that tourists undertake.' The entrance of the famous balcony of Juliet at Villa Capelletti in Verona being marked by thousands of chewing gum marks in different colours can be seen as an ironic appropriation and commentary to this specific place as a constructed tourist site. This example shows the relative freedom of tourists within the frames of tourist sites, but it also shows that the tourists are reacting according to the lack of objective authenticity. There is no referential balcony, which permits the ironic activism of the tourists. Such conduct would be unthinkable in historic real places.

Analytically, we can distinguish two kinds of performative authenticity. We call the first form an empathetic understanding of the other through the body and the second form a connecting to the world through the affected body as an instrument. In both ways the body is at stake and the medium through which the relation to the place takes place. The bodily character of the experiences of places is what points to a sharpened analytical gaze upon the body, as something more than a sign-producing and sign-interpreting machine, namely at different kinds of corporeal and sensuous investments and their mental and social implications.

(a) The empathetic understanding of the other through bodily performance

Empathetic understanding requires distance between the one trying to understand and the object of understanding (the cultural 'other', or the geographical or historical 'other'). Yet, this distance creates possibilities of feeling the bodily sensations of, as well as re-enacting, the situation of the other. The affected body is an immediate and physically direct way of perceiving and sensing authenticity. Our bodies may be affected in different ways according to technologies, genre (a war re-enactment that has the form of a role play (Gettysburg), a heritage visit that has the form of a reality show (1984 in Lithuania), a visit to a memory landscape such as the Memorial to the Murdered Jews of Europe in Berlin (2005) (Knudsen, 2006). But the central issue is that the body, as a thinking medium, suggests a dynamic relation between inner and outer. The affected body responds immediately and the physical response is the expression of the quality of the experience (Merleau-Ponty, 1945; Boltansky, 1999; Thrift, 2004).

Authenticity as the empathetic understanding of the world through the body can take place in cases in which the cultural 'other' is staged. This could be in screened encounters with the distant others, or in face-to-face encounters in 'exotic' places and designs. The authentic other can also be historical, or be spiritual in nature. Tom Selwyn, for instance, discusses the concern with self and other as a post-modern meta-narrative and a popular critique of consumerism (Selwyn, 1996: 25). We see the exercise of empathy as an expression of a longing for greater intimacy, for homeliness, and for historical and cultural truth and ethics.

All kinds of tourism and experiential designs that offer the possibility to live, enact, or re-enact the experience and living conditions of others are, potentially at least, offering the possibility to understand the other through the body. For example how to be a prisoner at the Alcatraz Island in San Francisco Bay is partially lived through experiences in the Alcatraz Island Prison Tours to the very site. Gulag Tourism, such as 1984, presents how to be a Lithuanian citizen in the 1980s during the Soviet Regime as a mixture of a live re-enactment (actors are playing the role of KGB, speaking only Russian to create the original atmosphere) and a reality-show (the tourists and their bodies take part in the play), bringing the glimpse of the past to live in a bunker, an original vestige of the past with original stage props from the days of the former soviet regime. Live re-enactments also offer the possibility of living through a certain period of an – often painful – historic time (always with a strong touch of mythology), as is the case in the re-enactments every year at Gettysburg remembering the Civil War in US, or the more heroic re-enactment sceneries of the Middle Ages throughout Europe (Torunn Selberg touches upon this aspect in her chapter Journeys, religion and authenticity revisited).

(b) The affected body connecting to the world

One of the privileged areas of theorising upon the affective relatedness between body and object is in art. As mentioned above, Roland Barthes pointed to the affective phenomenological relation between viewer and photo as a part of the ontology of the photographic medium per se. In contemporary art and art theory the purely cognitive approach (as in Immanuel Kant 1790) seems succeeded by relational aesthetics (Bourriaud,

1998); aesthetics implying the viewer/user interactively as well as aesthetics working directly on the body of the viewer/user. The feeling of authenticity has the expression of high intensity, affect, production and maintenance of energy; what Trilling (1972: 99) refers to as 'The capacity to affect the sentiment of being.' The increasing and decreasing of energy as a sign of aesthetic impression seems to have replaced the quiet contemplation of sublime or beautiful art. The high intensity and the strong bodily investment is often the case in extreme sport and adventure tourism (Chapter 18). In the cultural experience economy these forms appear in both high art and in more popular forms such as place design and tourism.

The desire for physical, sensuous experience occurs in many cultural spheres. The perception (from within) of the body at play, at risk, invested, intensified is the expression of a performative authenticity. The intensive experience of the body is in fact connecting the singular individual to the vitality of the world. In line with the non-human or inhuman thinking of Gilles Deleuze and Nigel Thrift we can say that the bodily perceived affects brings 'one's own vitality, one's sense of aliveness, of changeability [into play]' (Thrift, 2004: 63). The affected body (whether the stimuli are of a more emotional kind or a directly physical kind) appears to have three characteristics: it is open (to the world), it experiences an increase in vitality (I am so alive), and it is immediately contagious inviting to imitation.

For both kinds of performative authenticity the proofs of affection are many. They express themselves in bodily investment and affectedness of some sort. For instance, time-consuming labour affects could include the production of bodily fluids such as sweat and tears, together with arousal, shock, fear and trauma. Emotions and feelings are also produced such as hatred, shame, envy, jealousy, disgust, anger, embarrassment, sorrow, grief, anguish, pride, love, happiness, joy, hope, wonder etc. These proofs are important because on the one hand they are proof of the concrete investment, and on the other hand they provide 'a correspondence between the power to act and the power to be affected' (Hardt, 2007: x). The affected body is in some way solid proof of a future change (of a relation, of politics, of the society, of the world) different – in a phenomenological sense – from verbal guarantees of any kind. They become possible forerunners of a utopia. Indeed, we can take the argument even further: the affected bodies are moved bodies, a spatial metaphor expressing that some change already has taken place. The moved body has changed and can eventually influence others to change.

The Chapters

The 21 contributors to this volume are part of Scandinavian networks on Globalisation and Emotional Geography, and together these researchers represent a considerable range of disciplines including literary studies, media and communication studies, cultural studies, geography of the media, religious studies, ethnography, sports science, service management, creative industries research, history, area studies and business administration.

We have divided the book into several sections. The first section, entitled 'Staging and Practicing Authenticity' encompasses chapters positioned within the three main theoretical approaches that the book subscribes to: the cultural economy approach, the media–communication approach and the phenomenological approach. In Chapter 2, 'Staging Places as Brands', Anne-Britt Gran investigates two Norwegian case studies of the staging of authenticity in actual place branding. Using theatre theory she proposes two new forms: a 'look-a-like' authenticity and an alienating authenticity. The chapter 'City In-Between: Communication Geographies, Tourism and the Urban Unconscious' written by André Jansson sets out to explore theoretically what is in-between 'the concept city' and the 'thick city' in everyday encounters. He suggests two concepts – texture and fixture – in order to understand how touristic experiences of big cities can be authentic. Finally, Niels Kayser Nielsen in his chapter 'The Summer We All Went to Keuruu' explores the phenomenological dictum of being as embodying a perspective in the world in order to suggest a dichotomy of stasis and ex-stasis to describe a new tendency of 'topographification of identity' in actual tourism.

The second section entitled 'Branding and Materialising Authenticity' features three chapters on cultural place branding. All point to the inherent difficulties of constructed authenticity and all show how performative authenticity and processes are nevertheless part of branding strategy. The chapter of Can-Seng Ooi and Birgit Stöber takes as its point of departure case studies of Singapore and Berlin to highlight the issue of authenticity in place branding, and they consider the question of whether brand stories really reflect the places now that arts and culture are becoming so prominent in almost any branding exercise. This article proposes that place branding should be seen as part of the process of 'doing the place', creating new emergent authenticity. Søren Buhl Hornskov also has the perspective that brand management acts to frame and 'induce' culture in his chapter 'On the Management of Authenticity: Culture in the Place Branding of Øresund', he presents a case study of two Øresund modern dance venues in the development of the Øresund brand, highlighting the paradox that branding processes try to control and domesticate the social forces whose autonomy is crucial to the authenticity of the brand. The chapter 'A Ferris Wheel on a Parking Lot' by Hanne Pico Larsen explores the generic stereotyping of Old World ethnicity in the case of the 'Danish' town of Solvang in California, and how the authenticity debate has become very much a part of Solvang's identity. The fact that the citizens of Solvang are aware of Solvang as a themed space but are very afraid to appear as a theme park show that authenticity is still an issue.

The third section, 'Re-writing and Re-mediating Authenticity', presents chapters which illustrate how places are inscribed in texts and how places are 'pregnant' with narrations and texts. The section consists of chapters investigating in what ways people's experiences of places are enhanced by mediated narrations (TV series, film, computer-play, novels). In 'Travel and Testimony, Rhetoric of Authenticity', Dan Ringgaard explores the relationship between historically significant places and the act of witnessing – in writing – of three contemporary Danish travel writers. The article shows how the quest for authenticity and the danger of inauthenticity is rhetorically played out in modern traveler's texts. Karen Klitgaard Povlsen performs a cultural–archeological reading of the multiple layers of representation of Kullen – a Swedish visitor's site for 250 years. The chapter 'Cool Kullaberg: The History of a Mediated Tourist Site' shows how the authenticity of this particular place is produced differently in different historical periods. Kjetil Sandvik takes his point of departure in the notion of augmented place that represents an emotional enhancement of our experience of place by means of mediatisation. In the chapter 'Crime Scenes as Augmented Reality', Sandvik proposes five strategies for emotional value-adding to places. The chapter 'Murder Walks in Ystad' presents a case study of literary tourism in Ystad, Sweden, which is connected to the fictitious character Kurt Wallander depicted in films, TV series and novels. The article discusses the embodied experience of the murder walk in the exotically rewritten city of Ystad. Rosslyn Chapel in Scotland, as a media-augmented site, owing to the film *The Da Vinci Code*, is the case study for Maria Månsson who investigates the negotiation process between consumed media images and the tourists' embodied experience. In her chapter 'Negotiating Authenticity at Rosslyn Chapel' she introduces the concept of contested authenticity.

The section entitled 'Re-empowering Authenticity' encompasses three chapters showing how cultural change can happen through new medias and place-designs re-empowering minorities, remote marginal territories and ordinary people's travel experiences. The chapter 'Making Pictures

Talk' authored by Mette Sandbye explores how Danish photographer Pia Arke re-values and reopens the memory of a place through the means of photography. The re-opening is both critical and emotional in the artists 'ethno-aesthetic' approach. Sine Agergaard's case study of 'Globe1', a sports centre for ethnic minorities on the outskirts of a Danish provincial city, presents an analysis of the place, both as a discursively constructed place of integration and, as a lived space with 'non-political' recreational activities. Meanwhile, the chapter 'Online Tourism' addresses the phenomenon of online tourism via the internet using Virtual Tourist and Google Earth as prime examples. In this chapter Jakob Linaa Jensen shows how core users present, share and form communities around travels to physical places as a way of augmenting the tourism experience.

The fifth section of the book, 'Embodying Spatial Mythologies', features chapters which demonstrate how performative authenticity is connected to already existent place-narratives but also how new ones can be created so enhancing the place and re-connecting the tourist to the world. The chapter 'Journeys, Religion and Authenticity Re-visited' investigates place-narratives from New Age Tourism compared to ordinary tourism. The author Torunn Selberg argues that places-narratives about the sacredness and spirituality of places are common ways of emotional place-construction. 'Walking towards One's Self: Authentification of Place and Self' by Jesper Østergaard and Dorthe Refslund Christensen presents a study of postmodern pilgrimage as a way to merge landscape and body. Through the concept of 'ritualised authenticity' the authors describe the double strategy of the pilgrim: performing the landscape as authentic and performing the existential transformation the encounter with the landscape produces. Szilvia Gyimóthy's chapter, 'Thrillscapes: Wilderness Mediated as Playground' uses a case study format to look at how emotions like excitement and joy as well as kinaesthetic sensing are important in the construction of Voss in Norway as an unspoilt wilderness; a so called 'thrillscape'.

SECTION ONE

STAGING AND PRACTICING AUTHENTICITY

Chapter 2

Staging Places as Brands: Visiting Illusions, Images and Imaginations

ANNE-BRITT GRAN

Introduction

It seems like things – all things – are becoming more and more theatrical, as if they were staged and played. Authenticity is a popular thing to stage, which is a paradox since authenticity is also seen as the unstageable, the untouched and the real (thing).

Things are changing: today tourists and consumers are totally happy with well-made and properly staged authenticity. It makes place marketing much easier. Image has replaced identity, and making 'his-story' has replaced roots. Today places communicate in the same way as big companies do, and both places and companies seem very theatrical, but not false, as if the non-theatrical was the 'Real Thing' after all.

So what does it mean to say that places, and companies as well, are staged? Is staging a metaphor or a real thing? It could be both, but in this chapter it is neither. 'Staging' is rather used as a perspective: what do places look like if we see them as directed dramas and painted sceneography? Could a theatre perspective tell us something else and new about today's places? The aim of this chapter is to develop a theoretical theatrical frame for understanding places in the global tourist market (Gran, 2002, 2004).

I will connect the staging principles with some of the theories of brand building, corporate communication and place marketing. Theoretically, organisations and companies are more and more looked upon as communicational actors, rather than producing units.

> Contemporary organisations are – no matter what sector they occupy or what products and services they produce – in the communication business – that is the business of expressing themselves deliberately in their environments. (Thøger *et al.*, 2000: 247)

The focus of organisational theory on identity and culture, and the strong orientation of the marketing field towards branding and image, contribute to introducing a communication paradigm concerning the understanding of organisations (Brønn & Wiig, 2002; Kapferer, 2002; Moingeon & Soenen, 2002; Gran, 2006). This makes sign production and sensible effects part of these economic discourses.

Central terms for the organisation as a communicating actor are 'the aesthetic or beautiful organisation' (Strati, 1999; De Paoli, 2003) and 'the expressive organisation' (Schultz *et al.*, 2000). Today we also use terms as 'aesthetic management' (Thyssen, 2003); 'the aesthetics of marketing' (Schmitt & Simonsen, 1997); and 'aesthetics as organisational theory' (Guillet De Monthoux, 1998). In this perspective the term 'theatrical' is presented in order to display the aesthetic staged aspect of the communicating process of brands and places.

My focus will be on the relationship between identity and image in brand building, identity representing the authentic essence and image representing the superficial surface or the representation of the real. I have chosen to use well-known and traditional theories of brand building, because they demonstrate that thinking in terms of authenticity and essence is still going strong. In mainstream marketing mentality there is no room for poststructuralist insight or blindness.[1] In my view their metaphysical talking is subordinated a pragmatic paradigm: it is a question about selling the brand or not. The economic perspective is strictly instrumental, and if the economist is not happy with the identity or the essence of the product or the company, he will change also that. In my opinion talking of identity and essence in the marketing tradition is not real platonic talk, but platonic talk may sell really well. Even if brand building theory (as much other theory) rests upon the metaphysical distinction between identity and difference, the economic system is so pragmatic that it turns identity into many means.

I see the code of the economic system – to pay or not to pay – as more relevant here than the metaphysical heritage in the economic theories. In this perspective all brand building is always mainly construction work, created for communication and selling, as staging is made for communication and its audience. And all places have now entered the communication industry.

I am going to visit two places in Norway: Stiklestad in Verdal and Nordland. Stiklestad is where the Battle of Stiklestad took place in 1030, and the place is totally staged and based on this history. The second place is Artscape Nordland, a huge sculpture project in the wild and beautiful Nordland natural landscape. These places are chosen because they are visible illustrations and relevant examples in my theoretical framework; they are not cases in the tradition of field studies.

Theoretical Framework, Part One: The Shown and the Hidden Theatricality

As staging models we will use realistic theatre in the tradition of the Russian director Konstantin Stanislavskij and the *Verfremdung* principles of Berthold Brecht. *Verfremdung* has to do with *making strange* in a way that gives the audience new insight and a new way of seeing the same known phenomenon (Brecht, 1938).

Stanislavskij represents the staging of an illusion (Stanislavskij, 1994–1997). This principle tries to hide the theatrical instruments involved: I will call it hidden theatricality. This theatricality is found in its old-fashioned form in both realistic theatre and film, based on the principle 'as if it was real'. The actor has to play Hamlet as if he was Hamlet, and the ketchup needs to look like blood if that is what we want the audience to believe. The hidden theatricality implies mimesis of a true reality, and it represents the seemingly authentic. The aim is to get the audience absorbed in the stage, forgetting it is theatre. The more the acting and staging are hidden, the more the seeming authenticity is effective on us.

Brecht represents the opposite of hidden theatricality – always disturbing the illusion and showing the theatrical means, which I will term 'shown theatricality'. The actors comment upon their roles and the sceneography of a place may be shown by a sign: 'A new town' (no town to see, though). Another type of shown theatricality is masque theatre, like *Commedia dell'arte* (a popular theatre tradition from the Renaissance). When someone puts on a masque we are told all the time that this is theatre, this is true theatrical reality.

A model of the relation between shown and hidden theatricality is provided in Table 2.1:[2]

Both shown and hidden theatricality deal with creating effects and consequences for the contributors and/or the audience. The shown theatricality tries to seduce and move its audience through spectacular staging and visible acting. A carnival is pure masquerade, not miming anything, not being an illusion of something more real. Similarly, the city of Las Vegas and Disney World appear as pure staging, not miming or representing anything but themselves. They are genuine theatrical reality, created to be exactly that.

Hidden theatricality, on the other hand, leaves its acting and staging unspoken in order to achieve effects so genuine and real that they will

Table 2.1 Model of shown and hidden theatricality

Shown Theatricality	*Hidden Theatricality*
Staged artificiality	Staged reality/authenticity
Non illusion	Illusion: 'as if' it were real
Not mimetic	Mimetic: mimes the reality
Outspoken staging principles	Unspoken staging principles
Accepting being artificial	Hiding being artificial
Want to be spectacle	Want to look real/realistic/authentic
Examples	
Brecht-inspired theatre Masque theatre Carnival Las Vegas Disney World	Realistic theatre and film Historical reconstruction of buildings and towns Venice in Las Vegas Staged rituals

move the audience. It is only the context of the representation – the theatre, the cinema or a tourist context – which tells us that 'this is staged illusion'. It is the job of the director to make us forget this, while we are watching the play or the film. In the same way, the copy of Venice in Las Vegas is a pure illusion of the city in Italy, and the aim is to make the audience forget that fact. The staging principle, 'as if' it was the real thing, seduces the public. This is also the case when 'primitive' and 'authentic' rituals are given in tourist contexts; they must look real. The look-alike principle is what gives the hidden theatricality its meaning.

Theoretical Framework, Part Two: Theatrical Economy and Brand Building as *Mise en scène*

New terms in theories about contemporary economy often bring up theatre and aesthetics, as in experience economy and entertainment economy (Pine & Gilmore, 1999; Mossberg, 2007). A continuously globalised capitalism demands further differentiation of products and companies; both need to be visible amongst the competition in a fast growing market. In order to stand out one needs to draw attention. Both pure commercials and marketing, as such, deal with drawing attention to products and companies. The effects constitute a new resource in economics, a kind of aesthetic capital (Gran & De Paoli, 2005).

The term 'experience economy' was introduced in its full meaning in 1999 by B. Joseph Pine II and James H. Gilmore in a book bearing the same name. The subtitle of the book is *Work Is Theatre and Every Business a Stage*. One could presume this title to be metaphorical, both theatre and stage being images of how today's economy works. They're not. The authors make it clear at an early stage that theatre is not a metaphor for work and the stage is not a metaphor for all business; the theatre is rather looked upon as a model the business community needs to adapt itself to in order to stage experiences.

The value of the experience lies in its more or less intense existence in the moment, subsequently becoming a memory. The experience is an investment in our mental scrapbook. If our heads don't break, the product 'experience' can last as long as a human life. This way, the staged product both outlasts and proves more robust than traditional goods and services.

The obvious experience industries today are live concerts, all forms of festivals, the tourist industry and the restaurant industry. However, one of Pine and Gilmore's main arguments is that the experience economy is not industry-specific; it spreads out to all industries independently of the art of the production. The customer pays for the experience in the experience economy, regardless of the actual product. Only when a car is bought for the experiences it offers and not for its technical and functional abilities does a car enter the experience economy.

At the same time as the idea of experience economy breaks through, an intensifying in brand building happens in the subject of marketing (Olins, 2000; Kunde, 2000). Brand building becomes one of the most important measures for marketers for drawing attention to their product in the global market. Brand building is the art of making images; it is *mise en scène par excellence*, thoroughly directed and displayed for the eye of the viewer – the customer. Today it is not only products and companies that are built as brands, but also places, known persons and politicians. The marketing mentality is influencing all areas of society. To think about all things as brands has become a reception-modus in late modernity and late capitalism, and the brand has become holy. Brands function more like icons than like symbols; they are worshipped and you can't mock them without being punished (by the owners and the lawyers).

To make brands out of places has become a trend in marketing and in the tourist industry (Kotler *et al.*, 1999; Iversen, 1999; Buskoven *et al.*, 2002; Naper, 2002). Places have become of vital importance in the global economy, and marketers are turning places into images (Harvey, 1993). In so-called Strategic Image Management (SIM) one is concerned with such questions as: what determines a place's image?; how can a place's image be measured?; what are the guidelines for designing a place's image?; what tools are available for communicating an image?; how can a place correct a negative image?

> We define a place's image as the sum of beliefs, ideas and impressions that people have of that place. Images represent a simplification of a large number of associations and pieces of information connected with the place. (Kotler *et al.*, 1999: 160)

Image is not the same as a stereotype, but it is related to it: both being simplifications of a complex reality and both wanting to be the true extract of it. I will argue that brands and images are theatrical, put on a stage to be visible, but this does not mean that they are arbitrarily invented. They must relate to some relevant facts or reality effects: It is very difficult to put a middle age image on a modern town dominated by the architecture of international style. This means that a brand of a place must take into consideration what kind of resources and characteristics the place really has. For an image to be effective, it must, according to Kotler *et al.* (1999) meet five criteria:

(1) It must be valid. If the place promotes an image too far from reality, the chance of effect is minimal.
(2) It must be believable. To be valid is not good enough, if the visitors do not believe in it.
(3) It must be simple. If the place disseminates too many images of itself, there will be confusion.
(4) It must have appeal. The image must suggest why people would want to live, invest, work or visit the place.
(5) It must be distinctive. The image works best when it is different from other common themes.

These criteria tell us that the image must be related to some relevant reality that is unique, but what this reality is will differ from product to product, place to place. In branding theories this 'relevant reality' has to do with identity, essence and values. The image is seen as a representation of some deeper and true reality.

In theories about brand building and corporate communication, we find the old opposition between theatricality (staged and superficial) and authenticity (real and deep) in the concepts of image and identity. Brands consist of both images and identities (Brønn & Wiig, 2002; Van Riel, 2000, 2002; Schultz *et al.*, 2000). Image is perceptibly oriented and staged with the use of aesthetic effects, and it is always directed towards the world outside and its audience (Schmitt & Simonsen, 1997). Identity, on the other hand, is associated with authenticity and words like real, the core and essence. Image is meant to seduce the customer. Identity is what the customer is supposed to believe in. Products and places need both image and identity in order to form brands and added value. An added value is what the brand is worth beyond, and in addition to, its area of use and technical quality. Creation of added value is the aim of brand building. In our perspective a brand is as detailed in Table 2.2.

The distinction between image and identity in brands is an analytic separation; in practice it is difficult to separate a brand's visual logo from its inner values in the same way.

At the same time, the distinction allows us to see how branding theory rests upon a historical metaphysical inheritance, where the opposition/ contrast between the theatrical superficial and the deep authentic is central. 'Image' means our ideas and representations of things. One might argue that authenticity does not exist because it is deconstructed, or that it cannot be staged or that places are not brands. My point is that it does not matter that people (tourists) behave as if authenticity exists; that they accept that authenticity is staged if it looks real; and that they think about places as they think about other brands. In our theatrical perspective the brand as a whole acts more like Stanislavskij's illusion than Brecht's revealing of theatrical effects, and it relies on the idea that an image mimes the real thing. But the brand is made for selling, not for miming reality.

The concept of 'imagination' has the same etymological origin as 'image', meaning more free ideas about things, also called fantasy. Theories

Table 2.2 Brand: Added value

A brand consists of		
Image	+	*Identity*
Picture, surface	+	Essence, depth
Focus on the customer	+	Focus on value
Seductive	+	Believable
Visual (picture/image)	+	Invisible, but noticeable
Theatrical (staged/created)	+	Non-theatrical (is)
= Real added value		

about branding seldom or never make this point. 'Imagine' is a word full of dreams and future – 'all the people' (Brown & Patterson, 2000). The image of a place, in fact, plays on all these connotations: Our representation of what the place is, creative ideas about the place and our inner dreams and belongings associated with the place. When a place brand evokes the visitor's imagination, the image has been successfully effective. We are not only visiting physical places, but also our images of the place and our imagination about it – imagine visiting it!

Stiklestad in Verdal: Heritage Development

Stiklestad is located in Verdal in Nord-Trøndelag County and was the scene of the single most famous battle in Norwegian history.[3] The battle of Stiklestad, 29 July 1030 represents the christening of Norway, as well as the introduction of monarchy. The battle of Stiklestad is looked upon as a turning point in the history of Norway. Verdal apparently is the only municipality in Norway to keep its borders and local names unchanged as far back as we know. Verdal municipality's coat of arms is a yellow cross on a red background. In the battle of Stiklestad, King Olav Haraldsson and his army are considered to have used shields marked with a similar cross. Today, Stiklestad is a centre of activity consisting of an open air theatre, a church, a cultural centre and a number of museums. The main museum was moved to Stiklestad in the 1950s, and the cultural centre was finished in 1992.

The play of St Olaf, King of Norway (Olav Haraldsson) is the largest and oldest Norwegian outdoor play. The first performance of the play took place on 29 July 1954, called St Olafs Day or *Olsok*. Since then, 670,000 people have seen the play. The play most certainly has had a spin-off effect for the cultural life and the business community in Verdal. The play was a direct cause of the location of a national centre of culture in Stiklestad. The business community supports the play of St Olav, King of Norway through *Stiklestadsleidangen*, an agreement between a group of companies and the cultural centre concerning the development of Stiklestad and the financing of the play. A *leidang* was a system presumed to originate from Håkon the Good (*c*.950) concerning the organisation of a fleet for naval defence. The *leidang* was a tax paid by the farmers to provide ships, crew and provisions.

Olsok (19 July–29 July) in Stiklestad is a 10-day-long festival built around the play *St Olaf, King of Norway* (See Figure 2.1). The four performances form the basis, in addition to a Middle Ages-themed market, lectures, art exhibitions, the *Olsok*-profile, concerts, theatre, children's

Figure 2.1 Olsok Stiklestand Festival

activities etc. The National Heritage Museum in Stiklestad consists of 30 well-kept antiquarian buildings from the 17th century and after. The National Heritage Museum is also the arena for different events during all seasons of the year.

Stiklastadir is a farm under construction in Stiklestad (See Figure 2.2). Work on it began in 2007 and will last 15–20 years. Beside the battlefield from 1030 a yard is being reconstructed in order to retell the story from its early ages. The farm will consist of a long house, hall, stables, barn etc.

Stiklestad is staged as a historical drama (See Figure 2.3), not only the outdoor play, but everything that is happening there; the festival, the market, the building of new (old) buildings like Stiklastadir. Everything mimics the notion of the real Middle Ages, the real Vikings and the real battle. The aim is to look as realistic/authentic as possible, and to get the audience/the tourists absorbed in the illusion of the Middle Ages. Of course it looks theatrical: it is, after all, a representation of another Age, but the staging is based on the illusion principles to 'look alike' the real thing. What does the brand of the place look like? If we now try to combine the theories of staging with the theory of brand building, the result may look like the model below in Table 2.3. In the study of the

Figure 2.2 Stiklastadir

Figure 2.3 Stiklestad historical drama

Table 2.3 The Stiklestand brand

Image	+	*Identity (resource)*
Theatrical, picture, surface	+	Authentic, essence, depth
Staging the middle age	+	The historical Stiklestad battle in 1030
As an illusion of the real age	+	Where St Olaf the King of Norway died
= Real added value or 'imagine': The *aura* of the Vikings and St Olaf, King of Norway		

tourist industry (in an economic perspective) one calls the identity of a place a 'resource' (Lyngnes, 2007). A place must have a distinctive resource that can be developed in tourism and place marketing. The image is mirroring or miming the identity and the resource of a place.

The resource of the place is the historical Stiklestad battle in 1030. The authenticity of this fact is the ground on which everything else is built, and it is the brand's identity. The image is a picture of the middle age staged as a historical drama with true costumes and realistic sceneography. The brand of Stiklestad is built both on the authentic historical battle and on the image of the Middle Ages illusion. The fact that it is the historically correct place of the Stiklestad battle gives the place its aura and added value.

Is the Stiklestad image effective, according to the criteria offered by Kotler? The image is valid, because it is not too far from reality. It is believable too, because the visitors know the historical facts and enjoy the historical drama. The image is simple, Stiklestad does not disseminate many images of itself, only the Middle Ages-based one. The image must have appeal; the Middle Ages and the Vikings and St Olaf the King have such appeal. The image must be distinctive, and it is because it is the one and only: Oslo has the Viking ships, but Stiklestad has the battle, St Olaf the King, the outdoor play and many 'look alike' experiences to enjoy.

Trying to create and reconstruct a spectacular look-alike illusion of relevant historical facts is an effective strategy in heritage development, and heritage development is a very strong sector of the tourist market (Kotler *et al.*, 1999). This strategy suits the logic of experience economy: knowledge of history, also represented in the museums, is turned into heritage as staged entertainment. This transforms the museums from knowledge institutions to experience industry, which makes staging principles very important.

Artscape Nordland: Arts Planning

Artscape Nordland is an international art project. The project officially started in 1992, and was completed in 1998. At a cultural workshop arranged by Nordland county municipality, artist Anne Katrine Dolven launched the idea of turning Nordland county into the world's largest sculpture park. Dolven questioned the notion of how, in the world of art, something which finds itself in the periphery can take a central position by taking into consideration the specific features that are characteristic of the place (Indregard, 2006).

Originally, each of Nordland county's 45 municipalities was to acquire its own international, contemporary sculpture. Some 33 municipalities agreed to participate in the project. Finally, the world's largest sculpture park was a reality, despite furious letters to the editors of local newspapers, the base measuring 40,000 square metres.

A total of 33 artists from 18 different countries were involved in the project. The artists formulated a plan for the sculpture, and this plan was to be approved by the professional artistic committee, and presented for the municipality. The municipality and the project administration undertook a cost estimate and cooperated in finding both practical and economic solutions. After the cost estimate was approved, the creation of the work itself could begin.[4]

The idea of a work of art creating a place with its presence forms the basis of the Artscape Nordland project. The aim of the project was that the sculptures were to be created from the characteristic conditions of Nordland, and the artists should strive to use local materials and local workforce. The sculptures make the surroundings visible and offer a new dimension to the place.

The Artscape Nordland project is now in its second phase, a decision made by the county assembly in 2002. The project is to be expanded, with one new sculpture every other year until 2010. In connection with the project, a richly illustrated traveller's guide has been published with directions to all the sculptures. The guide is available in both Norwegian/English and English/German. Other project merchandise includes postcards with motifs from each of the 33 sculptures as well as a map where all sculptures are cited.

'Artistic Disturbances – Art in Nordland' is a continuation of the Artscape Nordland. It is a series of site-specific works of art developed by twenty international artists in close dialogue with municipalities, cities and villages in Nordland county during the period 2003–2005. The aim of the project was to question the local context, the communicative abilities of the art works and their function in real life, as well as to debate 'site-specific' as an artistic genre and strategy.

Many readers might find it much easier to accept the argument that the place, Stiklestad, is staged as a historical drama than to accept the idea that Artscape Nordland can be seen as staged at all. I will argue that this kind of arts-planning has much in common with Brechtian *Verfremdung*'s staging. But I am not saying that the people involved in this project thought about it in this way. This has to do with my experimental and perspectivist approach: what happens if we see both places and brand building as theatrical strategies? Will it be possible to see something new, to make new distinctions, to understand places and brand building better or differently? I hope so. The reception of this text will decide whether this perspective is relevant or not, in theory or praxis.

Why Brecht and the *Verfremdung* effect? *Verfremdung* is Brecht's German translation of the Russian concept, *Priem Ostrannenija*, used by the critic Viktor Shlovskijs. It can be translated as 'to make the known and homely strange'. This interpretation gives the *Verfremdung* concept a more general meaning than just being a political theatre style. Today we can find *Verfremdung* effects in performance art, in concept art, in site-specific art and in relational art. And the whole Artscape Nordland can be seen as a huge *Verfremdung* effect.

The sculptures are placed in a huge/vast area very different from a gallery or museum or a sculpture park (see Figures 2.4 and 2.5). The sculptures are created by known artists and visibly placed in the untouched nature of Nordland. The contrast and the dialogue between nature and culture are overwhelming. Every sculpture is made in relation to exactly the site it is placed. The sculptures do not mime nature, but they comment upon it, relate to it, in ways that make the audience see the *nature* in a new way – in relation to art and *as* art. Nature appears as the stage for the sculptures, and the artworks create a nature strange to the audience: As seen for the first time.

This must be understood in a Norwegian context, too. Tourism in Norway has been based on its beautiful nature, discovered by travellers in the 19th century at the same time as Norway became an independent nation. The wild and steep mountain nature is a resource in both Norwegian self-understanding and in the tourist industry. It has been and still is very difficult to sell Norway or a part of it, without this wild and clean nature image. Norway has a nature image, not a cultural image like Italy or France (which both have high mountains, too). In such a context the Artscape Nordland is somewhat radical in a region best known for its nature. This happens because the region has both artistic

Figure 2.4 Havmann, Antony Gormley, Rana Kammunes

Figure 2.5 Uten Tittel, Dan Graham, Vågan kommune

competence and a political will to put money in projects like this. The Nordland region has invested in and invented itself as a culture region, in opposition to, and as a supplement to, the well-known Lofoten nature. The brand of the place may be modelled as shown in Table 2.4.

Artscape Nordland is an interesting example of arts planning in town and region development (Evans, 2001). Competing to be attractive places for corporations and tourists, places are using architecture, museums, operas, festivals etc. as means to distinguish the town or the region from others. This has become a trend in Europe since the success with the Guggenheim Museum in Bilbao, and we can also see it in Gateshead, in Glasgow and in the new opera in Oslo. They are flagship projects, expensive and exclusive, and they are heavily supported by the public. In arts, planning the art – architecture and artworks – functions as a distinctive image in the development of both the place and the brand. Both the opera in Sydney and the museum in Bilbao play this role in the very well known images of these places.

Arts planning in Nordland has a totally different image than the heritage development at Stiklestad in Verdal. Artscape Nordland seems like a modernistic concept belonging to the 20th century, while Stiklestad is based on theatre principles from the 19th century. But they both function very well as distinctive images. And they both suit the experience economy, even if the experiences differ. Artscape may create the *Verfremdung* feeling and a kind of excitement, while Stiklestad may offer absorption in the illusion and an entertainment feeling. And maybe they tell us something representative about the staging and branding principles of arts planning and heritage development in general.

In this chapter I have tried to demonstrate that connecting theatre theories with marketing-thinking makes it possible to see how authenticity

Table 2.4 The Artscape Nordland brand

Image	*+ Identity (resource)*
Artificial, picture, surface	+ Authentic, essence, depth
Staging the nature through art	+ The Nordland nature
As art, through Verfremdung-means	+ Artistic competence and political will
= Real added value or 'imagine': The Nordland nature as an artistic place	

Table 2.5 Arts planning and heritage development as place brand

Arts planning as place brand	Heritage development as place brand
Artscape Nordland	Stiklestad in Verdal
The image of the exciting new	The image of the authentic old
Staging *Verfremdung* and the artificial	Staging illusions
Modernist experimental logic of the 20th century	Realistic 'look-alike' logic of the 19th century
Experience: *Verfremdung* and excitement	Experience: Absorption and entertainment

is a main capital in staging the images of place-brands. The image of authenticity is worth investment – financially speaking. I tried to show that both staging and brand building are basically pragmatic and constructive activities – *mise en scène* – looking for communicative effects. I have postulated that it is never enough to say that places (and other things as well) are staged; we must ask *how* and *in which way* they are staged. Different staging principles create different places and different brands. Theories about staging and directing make it possible to produce new distinctions between different kinds of constructed authenticity – as 'look-a-like authenticity' and '*Verfremdung* authenticity'.

I have tried to convince you that overlapping theories from theatre and marketing can give us new insight and creative concepts about how places are created and sold.

Imagine all the places!

Notes

1. My philosophical approach to authenticity belongs to the tradition of French poststructuralism – authenticity as identity is deconstructed – and American pragmatism, especially Richard Rorty, how does authenticity work in our daily life – because it is not dead.
2. This model is developed in *Vår teatrale tid* (Gran, 2004), and the original model also distinguishes between fictional and non-fictional forms in both shown and hidden theatricality. The level of fictionality could be relevant for staging places too.
3. See www.stiklestad.no and Idun Haugen: 'Ringvirkninger fra Stiklestad', http://www.spelhandboka.no/stiklestadeffekten.asp
4. See http://www.skulpturlandskap.no/Skulpturlandskap/Info/hist.html

Chapter 3

The City In-Between: Communication Geographies, Tourism and the Urban Unconscious

ANDRÉ JANSSON

Introduction

There are in the urban landscape layers of meaning and materiality we rarely think of or even notice. As urban dwellers we normally reflect upon just a very small share of the patterns of communication that surround us. We take for granted how (urban) technologies such as telephones, cash machines and traffic information systems operate – and that they function properly. We also take for granted the ways in which certain cultural forms or goods are circulated through certain areas or spaces of the city, producing a segmented geography of tastes and expressions. But what can we take for granted if we leave our own city and travel somewhere else? As tourists we often find ourselves lost and confused. Just small variations in transportation systems, signage and media circulation may shake our urban unconscious. Thus, albeit some organised trips are indeed made extremely 'smooth', the ambition to understand and/or overcome 'infrastructural obstacles' is to some extent always integral to the tourist gaze. It is partly through problematic encounters and coping processes, most likely to occur in big cities where areas of spectacle and *staged authenticity* (MacCannell, 1973) are interlaced with non-staged patterns of everyday circulation, we come to experience tourism as *real*, or *authentic* – that we have really been *somewhere else*.

Departing from the writings of de Certeau, Tuan and Lefebvre, this chapter sets out to establish a framework for exploring the opaque infrastructural spaces in-between the panoramic 'concept city', as represented in branding images, urban planning and popular narratives, and the immersive 'thick city', as experienced through everyday encounters. It is argued that the understanding of such intermediary urban spaces in general, and intermediary *communication geographies* in particular, has been underdeveloped in both media and tourism studies. A deeper understanding of these layers is crucial if we want to learn more about touristic city experiences, and how these are interwoven with prevailing notions of authenticity.

In order to make sense of intermediary communication geographies the concepts of *texture* and *fixture* are introduced. As shown in Figure 3.1, texture and fixture are intermediary concepts, mediating between (1) *the concept city and the thick city*; and (2) *sedimentation and circulation*. Texture refers to the sedimented *communicative fabric of space* – shaped as networks of/for circulation – symbolic as well as material in kind. Fixtures are the *strong points of textures*. Through sedimentation they contribute to the reproduction of textures, while at the same time working as nodes of circulation. They appear as both machinic infrastructural nodes (web servers, media centres, outlets, etc), and more hermeneutic loci (festivals, rituals, cultural scenes, etc.) with no clear boundaries between the types.

The study of the city in-between raises a research agenda that involves places, people and processes that attain an intermediary and often unexploited backstage character – phenomena that partly (and textures to a greater extent than fixtures) belong to the *urban unconscious* and therefore have rarely been the object of neither media studies nor tourism studies.[1] This does not make them 'authentic', 'genuine' or 'pure' in an

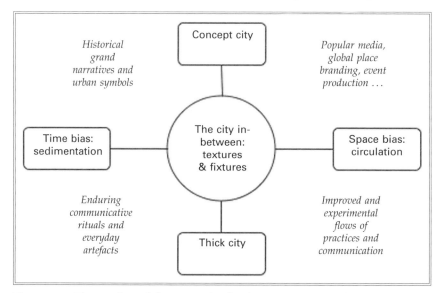

Figure 3.1 The analytical framework of urban textures and fixtures

objective sense of the word. But due to their embeddedness in urban everyday life, and their tendency to become somewhat more visible through the tourist gaze, they do carry a certain significance as to whether a city is understood as 'unique' among visitors, and whether travelling involves the experience of facing 'reality' or not. Indeed, more symbolically charged, or staged, spaces of the city rarely hold this potential (MacCannell, 1973). I will return to these questions later on. First, I will elaborate the model in some more detail.

The Concept City, the Thick City and the City In-between

Urban experience tends to alternate between two extremes. On the one hand, the city may be experienced as a sign or a panorama, through abstraction or geographical distanciation. This is the city of architects, planners, branding professionals, and gazing sight-seers. We may call it the *concept city*. On the other hand, the city is an immersive cultural forest, a city of walkers, waiting to be explored and navigated. It is a city to be absorbed by, and to lose oneself within. We may call it the *thick city*.

Human geographer Yi-Fu Tuan (1974: Ch. 13) holds that the polarisation of these two levels corresponds to a phenomenological gap among city dwellers. While experts on their own street, and skilled in the imagery of the entire city, most inhabitants have just vague, or incoherent, understandings of intermediate levels, such as the geographies of neighbouring districts. A similar gap might be experienced among tourists, albeit in a more ambivalent way. On the one hand, since their direct experiences and encounters with the thickness of a city are often conflated with promotional scripts and panoramic views, one might argue that the city in-between implodes. On the other hand, once tourists leave the 'tourist capsule' they may achieve very direct experiences of otherwise hidden urban structures (cf. Jansson, 2007).

The gap between *concept city* and *thick city* is also spelled out in Michel de Certeau's essay (1984: Ch. VII) 'Walking in the City'. In the opening of the text (1984: 91) he describes what it is (or was) to see Manhattan from the 110th floor of the World Trade Center:

> Beneath the haze stirred up by the winds, the urban island, a sea in the middle of the sea, lifts up the skyscrapers over Wall Street, sinks down at Greenwich, then rises again to the crests of Midtown, quietly passes over Central Park and finally undulates off into the distance beyond Harlem. A wave of verticals. Its agitation is momentarily arrested by vision. The gigantic mass is immobilised before the eyes.

It is transformed into a texturology in which extremes coincide – extremes of ambition and degradation, brutal oppositions of races and styles, contrasts between yesterday's buildings, already transformed into trash cans, and today's urban irruptions that block out its space. (De Certeau, 1984: 91)

As we can see, ascending the World Trade Center involves (or involved) a double metamorphosis. The street walker is transfigured into a voyeur, who is now in control of the landscape. His or her multi-sensory experience of the bustling city scene is replaced by a totalising gaze. The voyeur, a common figure among tourists, is not absorbed by, but measuring and reading the city. The city, in turn, transforms before the voyeur's eyes: it becomes an image, or even a text.

So what is in-between these levels? Where does the thick city end, and where does the concept city begin? Clearly, these spaces are not absolute, or objective, but operate above all on an *intersubjective* level. Nonetheless, or precisely therefore, they are important to (re)consider. They constitute and condition a great deal of social life, while simultaneously escaping the classifying forces of interpretation. As social subjects we tend to bracket off intermediary spaces and processes, in order to make the world more comprehensible. This goes also for urban communication geographies. Every city integrates more or less patterned infrastructures and symbolic flows. These are essential to the (re)production of both the concept city and the thick city – but they are also more or less hidden, belonging to the urban back-stage (such as places of maintenance, repair and monitoring – cf. Goffman, 1959), and/or taken for granted. We may imagine all the cables and wires criss-crossing an ordinary city district, providing us with information we do not problematise until we are off-line. Or we may think of the socio-geographic logic according to which artistic scenes circulate cultural products and hermeneutic energies in a city. We know that these infrastructures and nodes exist, but we have just a vague, more or less unconscious, understanding of how they are maintained. One may even argue that *they become more significant the less we notice them*.

In media studies there is, or at least has been, a tendency to reproduce the phenomenological gap between the concept city and the thick city – to concentrate either upon (increasingly global) flows of information, or upon local appropriations (in urban areas or elsewhere). Through such a dualistic view a lot of interesting and meaningful relationships tend to slip away. This is paradoxical, since one might presume that it is precisely within these intermediary spaces that processes of mediation may prevail.

Mediation represents what Johan Fornäs (2000) has termed 'the crucial in between'. My point is that intermediary communication geographies mediate in a dual manner (see Figure 3.1). On the one hand, they produce discernable paths and nodes that link the thick city to a broader urban context, and thus make it more comprehensible. On the other hand, they transfigure the concept city into more concrete and enduring sites of patterned experience and social practice. This process may be called *texturation* (see Jansson, 2006).

Texture

'The act of walking', Michel de Certeau (1984: 97) argues, 'is to the urban system what the speech act is to language or to the statements uttered'. This parallel is built upon three criteria. First, walking is a process of *appropriation* of the urban topography, just as the speaker appropriates language. Secondly, it is the *acting-out* of the place, just as the speech act is an acting-out of language. Thirdly, the mobile character of walking implies *relations* among differentiated positions, just as verbal enunciation actualises contracts between speakers. Walking, then, can be understood as 'a space of enunciation' (1984: 98). It is a space that emerges through the interplay between the possibilities provided by the urban system, and the selective actualisation of these possibilities on behalf of pedestrians. Urban movements may on the one hand produce durable paths, and on the other hand subvert the dominant order. As de Certeau concludes, urban life constitutes a 'wandering of the semantic' that makes 'some parts of the city disappear and exaggerate others' (1984: 102).

De Certeau's perspective illuminates the interplay between space and communication, through which a city is produced. And the argument does not restrict itself to the act of walking. We may understand all kinds of spatial practice occurring in the city as a 'wandering of the semantic', making the urban landscape thick of meaning, while at the same time impossible to fully represent. The bustling activity of the city cannot be translated, nor controlled. The only way to reach a sense of semantic control, as we saw, is through distanciation and abstraction, turning the city into a visual object. But the satisfaction generated from such a perspective, de Certeau (1984: 93) contends, is based on 'an oblivion and a misunderstanding of practices.' The *texturology* of the panorama, or the concept city, is just a phantom image.

It is not exactly clear what de Certeau means when he uses the terms *texture* and *texturology*. It seems like he refers to the visible patterns and urban inscriptions that surface through distanciation. At the same time, however, de Certeau insists on comparing these abstract patterns with a text – let alone a 'false' one. Hence, there is no clear distinction between text and texture (cf. Reynolds & Fitzpatrick, 1999). This, I think, reveals a limitation to de Certeau's view. The parallel between the city and language is brilliant in pointing out the communicative character of spatial practice, and the spatiality of communication. But it leaves out the material, sensory and emotional richness that exceeds the realm of speaking and thinking. To understand walking as a speech act is not to understand the full experience of walking. Nor is it to understand how certain spatial practices become attached to certain places and material infrastructures. In order to understand these spatial mediations we must think of them as something more than ongoing text-production.

One good way to do that is to apply Henri Lefebvre's (1974/1991) notion of texture. Lefebvre's point is that the repetition of practices produces meaningful paths and inscriptions that are at the same time material and potentially graphic. This is the very same observation that leads de Certeau to speak of the concept city – the city of cartographers and planners. But whereas de Certeau sees the illusiveness of such a perspective, Lefebvre sees an organic evolution of materialised meaning. Lefebvre does not link texture to visual abstraction and forgetting, but to an intermediary realm of social structuration and sedimentation. For Lefebvre, texture thus closes the gap between the thick city and the concept city, rather than producing it. We can see this in his discussion of spatial architectonics:

A spatial work (monument or architectural project) attains a complexity fundamentally different from the complexity of a text, whether prose or poetry. As I pointed out earlier, what we are concerned with here is not texts but texture. We already know that a texture is made up of a usually rather large space covered by networks or webs; monuments constitute the strong points, nexuses or anchors of such webs. The actions of social practice are expressible but not explicable through discourse; they are, precisely, acted – and not read. A monumental work, like a musical one, does not have a 'signified' (or 'signifieds'); rather, it has a horizon of meaning: a specific or indefinite multiplicity of meanings, a shifting hierarchy in which now one, now another meaning comes momentarily to the fore, by means of – and for the sake of – a particular action. (Lefebvre, 1974/1991: 222)

Texture is here understood as an intermediary concept, bridging the dualities between material and symbolic spaces, and between social practices and more solid spatial preconditions. The webs that Lefebvre refers to may be either symbolic or material, or a combination of both. The crucial point is that their meanings emerge through social enactment. Meaningful textures are like a network of well-travelled paths, made-up not only through spatial practices themselves, but also through the circulation of goods and information, whose mobilities are, in turn, produced through an interplay between structure and agency.

This brings us back to the problematic issue of intermediary urban space, and its vagueness (cf. Miller, 2006). If textures are to be understood as meaningful socio-material webs, can there be any other textures than those we see, or otherwise perceive through our senses? If some textures are recognisable only through spatial abstraction, can they still be understood as textures? My point here is that the very intermediary character of textures implies that they are not often seen, nor problematised, but taken for granted. Nevertheless, through structured sets of spatial resources and conventions they *enable* and *script* our social practices in ways that produce particular 'cultures of circulation' (see Lee & LiPuma, 2002). For instance, as Joshua Meyrowitz (1985) famously has argued, technological infrastructures not only enable certain forms of communication, but also impose the adjustment of spatial practices according to the anticipated presence and influence of these media. In the mediatised city people expect others to carry mobile telephones (turned on or off, depending on region); public behaviour is managed according to signage and surveillance technology, and so on.

This is to say that there is a social logic to the fact that intermediary textures operate largely unnoticed. We use them and feel them, but do not think very much of them. If we did, they would lose their intermediary character.

However, this is also a relative fact, which depends upon who the 'we' refers to. There are for instance people whose profession it is to operate and maintain textural webs and resources – people whose work the everyday citizen take for granted. To a great extent they occupy Erving Goffman's (1959) back regions, knowing where the telephone station is located in a neighbourhood, or how to use the back-streets for getting access to media infrastructure and delivery entrances. As Graham and Thrift (2007) point out, these people constitute the maintenance crew of intermediary communication geographies – and from their viewpoint the intermediary is both a visible and a thick space.

There are also tourists and other visitors in the city who feel and see things that non-foreigners hardly notice – often very mundane things. How do I buy a subway ticket? How do I open the bus door? Shall I give tip in this restaurant? Such obstacles are typically covered in guidebooks under headlines such as 'Getting Around', attempting to soothe the shock of novel infrastructures and cultural norms. While many 'authentic' spaces remain hidden to tourists, especially everyday work places and residential areas to which they are not recommended to go, certain textures may stand out and mark travel memories due to their mere difference. As Michel de Certeau (1984: 93) argues, city walkers make use of, and produce, *spaces that cannot be seen*, as long as the walkers do not transform themselves into voyeurs – or, we could add, *into tourists*.

Fixture

Urban fixtures can be understood as the strong points in urban textures. These strong points evolve through history, and are recognised as parts of tradition or institutional life. They cannot easily be invented or invoked, but emerge through *sedimentation*, that is, a 'thickening of space through time' (cf. Crang & Travlou, 2001: 167ff), or a solidification of certain nodes within the thick city. On the one hand, these nodes produce and are produced through increased circulation of material and/or hermeneutic energies in and around certain places. In this way, they structure urban practices and movements in a way that make thick spaces comprehensible. On the other hand, by means of cultural recognition, their solidification underpins the composition of the concept city. In this latter sense, fixtures are important to our visual and cartographic under-standing of the city as a social space. They help us getting around and coordinate our activities.

In a sociological account of urban culture Gerald Suttles (1984) argues that our academic understanding of it would benefit from a material turn, implying that more attention would be paid to the 'cumulative texture' of local culture. Suttles's argument is that the durability of a city can be understood largely through the materialised expressions of its historical values and narratives. As examples of such expressions he mentions not only urban monuments and museum collections, but also more mundane expressions, such as street names, restaurants, local sports teams, and what people put on their car bumpers and t-shirts. These objective artefacts, he argues, 'give local culture much of its stability and con-tinuing appeal' (Stuttles, 1984: 284). Through selective tradition, certain expressions will live on as a source of collective understanding. Others will fade away. Yet other cultural elements, once regarded as quite ordinary and undistinguished, will be transfigured into more enduring values or narratives. The step from these recognisable urban elements to the concept city is thus a short one (see also Borer, 2006).

What Suttles refers to as a 'cumulative texture' I would prefer to call fixture. The notion of fixture leads us to an understanding of intermediary space as a realm of socio-cultural dialectics – a realm in which organic solidification at a certain point is turned into abstraction. Memories of the local past are reproduced and fixed through materialisations within the urban fabric – named monuments, buildings, streets, public centres, etc. – or re-enacted through rituals, festivals, scenes and events, attached to certain recognisable time–spaces.

The strength of these fixtures, and the extent to which they are judged as 'authentic', depends upon the social relationship between naming and place-making, between the concept city and the thick city. In order to work as a node for circulation, this relationship must be widely recognised as meaningful to local identity. In addition, if it is to endure, the spatial marker must be anchored in a more general moral space. Therefore, as Yi-Fu Tuan has pointed out, there are only few spatial markers that can survive:

> The more specific and representational the object the less it is likely to survive: since the end of British imperialism in Egypt, the statues of Queen Victoria no longer command worlds but merely stand in the way of traffic. In the course of time, most public symbols lose their status as places and merely clutter up space. (Tuan, 1977: 164)

In spite of their time-biased nature, fixtures may thus come and go. Their structuring power both solidifies and dissolves over time. It takes enormous efforts to invoke new urban fixtures at the conceptual level, for example through place marketing, or what Tuan (1974, 1977) has described as boosterism (see also the classical writings of Wohl and Strauss, 1958; Lynch, 1960). While modern cities must create and nurture eligible symbols in order to become recognised in the global market-place, enduring place-values cannot be too alien to urban life forms. Place marketing always runs the risk of enhancing the gap between the concept city and the thick city, thus producing a sense of urban instability and artificiality. This logic corresponds to Dean MacCannell's (1973) under-standing of 'staged authenticity', referring to the local entrepreneurial ambition to make a place attractive to visitors through the exploitation and re-invention of local traditions. Touristic spectacles *can* and *do* indeed operate as fixtures, but they also contribute to an understanding of the city as less 'authentic', in the sense that spaces and events designed primarily for touristic consumption follow much of the hyper-representational logic of 'pseudo-events' (cf. Boorstin, 1961/1992), 'non-places' (Augé, 1995) and 'thirdspaces' (Soja, 1996).

This is a reminder that the thick city and the concept city must not be regarded as separate entities, but rather as two aspects of the continuous urban circulation of forms, meanings and materialities.

Urban Textures and the 'Authenticity Feel'

While there is little research on urban textures (and fixtures) in media and tourism studies, some interesting work has been carried out in urban geography, notably by Ash Amin and Nigel Thrift (2002, 2007). Their analyses also provide a necessary link to the discourse of authenticity, and to the question of how textures and fixtures contribute to the 'authenticity feel' of certain urban spaces, and certain touristic experiences. Speaking of an 'authenticity feel' is an attempt to reach beyond the commonplace debates regarding whether there *is* anything called authenticity, whether objective or not, and how *different types* of authenticity can be categorised (e.g. Wang, 1999; Cohen, 2007; Pearce, 2007). What I argue here is that most intermediary textures, since they attain a permanent, non-staged status in the city, contribute to experiences among visitors that go beyond the exclusively touristic realm. Coping with the textures of everyday urban life means escaping the tourist bubble and learning how to get around – thereby also exposing oneself to experiences that are not particularly designed for visitors.

The main objective of the works of Amin and Thrift is to re-evaluate the role of cultural factors in economic, material and administrative processes – from business making to infrastructural constructions. Through the concept of *circulation* they capture the close relationship between economy and culture in modern society, in particular how various forms of symbolic expression become significant to the accumulation of capital. In their article 'Cultural-Economy and Cities' (2007) Amin and Thrift seek to 're-imagine the urban economy [...] focusing on such influences as passion, moral values, soft knowledge, trust and cultural metaphor'. While the logic of capitalist markets and technological development are commonly (and often rightly) understood as the key forces of urban change, Amin and Thrift argue that culture is not just another force, but something that saturates all spheres of urban development. This argument corresponds to the perspective I have outlined above. Through their close attention to realms and orders that are normally taken for granted, and rarely problematised in neither economic nor cultural studies, Amin and Thrift touch upon the intermediary processes that constitute urban textures. The two following extracts show that these processes can be viewed from two distinct perspectives, corresponding to the notion of the concept city and the thick city:

> The urban – more precisely certain types of city – are being imagined as emblems of a new capitalist era. [...] Cities are coming to perform the script, to act as a particular kind of economic entity facing a particular economic inevitability, underpinned by a battery of associated investment preferences, and shifts in built-form, behavioural changes, and instituted practices, with very real and pertinent consequences flowing from this rebranding. [...] Symptomatic readings of capitalism generate symptomatic cities as the visualisation of the new, and then, as an expectation for all cities. (Amin & Thrift, 2007: 151–153)

The first extract points to how dominant ideologies ('globalism', 'informationalism' etc.) saturate urban decision-making and are concretely acted out through localised scripts – brands, regeneration projects, signature architecture etc. Ultimately, the circulation and adaptation of such scripts of 'successful urbanism' on the conceptual level lead to 'symptomatic cities', that is, what in certain theoretical contexts have been called simulated or place-less environments, aiming to fuel a place-brand with little or superficial ties to the sediments of local culture (cf. Castells, 1991; Sorkin, 1992; Augé, 1995). In other words, under such circumstances the city in-between is overlooked and potentially disrupted.

However, while the imposition of a global economic mythology may have tangible effects on urban textures and thus social life, textures themselves, and notably their strongest points of circulation, their fixtures, work as a balancing factor. Whether desired or not, these intermediary patterns are typically overlooked among strategists and decision makers, whose major concern is the direct transformation of concept into lived, thick urban experience. (Similarly, they are also overlooked in many critical academic notions of cultural annihilation or rupture, which tend to reproduce the same blindness that marks the ideologies they set out to criticise.) As the second extract shows, older and newer textural orders always co-exist, implying a multilayered cultural awareness, which among city dwellers is only slowly, and in various ways among different groups and in different areas, adjusted to new material/technologic conditions (see also Graham & Thrift, 2007). The cultural-economy of the city is dependent upon people's textural knowledge and trust, and how these taken for granted orientations may fit ongoing transformations:

> A silent architecture that regulates economic life [...] made up of many mundane objects of urban 'machinic order', including road signals, postcodes, pipes and overhead cables, satellite, office design and furniture, clocks, commuting patterns, computers and telephones. In the city, these objects are aligned and made to count through all manner of intermediaries such as rhythms of delivery or commuting, traffic-flow systems, integrated transport and logistics systems, internet protocols, rituals of civic and public conduct, family routines, and cultures of workplace or neighbourhood. This thick stratum of objects-in-relation, much of which provides the vital repair and maintenance that keeps cities going [...] can be described as a 'technological unconscious'. (Amin & Thrift, 2007: 153–154)

The impact of economic imperatives can thus not be interpreted in isolation from sedimented patterns of circulation and social interaction. Similarly, in public discourse the 'truth' of a city, its 'real meaning' or 'soul', is rarely associated with the attributes of place marketing, touristic events or high-profile regeneration projects, but rather with institutions, infrastructures, and cultural scenes that manage to link the thick city to spatial discourses in a socially meaningful and durable way. That is why, for example, the rapid transformation of a former working class area into a tidy centre for the circulation of design, media and touristic capital will necessarily involve an enduring discrepancy between many people's textural understanding and the cultural-economy of the area itself.

This does not mean that urban transitions by definition lead to the abolishment of 'authenticity'. There can be many diverging understandings of what is authentic and not. For instance, what an urban dweller might regard as an inauthentic space, alien to local history, visitors might ascribe 'symbolic authenticity', as long as it lives up to the promises of media representations (see Wang, 1999; Jansson, 2002). This is why I prefer to talk about an 'authenticity feel' that arises when visitors encounter spaces that exist beyond and relatively independent from the touristic realm.

As seen in the analyses of Amin and Thrift, urban textures and fixtures provide the preconditions for such a feel through their capacity to integrate the city and *make it work* on a day-to-day basis. Textures and fixtures provide continuity to the everyday lives of urban dwellers. They enable city people to establish routines and rituals as well as mobility and social connectivity, that is, to lead a structured life in resonance with others, at work and at home, in the streets and in the transit systems, in spite of the masses of people and unforeseen events that always co-exist. The machinic and symbolic orders that Amin and Thrift refer to cannot be rejected nor avoided, nor do they cause any trouble to the natural attitude of daily life – until something is 'out of order'. Speaking of an 'authenticity feel' in relation to textures and fixtures is to address the relationship between, on the one hand, the intersubjective layers of urban understanding – and the urban unconscious – through which urban inhabitants manage their lives, and, on the other hand, the relative lack of such more or less site specific understandings among temporary visitors. The 'authenticity feel' is thus tied to *the awareness and enactment of non-staged local textures and fixtures*, albeit these are sometimes hard to distinguish from one another.

This is also why textural analyses may inform the authenticity debate in tourism studies. As I noted in the beginning of this chapter, a common source of touristic satisfaction is the experience of having understood the codes and systems, and grasped some of the 'ordinariness' of a destination. Managing to use public transit gives more 'authenticity feel' than going on a sightseeing tour. Finding a nightclub that is part of the local jazz scene gives more 'authenticity feel' than spending one's time in the hotel lobby bar. Of course, searching for 'authenticity', getting a feel of the urban weave, may not be important among all tourists and in all forms of tourism. Nevertheless, being able to comprehend and master foreign textures and fixtures, which from the beginning may seem incomprehensible (such as a transit system or a huge shopping mall) or belonging to the urban back-stage, implies that one gets somewhat closer to the everyday life of permanent dwellers. Environments that are staged and arranged primarily for visitors (including their own 'touristic texture' (see Jansson, 2007), as well as many attention gathering urban fixtures) are much less likely to generate this particular experience.

Then, to conclude, textural awareness and enactment (whether success-ful or not) contribute to the touristic experience of authenticity in two ways: First, it is something that gives the tourist a feeling of having experienced the 'reality' of a city – *structured and non-staged ordinariness*. Secondly, it is something that gives the tourist a feeling of having experi-enced the 'reality' of travelling – *cultural and machinic friction*. While the thick city will always escape the tourist's full understanding, like a 'wandering of the semantic', and the concept city will never satisfy the tourist's desire for real life experiences, the city in-between can provide a gateway into the transformative authenticity of a *lived space*.

Note

1. My notion of the 'urban unconscious' is inspired by Amin and Thrift's (2007) description of a 'technological unconscious', referring to the taken-for-granted and largely invisible infrastructures of the city (see also quote in Section Four). The 'urban unconscious', as we will see, includes also other phenomena than technical ones.

Chapter 4

'The Summer We All Went to Keuruu': Intensity and the Topographication of Identity

NIELS KAYSER NIELSEN

Introduction

In the 1990s, geography, just like other research areas, took a cultural turn, which implied that geography became occupied not only with physical and palpable spaces, like the forest or the city, but also with imagined geographies such as symbolic and mediated spaces. Literature, film, TV, art, postcards, stamps, music, and so on, became relevant topics to study. It was even possible to make maps of meanings to look at the distributions of meaning and even emotions in space (Gren & Hallin, 2003: 174). However, around the turn of the millennium this cultural turn began to be criticised in the fields of history, cultural studies (Frykman & Gilje, 2003: 22) and geography. A common point of critique was that it was too reductive to define culture, and geography, as entirely systemic, symbolic or linguistic (Bonnell & Hunt, 1999: 26). Instead, the focus was on practice and embodiment, as can be seen, for instance, in the anthology edited by Victoria Bonnell and Lynn Hunt entitled *Beyond the Cultural Turn*. One of the points made in this book is that whereas the body has drawn a great deal of attention – a large number of books were written on the construction of the body in the 1990s, not least in the UK – the cultural turn produced relatively few investigations of the self. The self was reduced to an entirely constructed and therefore empty and plastic nodal point (Bonnell & Hunt, 1999: 22), just as the visceral part of the body was totally neglected (Kayser Nielsen, 1997).

So, today we are witnessing a topographical turn instead, in particular in ethnology and anthropology (Hastrup, 2005: 143); this topographical turn implicates investigations into the materialism and meaning of space; also included is often an interest in describing and analysing concrete places – *topoi* (Kayser Nielsen, 2005). There is a renewed interest in the actions, practice and environment in which identities function, including a turn from how identities are constructed towards how they are experienced from 'within' and what 'within' really means (Frykman & Gilje, 2003: 9). And what does 'meaning' actually mean? Instead of dealing with a reflexive attitude concerning the meaning of space and place, it might be more relevant to speculate about how bodily grounded images, fancies and dreams precede thought, logic and language (Frykman & Gilje, 2003: 37).

Concomitantly, this chapter, inspired by theories of phenomenology and bodily experiences, focuses on tourism as an embodied practice by where the body – endowed with textual and linguistic schemata and pictures – appropriates landscape. Due to its historical branding as a 'nation of landscape', Finland is chosen as a case in order to show how an embodied tourism is able to create experiences of intensity and a multi-layered identity which a holiday in a great city can hardly promote or deliver. Tourists, it is argued, carry narratives in their minds when travelling to their chosen destination, but it is the body which vitalise these narratives in a subtle interference between an 'absent' body that only lives, so to speak, and the awareness – contextualised by narratives – of bodily activity (Selberg, 2007; Hoem, 2007).

As concerns methodology the article will make use of written material and own as well as others bodily experiences of being a tourist in Finland. The combination of written narratives and phenomenology is essential in so far, it is further argued, that while texts necessarily are bodiless abstractions and bodily practice is 'out of language', the hybrid of narratives and bodily practices is the precondition for making conscious experiences, i.e. embodied imagined practice.

Body and Emotion

In my (admittedly selective) point of view, emotion has to do with being embodied. This means that emotions, needs, desires, affect, and so on, well up from a corporeal self which also consists of a visceral body. Our relations to other persons and to nature are based on our mutuality and face-to-face relations through gazing and touching – or, if writing, the movement of our fingers and shoulders; if reading, by means of our eyes and spine. Our resonance of feeling and perspective cannot but be connected with our final and embodied state of being.

But what does this mean? In order to answer this question, we may turn to one of the books of the Chinese-American geographer Yi-Fu Tuan:

his autobiography *Who am I?*, in which he tells an interesting story from his childhood:

> When we were children and lived in Chongqing, we played soccer whenever we could. We made a ball of sorts by tying together a bundle of cloth. One day, Father gave us a genuine leather soccer ball. We were ecstatic: we played with it, ate with it, slept with it. The disadvantage, from my point of view, was that it was hard. I didn't want it to smash into my chest or face. I was more than a little afraid of it. (Tuan, 1999: 71)

The main point is, of course, that the symbolic value of the ball does not compare with the physicality of the body in its facticity.

However, emotions are of course always combined with matrixes and inherited visual representations – in short, 'pictures', produced in a context of more or less mediated experiences, including a certain symbolically orientated reduction. However, these inherited, mediated 'pictures' are never outside our body like a ghost walking beside us. They are also embodied. Our arms and legs, belly and hands are full of memories of pain and pleasure and other emotions. In other words, our body knows, but always tacitly and silently. Normally the body does not even tell us that it knows. But still, emotions are grounded in the body and filtered through the body's capacity for knowing – for instance, the knowing of emotions. This goes without saying for both hip hoppers in Norway and farmers in Sicily.

My point of departure is in other words phenomenological. This implies that the body is seen not only as an object in the world – in German, a *Körper* or a Cartesean *res extensa* – but also as a German *Leib*, i.e. a lived body, and the very medium whereby our world comes into being: a Cartesean *res cogitans* (Leder, 1990: 5). It is intrinsic to lived embodiment to be both subject and external object available to an external gaze, but the distribution of these two bodily aspects depends on the situation. Sometimes we are able to forget our body; at other times it is impossible. Normally most of our body is out of mental reach: we do not recognise, say, our combustion and digestion or our breathing, just as we cannot see ourselves seeing, touch ourselves touching or hear ourselves hearing. But in certain circumstances parts of our body can be brought in the foreground – through pain or pleasure.

On such occasions, perhaps especially when in pain, we are tempted to use our language and call for help; we cry out 'it hurts'. This is, however, not a piece of factual information, but rather means 'come and help me' and refers back to our body's intentionality and outward-directedness.

In a seminal article concerning this symbiosis, Hans Peter Dreitzel has pointed to the fact that unlike a purely symbolic system such as mathematics, in our daily language words are always accompanied by a certain bodily activity. Our language, or rather our words, is context dependent. This means that in order to keep communication going, the words we listen to and speak are always 'open', partly vague and ambiguous. We use the whole context, not only the words, but also gestures, carriage, voice (the connection between 'Stimme' und 'Stimmung' in German is noteworthy). We use bodily activity to both regulate and illustrate (Dreitzel, 1983). This results in neither a frozen objectification of the message nor a complete and total assumption or adoption, but rather a state of 'movement' or, as Hans-Georg Gadamer would say: a situation of 'understanding'. This understanding is due to the fact that perception and communication overlap and intertwine (Crossley, 1997: 26).

Body and Tourism

It is our lived body *in toto*, not the intellect, that first perceives objects and knows its way around a room or a street. However, there is a risk of becoming too phenomenological and paying too much attention to these sensomotoric abilities and capacities and neglecting 'higher' forms of cognition. In my view, one of the best solutions to this problem is provided by Pierre Bourdieu's concept of habitus, which refers not only to the layering in our body of certain experiences, but also and much more importantly, the body's intuitive preferences and selections, i.e. a basic form of knowing and cognition by means of difference.

Normally we do not pay much attention to our body. It seems to be a crucial part of being embodied that we do not always need to pay attention to our body and to the actions of its different parts. When writing this paper I do not decide to use my fingers – they just move. They are in a state of what the American philosopher Drew Leder calls 'bodily absence', as is our liver and feet. But in spite of that fact, or rather, just because it is a normal thing I am doing, a habit, it is out of focus and unattended. In such a situation my body is *Leib* more than *Körper*.

But we are not always writing and located in habitual situations in which our body is absent and in a state of focal disappearance. It happens now and then that we find ourselves in situations where the body is attended to and in focal appearance – for example, when we are ill or if we learn a new dance. One of the main treats of the highly popular TV broadcasts showing non-professional dancers' difficulties learning how to dance is seeing the tension between dance as a habit and dance as a way of using our body reflexively and in an attended manner. We feel pity or laugh when we see the poor devil paying too much attention to the dance steps.

Another such situation is tourism. Not every kind of tourism; but the more bodily orientated kind. By tourism I mean unique experiences and newness. Tourism is like fashion in the sense that Walter Benjamin dealt with fashion – i.e. tourism, like fashion, has death in it. Once fashion becomes popular and is repeated and standardised it is not fashion any more. Fashion is volatile and is the opposite of habits, as is tourism. As soon as we have visited the same place several times, we are not tourists any more, but only strangers more or less familiar with the place. We cannot be surprised any more and run the risk of getting bored, whereas as real tourists we get surprised – or rather, our body is not on safe ground. But what does this mean? Is it a quality or a danger – or something in between?

Material

Most of my empirical material is from Finland, which is a bit odd as there are places in Finland where I am not a tourist anymore, but an anonymous stranger also very familiar with the surroundings. I simply know these places too well. However, I will draw examples only from those parts of Finland where I would definitely be a tourist if I went there. The majority of my material consists of tourist brochures and books for tourists, mostly versions written in English and Swedish. Some of the material goes back to the middle of the 1990s, when I was doing research on the representation of Finland; other parts of it date from the summer of 2006. The material is chosen in order to focus on the peculiarities of Finland's way of branding itself as a 'country of landscape where nature invites you to making bodily experiences, guided by narrated models of imagery'.

National Awakening and Landscape

In contrast to the old nation-states, Finland, as a young nation-state, has always had difficulty knowing how to sell itself as a tourist destination. Finland had to sell itself as nature rather than history because it was far too influenced by Sweden and Russia. The real and authentic Finland was in the countryside – in the outlying fields (Palin, 1999). Tourism in Finland was thus equal to nature tourism. If it was a matter of visiting royal palaces, medieval towns or 18th-century civil culture, there were other places in Europe where it was more obvious to go as a tourist. But if one wished to see unspoiled wilderness and authentic national culture – flanked by something as healthy and authentic as a sauna – Finland was the obvious choice.

The promotion of the Finnish forest and lake culture and of the national costumes and wilderness as the incarnation of Finnishness is radically distinct from Kölner Dom, Hermansdenkmal and Sans Souci in Potsdam. The people and the landscape are far more in focus in Finland.

Representation by landscape and nature representation has always played an important role in Finland, encouraging primarily 'lay geography' and the use of the senses; not only the sense of sight but also the senses of smell, touch and hearing, i.e. the senses facilitating the intimacy between subject and object and reducing the aspect of cognitive meaning (Urry, 1999). As has been said by David Crouch about leisure in general, 'it would seem that leisure space is not practised merely semiotically' (Crouch, 1999: 258). Besides, it seems, such practice has to do with 'a desire to know what cannot be seen', but rather be felt 'with both feet' (Crouch, 1999: 258), i.e. our bodily interaction with our surroundings. We will see examples of this in the following.

The Tourist Trade's Representation of Finland

We must distinguish between major and minor tourist spots. To the former belong, in part, the official ones such as national galleries, castles, the capital city, and specific wilderness areas that have been proclaimed as particularly national. To the latter belong the provincial towns, landscapes, cultural events and institutions that are 'typical' and common – ordinary. They do not consist of localities that one 'must' see, but are focused on the self-representation supplied by any small town with respect for itself and its visitors.

Let us start with something in between: the presentation of Finland in the Silja Lines catalogue from 1990, which the boat tourists travelling between Stockholm and Helsinki were given on the ferries sailing between the two capitals. This catalogue presents the Swedish painter Carl Larsson from the turn of the century, a popular Swedish novelist, ballet in Finland, fashion and jewellery, and the many high-brow summer festivals held at various places in Finland. The texts are written in either Swedish or Finnish. Besides the advertisement for Silja Line itself, the only article that is written in both Swedish and Finnish is about Finnish wildlife; entitled 'The Exoticism of Fresh Air', it is accompanied by pictures of a solitary man fishing in a forest lake, a forest-bordered river, and a characteristic Finnish town with the typical red or white wooden houses and hay barns in the middle of a field. The approach is established: 'In our marketing we have concentrated on the main message that truly unspoiled nature only exists in Finland', states Peter Doll, head of the Silja Lines office in Lübeck. Finland is primarily equal to nature – but not only.

Let us take a look at a couple of the 'great' venues, or national landscape icons, one of which is Aulanko, in Tavastland in central Finland. In a Finnish national travel guide to Aulanko, besides relating the history of the establishment of Aulanko as a national park, it says that it is possible to play tennis and golf here, as well as to ride horses, row, and water ski – and fish (Mäkinen, 1988: 32). Thanks to the many paths, it is also well suited for hiking. Today the place not only insists on being seen, but also on physical activity. The newest leaflet informs visitors that they may 'walk, jog and ski freely' as well as cycle on gravel roads and pick wild mushrooms and berries.

This also holds true for tourism in the archipelago on the west coast. But on the island of Replot the visitors are told that the area is stony and the surface uneven, so it is important to bring solid boots or rubber boots. In wet places there are small wooden bridges, but they might be slippery – and then there are the mosquitoes. It is a good idea to bring the right outfit. This almost appears to be an invitation to non-normal bodily experiences. Here we cannot trust our normal bodily unawareness; instead we run the risk of feeling that we are not just a body, but also have a body. We had better watch out and be reflexive while enjoying nature – in order to enjoy it even more.

Another one of the major tourist attractions is Mt Koli in northern Karelia, in eastern Finland. This 347-metre-high mountain offers a splendid view over Lake Pielinen, which has been painted by several Finnish artists, in particular Eero Järnefelt, whose painting from 1899 is perhaps the most famous of them all. In the introduction to a brochure from the tourist office of the closest town, Lieksa, it is emphasised that the second largest open-air museum is located here, as well as the largest forestry museum in Finland. The text continues, 'The exhibition halls display the life of ordinary people from the late 19th and early 20th centuries, as well as the life of the gentry in Lieksa and Pielisjärvi' – a typical priority in a country of farmers and lumberjacks. Most of the brochure concentrates on presenting Mt. Koli and the view of the lake:

> Koli has been a renowned holiday destination for over 100 years, attracting visitors all year round. Picturesque scenery, good company and relaxation are the ingredients for a memorable holiday. Here you can hike, camp and do whatever you enjoy most.

The extraordinarily beautiful scenery – 'picturesque' – is obviously not enough. It has to be viewed while moving about in the countryside. Nature means activity, not just contemplation and aesthetic reflection. Furthermore, the text says that since 1994 the tourists have been able to witness burn-beating, a means of cultivation that became obsolete around the year 1900 but that has recently been resumed. Instead of referring to history as impressive buildings or glorious pictures of generals or admirals, it is presented as the hard work of humble people in and with their natural surroundings in order to improve their living conditions. But, once again, history is presented not only as a matter of presenting and reconstructing the past, but also of bodily experiences and appropriating history by means of sensual activities. The text informs us that the lumberjacks' paths and ski tracks through the forest 'have now served nature-lovers for decades. Services for hikers have been improved and the network of trails expanded since the National Park was established'. Furthermore, it says that there are twelve campsites in the area, each of which is provided with benches, a spring/well and an outdoor toilet. All bodily needs are taken care of. Visiting Mt Koli is first and foremost a question of the body, a matter of accepting the invitation to be embodied.

This self-representation is not exceptional; the same is true of less distinct and famous parts of Finland with less spectacular national icons. In a brochure on going on a 'blue and white holiday' – with reference to Finland's flag – in the regions around Hämeenlinna, Tampere and Jyväskylä, it says that going on holiday in Finland 'is tasted, smelled, heard and affects'. Certainly the scene is laid for a most sensual holiday.

In Kuhmo, in eastern Finland, all of this exists in a concentrated form. In a beautiful tourist brochure made out of rough paper, so that the reader can touch the wood in it, it is reported that in 'Kuhmo culture is dressed in IT-shirts' – with a clear reference to the world-famous production of IT in Finland. In addition, it states that there are 5555 cars in Kuhmo, 5627 telephones, 4421 television receivers and, perhaps, 5558 chair sleds. To emphasise the proximity of nature there are photos of saw blades, wood-chips and wood waste, the forest itself – all of this under the heading 'In Kuhmo there is work for the axe'. The last section is entitled 'the population of Kuhmo may be lazier than average', and is accompanied by drawings of bears, wolves and reindeer along with a photo of a hunter who has shot a grouse and is now enjoying a cup of tea in the wilderness.

Summer life in Finland is characterised by activities where the best of the best is offered – for the Finns themselves and for the tourists. The outdoor dance floors are not far apart – for bodily pleasures and for representing themselves and Finland. As it states in an essay by Merja Saarnio (1994) in an issue of Finnair's magazine *Blue Wings*:

> An outdoor dance floor is something very Finnish, organically linked with the fleeting beauty of summer and the nights when darkness never really falls. Year after year, the Finns commune silently with the nature that surrounds them. Every week must be lived to the full, and it is as though summer gives permission to relax and take it easier. The long, cold winter lies behind, it is time for warmth and lighter clothes.

But enjoying the Finnish summer is not only associated with contemplative and reflexive abandon, rather it is linked to dancing, entertainment and activity. Rather than sitting still and enjoying, one moves and takes part. Part of the dance repertoire consists of tango. Finnish tango is not as dramatic in its gestures as Argentinean tango, nor is it tied up with any particular machismo. But it is just as melancholic. In the texts, one tragic love story after another is played out – often focusing on people situated in natural surroundings, where the sea in particular is important. As Koivusalo remarks about the tango lyrics, 'the sea has a special significance, symbolising a longing for something better and more beautiful'. In this way they differ from, say, the lyrics of the waltzes, in which life triumphs and love overcomes all obstacles.

Bodily Attention and Non-attention

But how are we to analyse all this information with the evident references to bodily experiences and challenges? One possibility is to look at them from a phenomenological point of view. Normally, our body, based upon what Husserl has described as a *Nullpunkt*, which might also be called the 'almighty' and absolute embodied point of departure, interacts with the outer world without difficulty and without reflexive awareness. We just act. We experience from our body and outwardly. This means that from where we stand in space we are directed towards the outer world; but nevertheless we still have our 'standing in the world', i.e. our 'stasis', as a precondition and a base. Otherwise we would be but a mind or a free flowing spirit. This implies as a point of departure a physical telos, which, though, is directed away from one's 'stasis' and corporeal base. So, this 'stasis'-state normally happens without acknowledging this 'stasis'. We are more absorbed with the surroundings and with our occupation with them. In such situations we are in a state that Heidegger has coined as 'ex-stasis', based on a state of 'stasis'.

The reason is that the 'stasis' normally is accompanied by an attentional telos directed outwardly at objects outside ourselves, which implies that our body is rendered subsidiary. Our actions are motivated by concerns situated outside ourselves. As Paul Ricoeur writes, 'actually, when I act I am not concerned with my body. I say rather that the actions traverse my body ... I am concerned less with my body than with the product of the action: the hanged picture ...' (Leder, 1990: 18ff).

In such situations the body is absent and is being used as what Drew Leder calls an 'unthematised substratum' upon which the world acts. Normally this is the case in habitual situations and in circumstances where we do not need to care much about your body: 'Though I may concentrate on the rhythms of walking, most of the physiology of the act remains resolutely hidden from my awareness' (Leder, 1990: 19). The body and concomitantly the mind are at ease. This is due to the body's third telos, the functional telos, implying that the body 'can', that it works without our attentional awareness. We rely on a set of abilities that we need not fully thematise. In such situations the body is absent and beyond our awareness. We do not care about it; it is simply there, functioning as a means for our aims and whims. In such situations we are absorbed by our actions in ex-stasis. We are out in nature or in dialogues with friends and colleagues. Our body disappears.

As tourists when we are absorbed by our surroundings, this is normally a sign of a good holiday. We are able to neglect our body and feel comfortable. But, unfortunately, this kind of tourism does not differ very much from everyday life, in which we also forget our body in different kinds of attentional and functional telos. While this kind of holiday is good, it lacks something. Just lying on a beach in Thailand and relaxing is like sitting in a deck chair on a boat or in an armchair at home. The body is not interpellated.

In Finland, many things are different. Of course, there are museums and an overwhelmingly amount of outdoor cafés in Helsinki. But just as in other capitals, like Paris, the chairs are placed in rows from which we can gaze at the pedestrian outside the outdoor cafe and notice that we ourselves are gazed upon. Suddenly we realise that we are a body being looked at, a body as object while at the same time a lived body, mingling with the outside, flirting perhaps. We are gazed at and have the opportunity for bodily awareness. This is different from resting in a deck chair at home in the garden. We behave just like Sartre's famous character who gets caught while looking through a keyhole, peeping into a room (Leder, 1990: 93). But unlike Sartre's Peeping Tom, who gets ashamed, this happens in pleasure and joy. We both see and are seen. We do not just gaze, but are aware of it – the result of which is intensity.

But this does not sell in itself Finland. It could happen at several other places. We never see tourist brochures about this phenomenon in the Tourist Hall in downtown Helsinki. Instead we are interpellated to use Finland as geography, to move and act and experience Finland by means of knowing by doing. In this way Finland is seen as a dead place that needs to be revived, by means of the body more than the mind, which implies bodily involvement.

In the first place this means that we are invited to move out into nature in order to get in a state of ex-stasis and to forget our body. First, this happens by the overwhelmingly number of invitations to experience nature and forget ourselves through our absorption in nature. More than in any other part in Europe, except perhaps for Switzerland and Norway, we are invited to go out in nature, to use it and make our body disappear through our bodily presence.

But in the next place we are also confronted with the possibility that nature is so strong that we will move out of our state of 'ex-stasis' with its bodily absence and intentionality towards things outside ourselves and return to a bodily awareness with focus at our 'being in the world' as bodies. We are, so to speak, invited to forget our forgetting and un-awareness of our body. Allow me to illustrate.

The Summer We All Went to Keuruu

In one of the brochures we see what appears to be a normal, cosy family holiday with people relaxing and doing things without attending to their body. Daddy is very active, behaving as a dad should by being absorbed with his boat and the sea; Mum is on the beach taking care of the little ones. The scene is all familiar. The family is totally absorbed with the surroundings and seems to have forgotten their bodies. They are all in a state of 'ex-stasis'. But, alas, in the next picture in the brochure you can see that something has happened: Daddy has got blisters!

He is no longer in an unattended, relaxed bodily situation in which the body disappears. His body is now in a state of dys-appearance. It hurts. Drew Leder tells us that this dys-appearance, which includes a bodily awareness, normally happens when the body is in dire straits and delicate predicaments – situations like birth, pregnancy, illness and physical danger. In such situations the tacid and silent thematisation of the body in a 'from' position and in its ecstatic projectivity is disrupted (Leder, 1990: 85). In such situations we are called to reflect back upon our bodily state. These perceptual as well as motoric difficulties may stimulate self-consciousness and bodily acknowledgement. Self-consciousness seems to arise at times when our 'ex-stasis' is disturbed, causing our attention to turn back upon our body (Leder, 1990: 87). It seems to happen when we are not any longer apart in a state of bodily 'absence', but in a state of bodily awareness and reflexivity. Some researchers have argued that the pain to which the body is exposed may be seen as a way to create a subject in the Foucauldian meaning of the word (Frykman, 1998: 15), where the torments act as a well of emotional differentiations and even as a cultural resource (Hydén, 1998: 49).

Leder points out other situations in which the attentional telos, the 'ex-stasis', and the bodily disappearance are not out of place (Leder, 1990: 91). To my mind, this is true of a lot of extraordinary situations in which the body is not taken for granted, but is precisely present as-remembered. In such cases where the body is dys-functional, attention turns back upon the body. The self can now take note of the body, acknowledging being both a lived body and a body as object. We may call it reflexive sentimentalisation of the body or a constructed intensification, referring to a situation in which the body at one and the same time moves around in a body-forgetting 'flow' and is aware of this. The result of this a permanent moving in and out of a 'comfort zone' exacerbating the knowledge and acknowledge of the scenery as a whole.

In his studies of allotments and caravanning in the UK, David Crouch has pointed out the fact that people occupied with such activities do not give priority to nature as such as part of what they do, but rather use it as a sensual backdrop for other events such as socialising with their leisure-time neighbours (Crouch, 1999: 264). Jane Zavisca, in her studies of the use of dachas in the city of Kaluga in Russia, has made a similar point:

> The dacha would be more profitable, if we didn't bring along so much sausage, cheese and vodka. Because you can't show up empty-handed; the neighbours will drop by, and everybody brings some-thing ... We wouldn't let ourselves do that at home. (Zavisca, 2003: 801)

Such events are very often about being someone else while still being oneself. In their allotments and caravan sites, these people feel at home, but not in the humdrum meaning of the word, which connotes repetitive and habitual activities where the body is un-attended, but rather in an attended way, combining, or perhaps rather contrasting, different possibilities of the self, embodied and social. People let themselves do things which they would not allow themselves to experience at home.

Such changes are very often concomitant with changes in space. Space becomes important in an imaginative realisation of the self, but still this self is both imagined and felt in doing (Crouch, 1999: 271). It could be called an embodied imaginative practice. This is just what we see in the pictures from Keuruu: Mikko, the son, is a bit scared because of the devil, i.e. a bit out of order.

Intensity and the Topographication of Identity

This dys-appearance happens especially in situations where embodiment radically diverges from the habitual. Is this one of the reasons why a new kind of tourism in general and bodily orientated tourism in particular are on the agenda these days: that what we are apt to call adventure economy is increasingly in demand? If so, the reason might be that it implies an intensity insofar as the body is in a both attended and un-attended state. We first move into a state of 'ex-stasis' and allow our bodies to be absent and non-thematised, based on a base of bodily 'stasis', but next – due to extraordinary circumstances – we are then turned back upon our bodily 'stasis', but now with attention on the 'being in the world' as a body. On the one hand, we just relax without paying much attention to our body; on the other hand, we are moved back to our body with awareness. Such intensification seems more and more relevant to tourism, but perhaps not only for tourists, but also for normal people in normal situations whenever a kick is needed.

It is thus not only a question of Finland and Keuruu; Keuruu with Daddy's blisters could be anywhere. It is a typical example of the new desire for a topographication of identity with bodies experiencing different forms of embodiment in different places. Instead of pain it seems more appropriate to talk about a situative identity caused by the ability of landscape and place to promote emotions through the body and its experiences of intensity. This touristic topographification is certainly volatile and ephemeral in a situation that does not last but for a short period, as tourism normally does, but it implies a greater scope of mind and a diversification that appears attractive. It looks like we all want to go and experience a landscape like that of Keuruu – as something nice to look at but also as a place that challenges us as bodies.

SECTION TWO
BRANDING AND MATERIALISING AUTHENTICITY

Chapter 5

Authenticity and Place Branding: The Arts and Culture in Branding Berlin and Singapore

CAN-SENG OOI AND BIRGIT STÖBER

Introduction

The Economist business magazine has a city 'liveability' ranking (*The Economist*, 2007). Relatively smaller cities, like Vancouver, Melbourne and Vienna are ranked the highest. Besides recreational and cultural activities, other factors such as crime rate, threat from instability and terrorism, healthcare and education availability, state of transport and communications infrastructure are included in this ranking. Big cities such as Paris, London and New York are not ranked highly because they face problems such as traffic congestion, higher crime rates and are also targets for high-profile terror attacks. Anholt and his city branding consultancy, on the other hand, ranks Paris, London and New York highly because of these cities' vitality, their people and facilities (Anholt, 2006). Florida (2003) offers yet another way of ranking cities through his Creativity Index. Florida focuses on three different criteria: technology, talent and tolerance. Urban places are ranked on the number of patents per head, the density of the population of 'bohemians' and gay people, the proportion of immigrants and the number of so called 'knowledge-workers' (Florida, 2003; Peck, 2005).

The ranking of cities has not only raised awareness that cities compete, but this also encourages cities to attempt to actively manage their image. This chapter compares the branding strategies of Berlin and Singapore. The respective authorities in these cities are actively marketing, branding and transforming their metropolises, so that these locations will be perceived as culturally vibrant, technologically advanced and attractive for investors, tourists and skilled workers. While Berlin and Singapore share the same goals, they also have similar problems – how can they convince a world that is critical and cynical about the commercial images presented through their place brands? How can they convince the world that their cities are really exciting and truly creative? Before going into the cases, this chapter will explain why the arts and culture – both popular and 'high' – are used in place branding, following which the discussion shifts to the problem of authenticity in place branding. An analysis on the concept of authenticity based on lessons learned from Berlin and Singapore will follow the two cases. Alternative ways of thinking about authenticity in place branding will draw the chapter to a close.

The Arts and Culture in Place Branding

A comprehensive place branding campaign usually entails three related tracks. The first branding track entails using professional place branding consultants, on behalf of municipalities, government ministries and/or tourist organisations, to package and promote a comprehensive brand image that tells a powerful brand story, so that outsiders can understand the place in a positive light.

The second branding track is based on the creation of high profile icons, such as hosting internationally popular sporting events or celebrating iconic features. Barcelona and Sydney are successful in associating them-selves with their Olympic Games. The Eiffel Tower and the Pyramids are iconic sights. These icons focus people's mind and promote the associated places. Places are increasingly being marketed and branded via new and spectacular icons.

The third track is to brand the place through endorsements and recognitions from other authorities. The above-mentioned rankings of cities inadvertently endorse some cities. UNESCO heritage sites accentuate the historical and cultural values of selected places. Similarly, the very presence of major banks in London and New York inevitably endorses these cities as global financial centers.

Regardless of the tracks used, the branding of cities and countries, increasingly, incorporate the arts and culture into the brand stories. There are several reasons why the arts and culture are used in place brand-ing. The first reason is that the arts and culture offer special messages for the place. History, heritage and popular cultural life are often unique to the place because of their intertwining historical, contemporary, social and geographical circumstances. Uniqueness in the place brand is essential in making the place stand out in the competition – arts, culture and heritage serve that function well in most instances.

The second reason is that most place branding messages want to present a humane, though selectively packaged, picture of the place.

For instance, Germany is well known for its technological products but in its new branding launched before and during the football World Cup 2006, the main place branding authority FC Deutschland GmbH told the world that Germany is also a people-oriented country. They wrapped a naked Claudia Schiffer with the German flag (Land of Ideas, 2006). The image portrayed a less than respectful attitude towards a national symbol, the German flag. Claudia Schiffer, as a pop icon and famous supermodel, was explicitly associated to Germany, thus challenging the dowdy image Germany may have.

The third reason why the arts and culture are used in place branding is that performances, exhibitions and various art and cultural activities communicate vibrancy, excitement and happening. A dull place is less likely to attract tourists, talented workers and investors.

The fourth reason is that residents want to perceive their places as spaces for the arts, culture and life. Place branding is not just about communicating with the outside world, it is also an internal search for a local identity. Branding authorities inadvertently encourage residents to imagine their own society through the promoted brand stories (Ooi, 2004a).

While the arts and culture are accentuated in almost all place branding exercises, do the brand stories really reflect the place? This is an issue of authenticity. How do branding authorities convince residents, foreigners and tourists – that their stories are 'real'?

Inherent Authenticity Challenges in Place Branding

Although a place brand will tap into the arts and culture to support the image of excitement, the issue of authenticity of the brand still surfaces: does the brand describe the place accurately? Is the brand just a ploy to seduce investments, tourists and foreign workers? There is a difference between the place and presented images of the place. Authenticity is an inherent issue in place branding. Branding authorities often present the place brand as the identity of the location, this means that the brand story should accurately reflect the place's culture (Kavaratzis & Ashworth, 2005). This is difficult, if not impossible, for three interrelated reasons.

Firstly, a place brand cannot provide a complete and honest story of the place. Because place brands, like brands for other products, tell stories, sell emotions and stimulate the imagination. Places are branded to attract tourists, talented foreign workers, investments and businesses (Lund-Hansen *et al.*, 2001). For a place brand to achieve its commercial and image modification goals, it packages the society and presents only nice parts of the location. For instance, Denmark is promoted as modern and trendy, a creative country at the fore-front of technological break-throughs. Marginalised are the social problems such as gang wars, drug abuse and racism (Ooi, 2004a). So, just as cities can be measured and ranked in different ways (e.g. *The Economist*'s ranking differs from Anholt's), place brands are inevitably selectively framed to seduce different markets.

Secondly, the place branding campaign may eventually destroy the original spirit of the place. Besides selecting brand images that make commercial sense, the place brand may also lead to 'commodification' of life in the community. Events, activities and locations may be promoted as brand icons. Popular local places may become expatriates' and tourists' haunts; the social make-up of the place would change and may lose its local appeal. In other words, brand icons may lose their authenticity because they have become popular and have been transformed into objects that no longer relate to the wider local society.

Thirdly, a place brand is also normative; it can function as a vision that transforms the location. Activities and attractions are created to support the brand. In tourism research, MacCannell observes that not only does 'commodification' and touristification destroy the 'authenticity: corruption' of local cultural products and human relations, but a surrogate, covert 'staged' authenticity ('authenticity:as staged') emerges (MacCannell, 1976). Cultural products are invented and re-invented, and eventually staged as authentic for visitors who may not be aware of alternative conceptions of a location.

In sum, the issue of authenticity arises because of the fear of forgery and fabrication – 'fabricated' when the consumption of culture is increasingly appropriated for economic purposes (Richards, 1996). The higher purposes and values of culture will then succumb to the logic of the production process and the market (Featherstone, 1991; Watson & Kopachevsky, 1994) – 'Kopachevsky'. The place brand may then lack evidence and local support. The place brand may also eventually transform the local society and thus change the relationships that local people have with their own location (Ooi, 2005).

Branding authorities are aware of these concerns. If the brand is not considered authentic, then the messages will not be accepted and the campaign is a failure. The global country branding consultancy Future-Brand, for instance, highlights that authenticity is a key branding component because people demand it (FutureBrand, 2007). The branding authorities of the cities of Berlin and Singapore are no different. How these cities brand and maintain the authenticity of their brand stories will be discussed next. After the presentation of the cases, this paper will re-visit the idea of authenticity and argue that the concept has to be contextualised.

Brand Berlin

Berlin is both Germany's capital and one of the country's 16 federal states (*Länder*). In the German system, policies related to culture, education and science are under the jurisdiction of the federal state. There is thus no national German cultural policy but instead, a policy framework that is open to different interpretations and actions by the 16 German federal states. Berlin, however as a capital city and also a federal state, has attracted the attention of both the local and national governments. Many German cities want to be more culturally vibrant, and scholars such as Gorning and Häussermann view Berlin as the most liberal and diverse in the country (Gorning & Häussermann, 1998).

The image of Berlin has evolved over the years (Cochrane & Jonas, 1999). In the last hundred years, Berlin's image changed from a glamorous and wicked city in the 1920s to the power centre of Nazi Germany. And during the Cold War, Berlin was seen as a devastated and divided city par excellence (see Stöber, 2008). With the fall of the Berlin Wall in 1989, Berlin's situation changed drastically, not only politically but also economically, socially and culturally. While the Western part of the city lost the financial support previously granted to it by the West German government to retain firms, East Berlin lost its special trade relations with Eastern Europe and its state-subsidies for manufacturing production (Häussermann & Colomb, 2003). The initial euphoria after reunification was coupled with high expectations of economic growth and expansion but the excitement was short-lived (Gorning & Häussermann, 1998). The city lost a large number of traditional industries, which led to an enormous increase in unemployment (Krätke, 2004). The image of Berlin was fast becoming that of a down-trodden, rust-belt city. The city authorities deployed a new plan to revamp the city economically. Berlin is to move away from the sunset industries and into the service and cultural industries. The city has embarked on a programme to reclaim its lost roots and cultural role in Germany and Europe. Such a strategy requires a new image modification programme of convincing Germans and the world that Berlin is again a cultural centre. This process is ongoing. The art market, music, publishing and journalism, film and TV, architecture, advertising and software developing sectors are currently generating around twenty percent of Berlin's gross domestic product (Berlin, 2007).

Today, Berlin is a city that is winning the world over through its promoted images of trendiness and effervescence. As a result, for example, a high number of foreign artists are moving to the city (Andreasen, 2005). The road to its current status has not been smooth; resources were and are used to rebuild the city into its current glory. Branding the city is part of this city's rebuilding strategy. Today, Berlin is being branded as 'Berlin – City of Change' by the private-public setup, Berlin Partner. This organisation is also the *de facto* branding authority of the city with a branding strategy that focuses exclusively on the contemporary aspects of the city. The then-marketing manager Joachim Grupp confirmed (personal communication with Birgit Stöber, 2004):

> We are not a historical organisation. [...] Primarily, we are interested in the development after 1989 and the potentials developed from that. [...] Our job is to ensure the positive impulses are underlined and visualised. The communication of advantages is our job. Disadvantages are known enough through the press.

Knowing that people are often critical and cynical of marketed images, Berlin Partner tries to make the promoted brand story believable and plausible. There are two related authenticity-enhancing strategies used to validate and strengthen Berlin's brand messages. The first strategy is to show that Berlin is indeed a culturally exciting city. The city re-claims and promotes existing cultural icons and is producing new ones. For example, *Reichstagsgebäude* – Parliament House – with its dome designed by Norman Foster has become an icon of the city (see Figure 5.1). The City Mayor of Berlin, Claus Wowereit, has become an iconic personality, a celebrity representing a tolerant and energetic Berlin. He came into office in 2001 by declaring: 'I'm gay and that's a good thing!' (Crossland, 2006). These icons and memorable instances allude to a truly exciting Berlin. The second way that the branding authorities are strengthening the message of Berlin as an authentic art and cultural city is by boasting of the city's many international recognitions. For example, UNESCO awarded Berlin the title of 'City of Design' in January 2006; it is the first city to be awarded in continental Europe. Today, the UNESCO logo is conspicuously used in city marketing by Berlin Partner. Such independent endorsements are useful in ascertaining the authenticity of the brand stories. On endorsements from the music industry, Universal Music moved to Berlin in 2002, which also let to MTV Deutschland moving from

Figure 5.1 Berlin city images

Munich to Berlin. In the same year, Popkomm, an international fair for the music and entertainment industry founded in Köln, also moved to Berlin. These events built up the city's creative image (see Lange *et al.*, 2008: 536). In this context, Berlin Partners asked MTV Deutschland's CEO Catherine Mühlemann to participate in an image campaign to promote the Creative Capital City. The campaign aimed not only at promoting the city, but also at highlighting the settlement of MTV in Berlin. This testimonial campaign, which started in 2001, was promoted through various media, including *Time, Business Week, Newsweek* and *Der Spiegel.* Prominent Berlin entrepreneurs vouched for Berlin as 'a major capital city and decision-making centre as well as a strategic location for young and creative industries' (Berlin Partner, 2008). Such positive messages affirm the authenticity of Berlin as a creative cultural city.

Berlin Partner wants to showcase the city's creativity internationally; the brand therefore focuses, among others, on contemporary art, music and fashion (Berlin Partner, 2007). While the Berlin place branding strategy is closely tied to the city's plan to promote the creative economy, the Singapore case will show that the relationship can be much tighter.

Brand Singapore

Singapore is a tropical island city–state. It has no natural resources, and is only 700 square kilometers in size. Although the Singapore economy is doing well and is the wealthiest in the region, the authorities are steering the economy away from its manufacturing and electronic bases and towards the financial services, telecommunications, life sciences, tourism and the creative industries (Ministry of Information and the Arts or MITA, 2005). Singapore is being re-branded to reflect the new economic drive.

Over the years, Brand Singapore has celebrated the city's multicultural population and has embraced the city's blend of the exotic East and efficient West (Ooi, 2004b). Competition from neighbouring countries such as Malaysia, Thailand and China, however, have made the branding of Singapore more challenging because these countries are making similar claims and have learned from the Singaporean experience. Singapore is no longer a cheap investment destination. As a result, the government has formulated a new 'East + West plus' approach to branding Singapore (See Figure 5.2). The 'plus' refers to unique Singaporean qualities, which include 'the trust others have in Singapore's ability to get things done; its knowledge base; its global network of transport and people links; and the high standard of living it offers to those who make their homes [in Singapore]' (*The Straits Times*, 2007). The Singaporean government has set up a National Marketing Action Committee to 'guide government agencies in designing marketing campaigns that balance the harder aspects of Singapore, like efficiency and technology, with the nation's softer side, such as lifestyle and innovation' (Goh, 2006).

Brand Singapore may tell of an exciting place but Singapore is frequently seen as a cultural desert; the authorities acknowledge that Singapore is inadequate in offering cultural activities to draw highly skilled foreign workers to work in the city-state (Yusuf & Nabeshima, 2005). Promoting the arts and culture is part of the push to develop Singapore's creative economy (Economic Review Committee: Services Subcommittee Workgroup on Creative Industries, 2002; Ooi, 2007). This is not only a new brand image for Singapore but also a vision for the city-state. Based on the government's blueprint to re-make Singapore, there are at least four inter-related brand authenticity-enhancing strategies to bring the Brand Singapore story and the goal of an exciting Singapore into reality.

First, in recent years, the Singaporean government has relaxed its regulations to encourage a livelier cultural scene. Members of Parliament voiced their worries about the loosening up of regulations in Singapore to attract foreigners and to present a livelier image of Singapore. The

Figure 5.2 Contrasting cityscape in Singapore

then-Minister of State for Trade and Industry, Vivian Balakrishnan, replied *(Singapore Parliament Hansard, 2004)*:

> There was an article that Professor Richard Florida wrote, entitled 'The Rise of the Creative Class'. [...] His research found that cities, which are able to embrace diversity, are able to attract and foster a

bigger creative class. These are key drivers in a knowledge-based economy. The larger lesson for us in Singapore is that we need to shift our mindset so that we can be more tolerant of diversity.

Second, various governmental authorities search for, and bid to attract, major events to the country. Subsequently, spectacular activities are frequently staged in the city. Besides hosting pop concerts by international mega stars, popular musicals and block buster exhibitions, Singapore hosts big events, for example, the 2006 World Bank and IMF meetings, the first ever Formula One night races in 2008 and the debut of the Youth Olympics Games in 2010. Such events generate extensive media publicity for the city-state.

Third, like Berlin, the Singaporean authorities seek investments and endorsements from the private sector to brand Singapore as pulsating. Besides searching for events, state agencies actively seek out opportunities to make Singapore into the hub of global and regional organisations, including those in the media, design, telecommunication, pharmaceuticals and financial sectors. Singapore is already a regional hub for the global media industry. MTV, Discovery, HBO and BBC have made Singapore their regional headquarters. The goal of the Singaporean authorities is to offer a truly conducive business environment for the creative industries.

Fourth, to become a respected arts and cultural city, Singapore has also established a number of cultural institutions. Three national museums were established in Singapore in 1997, and in 2002 Esplanade (Theatres by the Bay) was opened. The Singaporean government wants the city-state to be the cultural capital of Southeast Asia (Ooi, 2007). As Singapore is to offer the best of the East and West in its brand story, the various cultural institutions will showcase and promote cultural events that reflect the multi-cultural, cosmopolitan city (See Figure 5.3).

In Singapore, living the brand and realising the brand is part and parcel of promoting the arts and culture industry in the city-state. The brand is part of the vision and blueprint of what Singapore is to become. It asserts a future Singapore. Armed with regulations and resources, the authorities are determined to realise a new funkier city-state. With all the grand plans, it would seem that Singapore is plastic-fantastic.

Discussion

Earlier in this chapter, three inherent factors that give rise to the authenticity issue in place branding were highlighted: (1), a place brand cannot provide a complete and honest story of the place; (2), the place branding campaign may destroy the original spirit of the place; and (3), a

Figure 5.3 Singapore Esplanade hotels and offices

place brand is also normative, it often functions as a vision that may eventually contribute towards change in the location. Let us review these factors from the two cases and reconsider the notion of authenticity.

Based on the first factor, can a place brand be honest and present a comprehensively accurate picture of the location? This concern assumes that a place brand must be comprehensive and honest before it can be considered authentic. But place branding, by definition and purpose, is always less than authentic because the positive brand messages sent will always be limited. On the other hand, criticising that a place brand as engendered and can never be comprehensive is trivial because no message – whether it is a brand slogan or an encyclopedia-length book – can actually present a totally comprehensive and accurate picture of the location. Any story of a place will remain a representation, and that representation can only approximate the reality in the location. As Foucault's archaeology of knowledge points out, a message is always embedded in a context. In the message, some ideas and knowledge are accentuated, while others marginalised (Dean, 1994; Foucault, 1972). From the two cases on Berlin and Singapore, we see that place branding is tightly linked to the social, economic and cultural policies of these cities which are actively pursuing the creative economy, they want to attract investments, visitors and workers; place branding and the enlivening of the arts and culture in these cities are part of the marketing strategy to achieve the said goals. The branding campaigns are never meant to be frank, independent and separated from commercial interests.

Is the concept of authenticity still meaningful in place branding? As shown in the two cases, the city branding authorities are still dealing with the issues of authenticity and credibility in their branding campaigns – they seek endorsements and intensify the presence of these cities in the global media, for example. Audiences are often aware of the commercial agenda behind marketed messages. It is essential for scholars not only to contextualise the place branding campaign in the social, commercial and political milieu, the concept of authenticity must be framed in a way meaningful and relevant to the practice of place branding. This takes us to the next point.

Moving to the second authenticity-eroding factor, to what extent does a society lose its authenticity through the processes of commodification and commercialisation? In studies that deal with host societies and how these societies are affected by touristification and commodification, many researchers call for a balance between the preservation of authenticity and 'commercial interests' (Newby, 1994; Teo & Li, 2003). The attempt to enhance and revitalise the arts and culture in a city to attract investments, tourists and foreign workers – as in Berlin and Singapore – may mean that resources are available to keep less popular art forms alive. Traditional cultural forms provide the unique selling proposition for the marketing of the city. In Singapore, for instance, vanishing Asian art forms such as Teochew operas and Malay street shows are being staged and publicised. The separation of culture and business is not meaningful when one considers the intertwined relations between commerce and culture.

The entanglement of commerce and culture is also felt deeply in the age of globalisation. Around the world, people consume 'global' products which have become part of local everyday life; the differences between what is constituted as cultural and what is commercial, and what is local and what is foreign are fast dissolving. Commercial cultural practices are actively 'localised' and made meaningful not by rejecting intrusive 'global' structures of 'political economy' but by consciously engaging them, appropriating what is available within them and making it part of local life (Robertson, 1995).

Societies have always evolved with the merging of social, cultural, political and economic forces, which may originate locally or from afar. It would be a rather inauthentic picture if a modern society is presented as static or one that it is changing without commercial influences or foreign engagement. Place branding commodifies society but this exercise is contributing to an 'emerging authenticity' (Cohen, 1988). The concept of authenticity in place branding then must acknowledge place branding as one of the socio-economic processes that is part of the evolving society.

The last factor that gave rise to the fear that place branding will destroy the authenticity of the place is that the brand is also normative. To what extent then does a society lose its authenticity when social changes are engineered and directed to a desired goal? The place branding processes of Berlin and Singapore are part of the strategies by the authorities to improve and enhance these cities. Culture – 'culture as evolving' – and place are ceaselessly reconstructed' (Hobsbawm & Ranger, 1983). Brand Singapore and the promotion of the arts and culture are part of the creative-turn that the government wants the country to move towards. Similarly, in Berlin, the authorities want to revive the flagging economy. By embracing commercial and popular cultures, new cultural forms are promoted. If a place brand is normative, then it is also one of the social engineering processes in the society. All governments are engaged in social engineering – through the education system, mass media, policies and regulations. As we can see from the cases of Berlin and Singapore, place branding is part of the intended strategy to transform these cities.

The fear that the place brand is not authentic or that the place branding campaign will destroy the authenticity of the place holds various assumptions: (1), a place brand must be comprehensive and honest before it can be considered authentic; (2), a society would lose its authenticity if commodified and driven by commercial activities; and following which, (3), a place brand should only be descriptive and cannot inspire and direct changes to society, otherwise the society would lose its original authenticity. These assumptions are problematic. The concluding section will explicate the lessons learned.

Conclusions

Places get branded because the authorities want to promote their places. But the authenticity issue is still of paramount importance in place branding; branding authorities are concerned with it. One must however contextualise the concept of authenticity to reflect the emerging reality of society. The authenticity debate will not be fruitful if one views the branding campaign in isolation and extracted from the entangled social, economic and political issues behind a place branding campaign. A place does not lose authenticity if its culture and social life are influenced by economic and political forces – in fact, these changes in society are the reality. To what extent and how should a society change is a decision made partly by leaders, partly by residents and partly by the influx of external influences. As we can observe in the cases of Berlin and Singapore, the authorities in Berlin seek endorsements and try to promote a good image of Berlin and the Singaporean authorities do the same but engineer Singaporean society further. The Singaporean authorities change regulations and establish numerous cultural institutions to promote a livelier image of Singapore. These plans are inextricably part of the move to develop the local creative economy. The place brand is then part of the making of an evolving society, embedded in the various social, economic and political forces. Instead of seeing place branding as a source of authenticity corruption, the place branding process is part of the emerging authenticity.

In the various ranking of cities mentioned at the start of this chapter, the main issues addressed are on the contemporary and current quality of the cities. As cities attempt to climb up the rankings, they are intentionally trying to lose their past and become better. Having a livelier art and cultural scene is now essential in making a city more liveable, more attractive for residents and to receive the attention of the global media. The authenticity of the brand messages rests in how these messages measure up in the present, not in how the past has disappeared in those cities – these in fact are positive, according to the desire of the branding authorities and many local residents. Place branding and the resulting changes that come about from the place vision is part of the emerging society. That surely makes place branding an intrinsic process of society.

Chapter 6

On the Management of Authenticity: Culture in the Place Branding of Øresund

SØREN BUHL HORNSKOV

Introduction: Authenticity and Culture

Branding research emphasises what phenomenology has always known: subjective experiences of places have a range of different origins and qualities (Caldwell & Freire, 2004; Olins, 2003; Pedersen, 2005). As an effort to make the most of this range of different sources and kinds of experience for the commercial and political construction of places, a particular kind of sentimentalism makes an impact in the branding literature, namely the focus on authenticity.

The focus on authenticity has drawn place branding theory to culture. The interest in culture as the source of origin, truth and meaning has become a dominant streak in marketing and in place branding (Pine & Gilmore, 2007; Saren, 2006). The interest in culture marks the difference between concerns with the surface of things and the belief in a deeper, authentic level of reality. Place branding hence deals with issues that are, as Anholt puts it, 'considerably [...] *deeper* than most that advertising or PR agencies have to tackle' (2003: 60, emphasis added).

This notion of depth is the focus of the present paper. The argument is that the social and cultural conditions that influence a branding process are dynamic in important ways. Branding often aims to influence these conditions, but in fact relies on patterns of social interaction that are not only beyond its control, but (and here's the paradox) the autonomy of which is crucial to the authenticity of the brand. Branding thus aims to balance social forces with management strategy (Lury, 2004), but often fails to recognise the potential and challenges of these social forces.

This chapter looks at a case study of how the composite reality of the brand is played out, namely the role of two Øresund modern dance venues in the development of the Øresund brand. From the case it becomes evident that place branding requires a model of culture sufficiently complex to host the non-consensual and paradoxical. The ambiguity with respect to the authentic and the struggles against brand management by actors in the cultural field indicates that brand management is facing a major challenge when it comes to constructing cultural authenticity.

Method

The work presented here is based on research data on the regional branding of Øresund (Pedersen, 2005). These data include a literature review of the place branding, document analysis from Øresund organisations and 25 qualitative interviews. The methodological aim was to look at the ways in which knowledge and awareness of Øresund – its naturalisation and authentication, in other words – was constructed by local actors, predominantly managers, in cooperation with external branding consultants.

The problem of the relation between culture and place branding surfaces in many different forms in actual social processes. 'Culture' may be the object of place branding; it is something management seeks to influence and change through dialogue, interaction and formalisation. Yet, at the same time 'culture' is the prerequisite of brand management as a reference or a passive resource.

The case study presented in this paper is based on seven personal interviews with directors and members of staff of two regional organisations. In this case, the construction of Øresund took place in local organisations within particular value systems. We call these 'cultures'. The conflicts between these systems (and we may add the clashes and contacts of many other organisations) were, in effect, the primary drivers in the construction of the Øresund region.

The data for the study of the Kulturbro biennale were collected from the dance venues, which were so kind to allow three interviews with the directors and provided contracts, correspondence, programs and other material. The author wishes to thank the respondents for their engagement and time.

Manageable Culture?

Authenticity has become a label for a valuable, deep level of reality. Indeed, authenticity has been established as a key competitive factor in contemporary economy (Pine & Gilmore, 2007). Yet, to access culture in practice often means dealing with the guardians of culture; the cultural *aficionados* or professionals.

The necessity of this dealing-with (sometimes, but not always inseparable from culture as such) has made branding increasingly concerned with the management of various kinds of participation (Arvidsson, 2006; Ind, 2001; Kotler & Keller, 2006). This concern implies not merely an interest in the immediate positive forms of sociality (such as participation) but also in forms that are ordinarily perceived as negative, i.e. resistance and opposition. Indeed, as I will argue, to make the best of the *potential* of resistance is the biggest challenge of brand management.

Given this paradoxical character of place branding it is worthwhile to look into the conflictual relation between management and the cultural field. The question of participation in practice deals with a host of perceptions on how to prompt and sustain participation. The status of branding as a practical social organising of the cultural affect of belonging is frequently reduced to a view on the representational aspect of brands. Examples of this reductionism are Hannigan's (2003) and Evans' (2003) definitions of branding as merely the practices of writing slogans and designing logos. Yet in the case of place branding, strategies of organisation are indeed distinguishing features.

In the present paper, the organisational aspect is dealt with in a dual analysis. On the one hand, the intervention in 'culture' to touch and influence the social fabric of places is analysed. On the other hand, the analysis addresses networking strategies that attempt to nurture social relations around a common interest and value base. The paper looks at a dance festival to discuss the network aspect of place branding. This turns out to be a narrative on the clashes between powers of authentication, strategies of participation, and the impact of the local resistance to place branding.

Challenging the Notion of Culture as Essence

To think of culture as a means for the manipulation of the identity of places is to challenge the idea that culture is ontologically primary to any management effort. In social theory, 'culture' has been described as a resource outside the reach of management.[1] Correspondingly, parts within the branding field consider cultural essence an immutable resource for the construction of brands (Bedbury, 2002). The present paper aims to turn this contention on its head. Rather than holding culture to be separate or even distinguished from management and the market, I will follow Zukin's observation that 'culture':

[...] has become an abstraction for any economic activity that does not create material products like steel, cars, or computers... Because culture is a system for producing symbols, every attempt to get people to buy a product becomes a cultural industry. (1995: 12)

Place branding, then, cannot be studied without paying attention to the cultural industry of persuading people to recognise the legitimacy of the place brand. Adding to the attractivity of places, in other words, involves 'the conscious and deliberate manipulation of culture' (Philo & Kearns in Teo, 2003).

'Culture' can therefore be conceived as a certain register of place branding, an aspect of its interventional strategies in social life as well as its promotional strategies on the global market (Zukin in King, 1996: 45).

The Øresund case invites us to look at place branding processes in which 'the cultural' is a way of thinking, framing and communicating a new 'authenticity' for a place. The object of analysis, in other words, is a specific discourse within which the term 'culture' is used to define phenomena according to their degree of authenticity. 'Culture' is a way of labelling a sign regime and belief-system that has the power to authenticate social phenomena, that is, according to which there is a difference between a 'real identity' and its more derived or even 'in-authentic' representations. Identity, thus, is a concept that indicates a certain gravity of the cultural. In the following I will approach a particular case in which the idea of the authentic has been of central importance.

The goal is to discuss the productivity of the forms of resistance and anticipation of participation that pertains to the organisational dimension of place branding. How does branding aim to organise and encourage forms of participation in order to transform the character of a place? And, does place branding foster new spaces for productive cultural relations as unintended effects rather than as its intended goals?

Introducing Øresund: A Brief History of an Emerging Place Brand

The Øresund Region is the outcome of a political and commercial desire to bridge, both physically and symbolically, the narrow sound between Denmark and Sweden. The physical link was realised on 1 June 2000 with the opening of the bridge between Copenhagen and Malmoe (Ek, 2003), while the construction of cultural coherence between the two countries is an ongoing process.

The Influence of Place Brand Consultancy

The opening of the bridge took place in parallel with a process in which trade, state administration and industry began to work together to organise the marketing of the region on the global market. Emphasis was placed on industries such as medicine and informational technology, while using the cultural assets of the area as a motor for raising the global recognition of the Region. At the same time, the outward ambition came to be accompanied by an inwardly directed ambition to genuinely integrate the Øresund Region. The aim, for instance, was to facilitate the cooperation of Swedish and Danish companies and institutions.

The early stages of the regional organisation involved the expertise of the Wolff Olins consultancy. The ideas of the Wolff Olins consultancy represented a major source of inspiration and hands-on tactics for the ways in which place branding was organised and exercised. One of the major challenges of the process was to bridge the gap between formal and informal processes of regional development. How, for instance, could the harmonisation of tax systems go hand in hand with the creation of shared cultural values? And how could local actors be engaged as participants rather than being discouraged or even alienated by the methods of the consultants and the regional innovators in politics and business?

Authentication and the Heteronomy of Emergent Identities

In place branding the processes of authentication are driven by the tension of the performance of the essential and of becoming. Sharon Zukin puts the relation between the official acts of government and the experience of places – in her case cities – as follows: 'The look and feel of cities reflects decisions about what – and who – should be visible and what should not ...' (Zukin, 1995: 7).

This perception of authentication is recurring in nationalism and other discourses based on ideas about the primacy of cultural essence.[2] 'Culture', when constructed politically, becomes something that can be distinguished for its degree of authenticity. 'Culture', as 'identity', is always something particular and seen as opposed to universal or global media, norms and institutions. The literature on cultural resistance to capitalism and state domination often focuses on 'identity' as a source of resilience, an order of symbols with the potential to empower actors (cf. overview in Castells, 1997). Kevin Hetherington sets out to explain this peculiar mechanism:

> Identity is both about similarity and difference. It is about how subjects see themselves in representation, and about how they

construct differences within that representation and between it and the representation of others. (1998: 15)

Moreover, Hetherington emphasises the importance of a theoretical focus on the emergent character of identity and thus of resistance as located in sub-cultural positions: 'Identity formation as a process of identification is a spatially situated process. It is, however, about creating symbolic spaces rather than always adopting established ones' (1998: 17). The central issue is whether identity is established by subscribing and identifying with symbolic orders that appear to be *already there* – such as the brand in an authoritative and fixed form – or whether identity is created in a process in which the symbolic order is part of the output rather than the input.

Lash and Friedman (1992) discuss the history of the social formation of identity with the aim to arrive at a narrative about the freedom of modernity. In pre-modern society, they argue, identities were produced in centres of authority that were not really part of social life. Lash and Friedman admit that 'in modernity, heteronomous definitions of identity persist', i.e. asymmetrical distributions of power are still the political reality. But, they continue: 'Also in modernity, with the demise of both God and Caesar, social space opens up the way for an autonomous definition of identity. In modernity we are fated to be free' (1992: 5, emphasis added).

Place branding arguably deals in the construction of this freedom. To a certain degree, place branding obscures the division between power and resistance by joining up management power and the autonomy of participant citizens in the very process of producing identity.

With the case of place branding as a complex authentication process it becomes impossible to uphold the dichotomies of autonomy and government that marks the positions of Lash and Hetherington, Friedman, and Giddens. Yet, in practice dichotomies are significant because the people and institutions to which place brand management appeal may be reluctant to accept the idea that place branding is perfectly legitimate. Criticism, thus, may no longer consist in lamenting the loss of 'autonomous' culture (Lash, 2002: 80ff), but may seek to challenge the initiatives of place brand management.

The notion of authenticity in Øresund suggests an improvement in the sense of more compatible, local identities in the face of global competition on image. Yet, an emphasis on the authentic finds its way into the Øresund construction process as a key factor in the formation of the regional identity.

Brand Imagery and the Resistance of Social Space

Place branding suggests a revision of definitions of place and a comprehensive strategy for the communication of the definition of place. The ambition of place branding can be perceived as a new order of authentication, a re-writing of the history of the place in question.

Brand management thus seeks to influence a two-fold reality: first, it focuses on the conception of the brand as totality, including both representational and organisational elements. The success of attempts to realise the conception of the brand in practical social life is crucial to the strength of the brand idea. Secondly, brand management aims at the construction of a space for the interaction of actors outside the brand owner organisations. It is arguably this potential of resistance that marks the biggest challenge of brand management.

On the Choice and Analytical Strategy of the Case: Reading for Resistance

The *Kulturbro* 2000 and 2002 was the outcome of an explicit political intention to balance management and emerging culture in the Øresund Region. The *Kulturbro* was born from a governmental vision of engaging not only business and political organisations but also cultural institutions in the region building process. As such, it illustrates the cultural scope of the negotiation of belonging: the history of the dream of the region is dominated by ideas about the region having to be or become *popular* and anchored in a genuine cultural basis.

The Kulturbro Foundation: The Unintended Productivity of Resistance

The *Kulturbro* Foundation funded two ambitious biennial festivals of 'regional' culture – in 2000 and 2002 – as part of a comprehensive political ambition to develop cross-border interaction and a new collective identity for the region. The Foundation was designed to work as a place branding organisation with the specific goal of strengthening the regional culture. This strategy was based on an understanding among regional leaders that what was loosely conceptualised as the cultural sector was the most genuine expression of the 'authentic' region. Thus, the formulation and manipulation of 'regional culture' was seen as a necessary step towards the realisation of the region. The Foundation sprung from this regional ideology, which would shape a host of public and private initiatives in the region during the late nineties:

The Kulturbro Foundation's main task is to put the Øresund region on the map as an area that holds its own, strong cultural attractions. Likewise, the foundation aims at the promotion and development of the funding of cultural co-operation between cultural institutions in the Øresund region, thereby strengthening the region's position internationally.[3]

The statement expresses an idea of linking local culture ('own', 'strong', 'cultural cooperation') to the idea of international image. Arguably, this strategy has become dominant for cities, nations and regions in the emerging 'experience-economy' (Evans, 2003; Löfgren, 2003). As an example, the ongoing rebranding of New York after the 9/11 tragedy has provided the New Yorkers (or rather their political leaders) with the occasion to re-configure the relation between the local history, salient features of the particular culture of the city and the perception of this identity in the outside world (Greenberg, 2003).

Greenberg observes that New Yorkers have questioned the democratic legitimacy of the transformation of their city. In a similar way, the Øresund branding was contested by existing regional networks. The Kulturbro Foundation was set up to fund cultural projects, yet for its recipients this funding policy had its prize: it came with the obligation for existing cultural institutions to become cogs in the machine of the regional branding strategy. Cultural projects should, as far as possible, be developed in harmony with the themes and values of the Foundation. Louise Seibæk, director of Dansescenen, explains what she considers to be the fundamental flaw of the Foundation:

[...] the Foundation saw itself as too important. Kulturbroen was perceived as the goal, as the thing to be promoted, rather than the means [of the cultural projects that it funded].[4]

The case study of two dance venues thus provides an opportunity to discuss the consequences of and ambiguities between the overall branding effort, set against a self-proclaimed organic and autonomous, highly specialised art community. As the study will show, the meeting of the two interested groups created considerable tension.

The Tension of Immaterial Rights and Contractual Obligations

Cultural institutions applying for funds from the Foundation were faced with a demand to subscribe to a fully designed brand identity for the region, complete with logo, promotion photos, pay-offs and globalist ideology.[5] For the two dance venues in particular this meant that funding came with the obligation to use the logo of the Foundation on programs and tickets, to use the photos of the Foundation rather than their own and so on. This was an asymmetrical relation in the sense that while the Foundation had the *right* to use the material of the venues to promote the biennales, the venues had the *obligation* to use the logo of the Foundation on tickets, programs and other marketing materials. In other words, the branding-strategy *de facto* treated the dance venues as secondary to the construction of a new regional identity; the art was reduced to the promotion of the region rather than the region being the support of local art. This situation made the cultural institutions work out counter-strategies aimed at getting their funding without completely compromising their status as autonomous art institutions.

The practice arising from this contractual relation became highly conflictual in the course of the two biennales. Tension thus arose around the issue of what should be promoted; the dance or the Kulturbro biennales.

The counter-strategies of the dance venues were, to a large measure, fueled by the contention that their relation constituted an 'authentic' and 'original' network, historically and logically prior to the talk about a new regional identity. The cultural institutions describe themselves as pivotal to the foundation and their network and joint projects across the existing region as the 'real' region, defining is as being opposed to the glitzy, superficial imagery of the *Kulturbro* Foundation.

Authenticating the *Real* Real

Despite this improvement, the biennials and the Foundation as such have been regarded with a solid measure of scepticism by the directors of the two dance venues. The two venues considered their cooperation, which predated the Foundation, to be a more authentical regional project than the Foundation. As Seibæk puts it:

> [...] we had the cooperation that the municipalities and so on had been pushing for; that we should strengthen relations across the Sound. We did it, before anyone began talking about it. We built the real relations.[6]

Adding to this historical sense of autonomy, as articulated by the dance companies, any political intention to bind expressions of dance to any specific location aroused scepticism. The venues argue that dance is a profoundly global art form in the sense that there is a profound exchange of work, of shows, of choreographies and, certainly, of people – dancers and choreographers – across the world.

Dance thus understands itself as a de-territorialising art form. Dance performance creates affects that transcend political territories. A result of this self-description is that the regional becomes an artificial in-between of the local and the global stages of dance art. Dansstationen in Malmoe, however, does have a regional strategy. But rather than considering Øresund the primary territory, Dansstationen is preoccupied with the promotion of dance in the Swedish Region of Scania. The director of Dansstationen refers to this regional project as 'true' as opposed to the strained attempts to manufacture a regional identity in Øresund. The involvement of his venue in promoting dance within Scania is said to be a 'true' regionalism because it is based on a more radical concept of participation.

When asked if the venue is in it for the money or if there is more to it, Torsten Schenlaer shows no hesitation:

TS: It is only the money. It is about raising the attention to dance. The Kulturbro Foundation in itself is of no importance at all.
SBP: Is there a difference between the Foundation and regionalising?
TS: The Foundation is not regionalisation. I can compare it to another project ... which is a dance project for kids and young people. There, we built a network from scratch, where we educate people and apply for funding. *That* is to regionalise culture in Scania.[7]

At the same time, this forceful stance against the Foundation both furthers and impedes the goals of the regional branding. Concepts of regional identity are being formed in the management of the venues and in this sense 'the regional' is advancing. Paradoxically, this advance represents a refusal of the forms of authentication set out by the Foundation. The resistance of this differential space in other words supports the formation of the regional brand, however, without affirming the officialisations of the Foundation. Accordingly, the regional totality can be conceived as being a profoundly divided and conflictual social whole.[8] The regional 'habitus', defined as a collective body of discursive and material relations, is thus constituted by its difference to itself.

Learning to Resist and How to be a Foundation

The two dance venues both emphasise the importance of their relation as an asset in the negotiations with the political authorities. The two venues consider their relation to be pivotal for the necessary empowerment vis-a-vis not only the Foundation, but broadly speaking all authorities in their field.[9] Surely, strengthening of relations would also be considered a vital strategy of the Foundation, however, the two venues clearly unite with the objective to oppose the Foundation. They join together to become more powerful in order to resist to what they perceived to be the Foundation's attempts to influence the artistic content of their venues.

Yet if the two venues developed an appreciation of the value of their relation over the course of the two biennales, the Foundation learned its own lessons. Despite all the criticism, the directors of the venues emphasise that the Foundation improved their marketing and organisation skills in the course of the two biennale. As such, in a processual perspective the Foundation seems to have had the technological capacity to evaluate itself over time. We thus see how brand technology involves reflexive practices on a number of different levels and relations. As a side effect, the mutual branding project has strengthened particular participating organisations which, by mirroring themselves in the brand interface, became able to make themselves objects.

Conclusions: Fixation, Infatuation and Competing Ideas about the Brand

The organisations described above are players in the process of regional branding. They navigate in relation to positions of power and shifting priorities. In so doing, paradoxical relations are maintained, such as the ambivalent opinion that the two venues have of the Foundation, in spite of the fact that it makes their art possible.

Both the venues and the Foundation are in themselves cultures, marked by the regionalist vision. The case illustrates the managerial infatuation with the idea of the region, held at a problematic arms length relative to the cultural venues.

The vision of the regional future views it as a mere strategic reality, an abstract 'billboard identity' to which they refer in the effort to settle their differences or to legitimate their own existence. The infatuation with the region in other words seems to impede the ability of these organisations to relate to the surrounding world. Judging from the case presented, brand management begs a particular form of *enthusiasm at a distance*; an ability to energise processes without becoming too absorbed to be able to see the boundaries to the imaginaries of the importance of the regional that prevail in brand space. This frustration leaves the organisations with only juridical tools, forcing them to conceive the brand as a fixed asset.

The outcome is a forced authenticity that has little appeal for potential engagement of outsiders.

Brand management aims to render culture official. It aims to set up a specific framework within which a culture may emerge. In the case of the Foundation, the rigid strategies of brand ownership and specific authoritative obligations for participants, fuel the resistance of the dance venues. This makes cooperation difficult. Thus, even though the idea is for the two to work together, the Foundation competes with the dance venue's way of thinking regional reality. The two venues deploy strategies to define the *real* real as something that escapes the authentication effort of the Foundation. Thus, the Foundation loses its opportunity to create value for the Øresund brand through the dance venues.

As a consequence, it seems that the Foundation has failed to establish a close relation to the venues. It has repelled these potential brand ambassadors, and the lack of mutual understanding has reduced the relationship to a minimal one of a sponsorship. The Foundation seems to lack an understanding of the particular cultures and traditions of its partners. The Foundation insists on the fixation and 'solidification' of the brand, rather than the adoption of a processual approach that may allow the brand culture to emerge unforced.

Another way of describing this climate of hostility is to focus on the clash between the ambition to *include* and the obligations to formally *represent*. In the work of the Foundation, strategies to make the regional and the brand *representable* result in a formal *fixation*, a stasis of conceived space. In the case of the Foundation, the venues report that they feel as if they are merely tools to further the ideology of the Foundation, not autonomous organisations with activities that transcend the objectives of the biennales.

Yet, despite these conflicts and ambiguities, the Foundation has arguably been a relative success. The fervent resistance of the dance venues may not be productive to the proliferation of the Foundation brand, but it strengthens the relationship between the venues. And as such, it arguably strengthens a particular aspect of a potential regional brand.

Notes

1. See for instance Castells's influential trilogy *The Information Age*, which presents a concept of culture fundamentally opposed in its insistence on the primacy of culture to the postmodern perspective set forth in, for instance, Jackson *et al.* (2000). Castells believes that 'defensive identities' *vis-à-vis* the global have an 'autonomous' character as constructed around 'a specific set of

values whose meaning and sharing are marked by specific codes of self-identification' (Castells, 2000: 65)

2. See, for instance, Ernest Gellner's essay on primordialism versus modernism for an overview of the different concepts of authenticity in European nationalism (Gellner, 1997).

3. The excerpt is from the mission statement of the Foundation on www. kulturbro.com. The site is no longer accessible online.

4. Personal interview, 11 December 2003.

5. The contractual description of the sponsorship of Kulturbro specifies the conditions under which the dance venues and the Foundation are to endorse each other.

6. Personal interview, 22 October 2002.

7. Torsten Schenlaer, Personal interview, Malmo, January 2003.

8. In Callon (1998), this paradox is discussed as the question of producing market spaces: '[…] framing requires the mobilisation of entities, while their irreducible autonomy is a source of new overflowing' (p. 38). The dance venues can be perceived as such irreducible autonomies.

9. Personal interview, Seibaek, 11 December 2003.

Chapter 7

A Ferris Wheel on a Parking Lot: Heritage, Tourism, and the Authenticity of Place in Solvang, California

HANNE PICO LARSEN

Introduction

In this chapter, I will explore the fine line between real patina vs. constructed tourist appeal in a Californian multicultural tourist setting. Solvang, a well-known Danish-themed destination in Southern California that attracts about 1.5 million tourists annually, is the nexus of the study. The demand for authenticity in the tourist experience, as well as for the local residents, is a complex issue. The issue is further complicated by factors such as history, local economy and tourists' expectations. When the idea about a Ferris wheel was introduced, and even appeared on the ballot, members of the Solvang community had to decide between *quaintness* and *kitsch*.

While a particular definition of authenticity is not of primary concern in this chapter, the quest for authenticity and the authentic tourist experience continues to be an intrinsic concern within tourist studies (see for example Bendix, 1989; Boorstin, 1992; Bruner, 1994; Cohen, 1979, 1988; Culler, 1981; Enzensberger, 1996; Frow, 1991; MacCannell, 1973, 1999, 2001; Olsen, 2002; Redfood, 1984; Urry, 1990; Wang, 1999, 2000). The authenticity of the Solvang tourist experience has been discussed elsewhere (Larsen, 2006; Linde-Laursen, 1997), and it is obvious that Solvang is as aware of the buzz words *authentic* and *original* as most other tourist attractions. Solvang has been caught in the semiotics of tourism, and the overt manifestations of authenticity are mainly visual. The exploitation of heritage for tourism has been crucial for Solvang's economy, and as a consequence the city is full of various cultural markers, mainly architecture, with ascribed symbolic value. The several fake windmills and fake storks nesting on fake thatched roofs might seem a bit exaggerated and as paraded culture far removed from the original context (Larsen, 2006). My earlier conclusions emphasised the ease of forgetting to consider Solvang as a special *Danish* location and not just an American folkloristic creation placed in a Danish colony. The curators of the city are a mixed bag of financial backers and cultural brokers. It is not necessarily Danish ethnicity that is sold here, but rather generic (northern/western) ethnicity, or Old World ethnicity. In turn, the exhibited Danish-ness of Solvang, the presence of somewhat stereotyped cultural markers, reinforces a sense of being Danish to locals and visitors of Danish descent. Solvang is indeed a little bit of Denmark, Disney *and* something else. (Larsen, 2006). In this chapter, however, I will explore Solvang residents' struggle to maintain the town's status as a tourist attraction and the fine line between *quaintness* and *kitsch* as they perceive it. Where does authenticity stop and the theme park take over? I argue that the debate about authenticity has become part of Solvang's identity and the town's local folklore. It is articulated verbally, in print and through material objects. The Ferris wheel becomes a catalyst for making the political, the physical, and the cultural landscape of Solvang intersect in the creation of the social landscape and makes it apparent that the Solvang illusion was created *by* and *for* the Danes, and later reinvented and maintained *for* the tourist.

Solvang Discovered

Although Solvang was founded around 1910–11, it was not until January 1947 that *The Saturday Evening Post* published an article about 'Little Denmark' (Jennings, 1947).[1] This article was a watershed event in Solvang history, bringing nationwide attention to the small community. The article described a little, overlooked town with old-country charm and ruddy-cheeked citizens, and delved into the history of the area, the Danish customs that had been kept alive there, and the special Danish dishes consumed in this tucked away gem. Postcard pictures throughout the article showed blond children and adults in folk costume, the white-washed church, a baker in action, people folk-dancing in the grove, and the headmaster of the high school wearing a Danish outfit while cheerfully smoking a pipe and proudly displaying the guest-book. Below one picture was written: 'Near-by Hollywood could not have created a more exquisite setting than the founders of "Little Denmark" chose for themselves, in the lush Santa Ynez Valley against a backdrop of mountains' (Jennings, 1947: 28).

The article was not meant as a tourist advertisement per se, but soon became one. The image of a welcoming, idyllic, Danish–American small town with healthy, glowing Danes roused the curiosity of many travellers. The theme was on! Solvang decided to make use of this newfound national attention and stage an annual festival, *Danish Days,* with an open invitation to the outside world. The invitation was warmly accepted, and soon local merchants and civic leaders sensed the commercial value of emphasising Danish traditions. The journalist had made the comparison to Hollywood in an admiring way, not out of indignation, and Solvang played off the idea.

A week after the appearance of the article, the local newspaper related its effect:

> The *Saturday Evening Post*'s article 'Little Denmark', which gave a description of life in Solvang, had its REPERCUSSIONS throughout the valley, and in Solvang in particular last weekend. Visitors flocked to the valley and Solvang from all parts of California to 'see for themselves' what the Post article had so vividly described.
>
> Disappointment was the order of the day, however, as a greater majority of the visitors had their eyes bent for natives parading around in 'old country' costumes, Danish pastry shops going full swing and Danish stores, just chock full of wares typical of Denmark and the Danish people. (*Santa Ynez Valley News*, 1947: 8)

Several days later, a jogger of Scottish descent from a neighbouring community warned the Solvang townsfolk of all the changes tourism would bring:

> The pastoral quiet of your lives has been lost. Irrevocably, you have been 'discovered'. Since the day that 'Little Denmark' appeared in the '*Post*' each of you have found life a little changed. Even if it were only to the extent of having your morning cup of coffee at the Sunny Café a bit less leisurely now. (Southwell, 1947: 4)

Southwell described a jog through Solvang, where '[...] a friendly Great Dane trotted out from one of the ranches to have his ears scratched. (It actually was a German Shepherd, but the truth must go by the boards when a community is touched by the magic of glamour)' (Southwell, 1947: 4). The dog serves as an allegory of tail-wagging Danes drawn to the ear-scratching of immediate fame and already catering to the tourist. The dry comment about the substituted breed, however, hints at the insidious consequences of glamour, which could harm the earnest authenticity of a Danish place. Jogging a little farther, Southwell met two ladies in

Solvang: '[...] I [...] heard the following snatches of conversation, so, they asked me why we weren't wearing our Danish costumes today. "Oh well," replied the friend, "they'll stop coming and it will die down after a little while"' (Southwell, 1947: 4).

On the contrary, Southwell warned, the tourists would come again and invite friends. The empty lots in the town would disappear, prices would rise, neon lights would be required, and the festival would become a must to satisfy the growing hordes of visitors. In other words, change has already taken place and there remained only one alternative: 'Learn to live two lives, the exterior that pleases your visitors and in your dealings with others measure your lives as in the past by the golden rule [...] and "a private world of your own – where no eager tourist may ever invade"' (Southwell, 1947: 4). The double life would require a balance between a public life staged for tourists and a private, less spectacular community life.

Solvang and the surrounding valley had to decide what to do about the newfound fame: an editorial published on the same day warned against shifting from the closely knitted social and economic life based on agriculture to a tourist economy. 'That way lies a complete disintegration of community life, and a "feast or famine" economic life' (*Santa Ynez Valley News*, 1947: 3). He proposed that the community make a quick decision and then act upon it immediately:

> Off hand we can't think of any small community that has remained unaffected in a similar situation. Either they mushroom into a tourist resort with all the props and supports of a Hollywood production, or they are left with all the props and none of the audience. There is nothing quite so futile or quite so dead as a theater just after the audience has gone home and the lights have gone out. (*Santa Ynez Valley News*, 1947: 3)

In contrast to the article in the *Saturday Evening Post*, the allusion to Hollywood here has a negative ring. It is a production requiring props and audience. Solvang is now considered theater as opposed to a sincere place.

Echoes of the discussion from 1947 can still be heard in Solvang today. The fine balance between keeping Solvang for Solvangers while making room for tourists is hard to strike. The fear of selling out the Danish heritage and becoming too much of a theme park is prevalent. At the same time, the economy of Solvang currently depends heavily on the tourist industry. Voices are many and loud in Solvang, and the discussion about what Solvang ought to be is complex. The townspeople never really made the choice to become a tourist location, but due to the impact of a single article, Solvang turned into one.

It is hard to know whether pride of heritage, a calculated desire for a profitable heritage enterprise, tourist demands of various kinds, the inevitable organic growth of any small American town, or some combination of all of these factors together made Solvang into what it appears to us today. But the discovery of Solvang in 1947 became an important turning point for the community, happening literally overnight. Since then, Solvang has become a tourist destination in the heart of the Santa Ynez Valley. The debate within Solvang continues, however, about how to balance the *authentic* and the *theme*.

The Ferris Wheel in the Parking Lot

Between Solvang and the old Mission of Santa Inés[2] is a parking lot that functions as a liminal space and as a buffer zone between two different worlds, that of the Spanish conquerors and that of the Danish immigrants. In the recent past, a proposed Ferris wheel in the Solvang parking lot became a point of intersection between these two worlds. Placing a Ferris wheel between the two places, it was feared, would tip the image of both Solvang and the Mission from *quaint* to *carnivalesque*. A Ferris wheel, even if presented as a Danish icon, was not a Danish invention, but rather an American one, first built and presented at the 1893 World's Fair in Chicago by an engineer called Ferris (Anderson, 1992). In Solvang, the terminology was debated. The outspoken people speaking out against the structure insisted on calling it a Ferris wheel, whereas Gary Jensen, the local businessman and entrepreneur behind the wheel, introduced it as a Danish icon and called it a Tivoli wheel (see Figure 7.1). The old Danish amusement park, the Tivoli Gardens, has a Ferris wheel. The Danish wheel in the Tivoli Gardens, called *Ballongyngen*, is by no means tall or in other ways impressive, but it has an air of romance to it and has become one of the symbols of Copenhagen's romance, tourism, and pride.[3] When Jensen insisted on calling the wheel a 'Tivoli wheel', a critic promptly replied: 'Gary Jensen is emphatic that his proposed Tivoli wheel is not a Ferris wheel. However, in my book if it walks and talks like a duck it must be a duck.' And he went on '[...] The only basic difference in the Tivoli wheel are the balloon-like decorations suspended above the passenger enclosures, or "gondolas" – sure looks like a Ferris Wheel to me' (Mathiasen, 2002: A5).

Jensen meant the wheel as a gift to Solvang, and he argued that it would be a source of income for the town. Protesters argued that it did

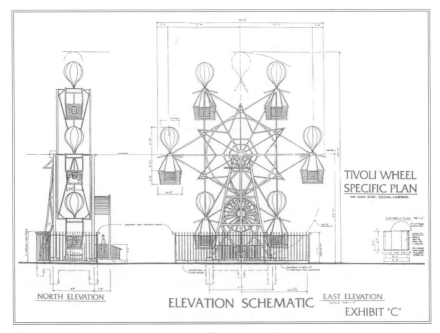

Figure 7.1 Gary Jensen's proposed Ferris wheel

not belong on a parking lot, it would cheapen the image of Solvang, and it would destroy the equanimity of the Mission. The Ferris wheel was on the ballot twice, and the discussion dragged out for 10 years. The image of Solvang became the key issue. While most people claimed the discussion was about location, it was as much about putting Solvang on the verge of becoming a carnival-like, noisy, colourful, kitschy place. In order to maintain the quaintness, Solvang needed the serenity and quiet of the Mission, devoid of flamboyant architecture.

From the point of view of the parishioners and friends of the Mission, the Ferris wheel would interrupt prayers and other religious services and disturb the peace, which Mission visitors so much appreciate. The Ferris wheel would stand between the two dueling tourist visions: Solvang and the Mission. Solvang mainly serves the white (upper) middle class and white (upper) middle class tourists, whereas the Mission draws many different types of tourist but which is also a stronghold for the local Mexican population, who are generally less affluent. Nonetheless, Solvang and the Mission of Santa Inés have learned to live side by side, separated by a parking lot, and to share the tourist's attention, as the

Danes and the Mexicans have learned to divide tasks and coexist in Solvang.[4] Whether you come to see the Mission or Solvang, you will inevitably get two different tourist experiences.

Elsewhere (Larsen, 2006) I have interpreted Solvang as three over-lapping categories, or landscapes: first, the *political landscape* encapsulates formal as well as informal politics. Who are the decision makers, who will people listen to? In Solvang, a white hegemony exists and the older members of the Danish Mafia often set the agenda.[5] Second, the *physical landscape* is the topography: the valley, the mountains and vineyards, but also the iconographic Danish-themed architecture, and the *Little Mermaid* fountain. Last, the *cultural landscape* reveals what the tourists see: the small-town idyll of bygone days. On the other hand, it is also a matter of the history and demography combined: the juxtaposition between the Danish and the Hispanic. The discussion of the Ferris wheel engaged all three landscapes in the evolution of the *social landscape* of Solvang. It was a political matter, and both formal and informal political rhetoric were used. As an architectural structure the Ferris wheel would have become part of the *physical landscape*. The location of the proposed Ferris wheel was planned to be in the middle of the two worlds that con-stitute the *cultural landscape* of Solvang. The *social landscape* is not as much about actual space, but rather about what the space symbolises. In this example, the Ferris wheel became the locus of all of these landscapes. It was the centre of a debate about what Solvang, as a community, wants to be.

When Gary Jensen first proposed the idea of erecting a Ferris wheel in the early 1990s, the local Planning Commission and the Solvang City Council rejected the project. Jensen hired public relations experts to promote the cause and the Ferris wheel appeared on the first ballot in 1994. When asked if an ordinance approving the Tivoli Garden Ferris wheel plan should be adopted, 1033 voters said 'yes' and 1278 said 'no', so the wheel was for the first time 'spun out at the polls' (Etling, 2002: no page). But the discussion was not over. Jensen had conceived the idea of erecting a Ferris wheel on the parking lot behind his own shops in Solvang. He envisioned a garden in which the Ferris wheel would be the main attraction. He wanted to fund the Ferris wheel with private funds; he did not ask the City of Solvang for financial support. He only asked permission to erect a Ferris wheel, which he considered a good gift to Solvang and a tribute to Danish heritage.

The counter-arguments were plentiful and predominantly focused on the unsuitability of the location rather than on the Ferris wheel as such. The parking lot between Solvang and the Mission was deemed an inappropriate spot for the wheel since it was too small and not perceived as a real park. Moreover, the presence of the wheel would threaten to destroy the serenity of the Mission and jeopardise the character and atmosphere of Solvang. While that was never defined, it was stated over and over again what Solvang does not want to become, but would become if the Ferris wheel (the amusement enterprise) was realised: a carnival-type town. The words *amusement* and *carnival* are in this sense loaded with negativity and in direct opposition to the serenity of the Mission. Furthermore, a concern was that if a Tivoli wheel was allowed, then Solvang would have sold out, and what would the next thing be?

In 1999 Jensen tried again, and for the second time the Solvang Planning Commission stymied him. A local journalist gave the following account of the building suspense:

> It goes around, and it comes around. The towering Tivoli Wheel, the Ferris wheel that refuses to die, is making yet another appearance on the Solvang stage, bringing with it more dismay than amusement at this point. Tenacious Gary Jensen, longtime local merchant and wheel promoter, has lost numerous battles over the wheel in the past. Jensen proposes to site the 49 foot, six gondola replica of a wheel in Copenhagen's Tivoli Gardens on his Solvang commercial property, about 60 feet west of the venerable Santa Ines Mission's gardens. (Etling, 2002)

Using the metaphor of a wheel spinning, the author mockingly unfolds the story of the wheel, reports on the reaction of Solvang citizens when the wheel gets its second whirl, and depicts Gary Jensen as one stubborn fellow.

> Bloodied but unbowed, the never say die Jensen has stepped into the ring again, and locals are sharply divided about the project. He managed to get the wheel on the ballot again through the initiative process, gathering 665 supporting signatures. 'Business is down in Solvang,' says Jensen. 'We need something to build business traffic [...] If it doesn't work, we'll take it down.' (Etling, 2002)

It was not only Solvang citizens and business people who protested about the wheel. Parishioners and friends of the Mission held meetings in a mobile home park outside the city of Solvang, and were active in the debate as well. 'Fr. Michael Mahoney of Mission Santa Ines says "directly in front of where the proposed wheel would be located is the Blessed Sacrament Chapel ... Can you imagine how the music and noise would interrupt the prayer? . . . I wish Mr. Jensen well. I just wish he would find a more suitable location for his wheel"' (Etling, 2002).

In a letter dated 12 September 2002, sent to those affiliated with the Mission, Fr. Michael Mahoney pleaded with them to join him in keeping the Mission 'a haven of peace' by not supporting the proposed Tivoli wheel initiative to appear on the ballot (Mahoney, 2002).

Whereas Solvang citizens were afraid of having the image of their city cheapened, the concern as seen from the Mission was about disturbance of the peace. The Tivoli wheel and its location were seen as irreverent by religious as well as commercial forces. The wheel would be too close to both the historical Hispanic cemetery of the Mission and Solvang, the Danish tourist destination.

The last twirl of the infamous Tivoli wheel was another defeat. This time only 859 voted 'yes', whereas 1317 voters, about 60%, said 'no' to noise at night, lights, a cheapened image of the town, and to the clash with the serenity of the old Mission. Still today, all informants insisted that it was not the wheel as such but its proposed location that prevented it from being built.

The story about the Ferris wheel of Solvang ends here. Gary Jensen is still in town, and four years after the last defeat of the wheel an informant speculates that the wheel could even reappear on the ballot: 'Some of us really think that he bought it and he was just hoping for a quick result, so that he could stick it up. We think he's got it in storage some place.'[6]

Amusement and Architecture

The Ferris wheel controversy is humorous in retrospect but also a serious debate with many layers of meaning. The discussion about the so-called Tivoli wheel is not the only discussion Solvang has had about amusement-related buildings. In the 1960s the discussion was about a Danish theme park, which was never realised (Praul, 1960). Later an outlet centre was built on the outskirts of the town. But Solvang did not want cheap outlet stores, and the place was left destitute.[7] Today the outlet centre houses a gym, a motorcycle museum, and a few administrative offices, but it stands mostly empty as a spectral monument of a Solvang dispute about quality architecture. Tourists never venture down there. The greatest asset of the outlet center was a very beautifully crafted merry-go-round, which is no longer there.

Currently, the Chumash casino and resort outside of town disturbs most Solvang citizens because it is generally assumed that it attracts the wrong people and brings crime to the valley. In 2007 the Santa Inés Band of Chumash Indians purchased the Royal Scandinavian Inn, the biggest hotel in Solvang. The fear is that the Chumash Indians will expand their gambling business and take over this ostensibly Danish place and put Indian stereotypes on display, and thereby confuse the image of the town.[8]

While discussing the image of Solvang with a prominent master builder residing in Solvang, I got another story. In spite of the fact that he himself had been instrumental in introducing the Danish theme in Solvang as well as the Bavarian theme in Leavenworth, Washington, he thought that the Danish theme had outlived itself.[9] To him, the place now attracted the wrong kind of tourists, mainly day-trippers who only buy cheap t-shirts. As the owner of an upscale inn, he of course would rather see upscale tourists coming to town. With the recent upswing in wine-related tourism, he suggested that Solvang should go French. Many wineries have opened up tasting rooms in Solvang, and the 2004 film *Sideways*, set among nearby wineries, also gave Solvang new and different attention. Danes drink wine, but they do not produce it, so there is no direct association between Solvang (or Denmark) and wine. However, grapes are locally grown, and wine is made in the valley. According to this master builder the wine theme would go well with the French: French cuisine, fine wine, a bit of golf, high-end antiquities, and a stay in a luxurious inn. *Voilà*. When I inquired about the four windmills of Solvang, in case Solvang would go French, he had the perfect solution. He would just take off the arms and then the structures would resemble the French pigeon houses of Normandy. The French pigeon houses were round brick buildings, often with thatched roofs. As they were not to be owned by commoners, they became a symbol of noble authority.

The master builder's idea shows the importance of Solvang's image because of the town's dependence on tourism. The suggestion to change the town's theme from Danish to French with no major adjustments except for cutting off the wings of the windmills signals that it is not only heritage but indeed the Old World reference that may attract tourists. The importance of tourism is a reality for Solvang, and the debate about upscale tourism versus ordinary tourism is imbedded in the story about the Ferris wheel as well. What should Solvang be and for whom?

The fear of becoming a mere theme park is also reflected in local legend. John Hoj, a local of Danish descent who grew up in Solvang, presents one version of the story as a childhood memory in an article he wrote for the magazine *Velkommen*: 'Danish Days in Solvang, 2006'. The reader is plunged right into the story. A car stopped a little Danish boy on his bike to ask for directions:

'Excuse me,' the driver said. 'Is this Solvang?' The young boy was caught unprepared, but he overcame his fear and responded: 'This is it.' 'No, no,' the man said holding up a colourful pamphlet that sparkled in the sun with pictures of windmills, storefront windows, and the *Little Mermaid*. 'We want to know where Solvang is!' The boy gave them directions to the downtown, the driver thanked him, and added, 'Oh ...,' 'by the way, what time do the gates close?' 'Gates, Sir?' 'It is getting late, we don't want to pay for admission and not have enough time to see everything.' I shook my head and began to pedal up Alisal hill on my way home, unable to muster any reasonable response. What did he think this place was, Disneyland? (Hoj, 2006: 42)

Solvang has no gates, and there is no admission fee. Hoj shows how it can be growing up between two cultures: that of Solvang, which is part of the Danish Diaspora in Scandinavian-American immigrant culture, where Danish traditions are emphasised, and that of the Californian *hyperreality* with an abundance of themed tourist attractions (Eco, 1986). However, this is Solvang, not Disneyland.

Conclusion

The parking lot where Gary Jensen wanted to erect his Tivoli wheel is on the eastern border of Solvang. It serves not only as a place for tourist buses and for other visitors to park, but it also marks the boundary of Solvang. A big wall separates the parking lot and the city from the beautiful old Mission of Santa Inés. It is an almost surreal experience to go through one of the two doors in the wall, the views from which in either direction result in such different scenarios. On one side is the parking lot of a Danish-looking themed city, and on the other side is the old Spanish Mission in the middle of a beautiful, fragrant garden. The Mission itself is a California state landmark, while Solvang can be interpreted as a Californian reproduction of a nation–state. As one informant observed, as you go into the garden of the Mission you can look back over your shoulder and see the dumpsters of Solvang, as if the Mission is hidden behind the (trash of the) city.[10]

The contrast between the two scenarios is striking. Whereas the Mission seems more adapted to the surrounding nature, and is a functional building, Solvang looks false and out of place in the Californian land-scape. Yet both worlds are constructed to produce a feeling of either early 20th-century Europe or the 19th-century Hispanic Capuchin Franciscan order. In both cases, seemingly authentic looks can be highly questionable. Achieving a balance between *authentic* and *simulated* or manipulated architecture is difficult. Solvang as it looks today was built to satisfy tourists. In Solvang there exists a deep angst for appearing as a theme park as well as self-awareness of the city as a themed space. John Hoj's story is a piece of folklore that serves as a warning, and it is usually evoked when locals comment on the image of Solvang. They do not want it to become a place where people believe they need a ticket in order to come inside.

A parking lot seems like a trivial place, and a Ferris wheel seems like a somewhat cumbersome symbol of amusement. This particular parking lot, however, represents a liminal space, a sensory threshold between two very different worlds. By unfolding the conflict and disentangling the layers of meaning that lay underneath the spoken, more obvious dialogue, one can see how a single amusement structure threatened to spoil the image of Solvang and the peace of the Mission. By placing a Ferris wheel on a parking lot next to an old mission on the border of a Danish themed town, three landscapes: the political, the physical, and the cultural intersected. The parking lot became the vortex of yet another battle about what values Solvang should represent. Sixty years after its discovery as a tourist destination, the debate goes on. Should Solvang stick with the theme or keep out of the lamplight and away from the beaten track of tourism? Should it become the 'Hollywood production', facing the 'dead [...] theatre just after the audience has gone home and the lights have gone out' (*Santa Ynez Valley News*, 1947: 3)? Or, will the Danes simply chop off the wings of the windmills and retrain themselves to say *Bon Jour*?

To be continued ...

Notes

1. *The Saturday Evening Post* was an American weekly magazine (http://en.wikipedia.org/wiki/Magazine) published in the United States from 1821 to 1969. It was a conservative mainstream publication often illustrated by the famous Norman Rockwell.
2. The Old Mission of Santa Inés is located on the border of Solvang in the Santa Inés Vally. It is one of the 21 Californian missions along El Camino Real build by Spanish missionaries. The mission represents the first arrival of non-Native Americans to California and is visited by many tourists. The mission also has a functioning church used mainly by the local catholic population.
3. The movie *Forelsket i København* (*In love with Copenhagen* or *In Love in Copenhagen*) was released in 1960. The plot is very simple: the beautiful,

young Swedish actress - Siw Malmquist - comes to Copenhagen, where she falls in love. The object of her affection is a Dane, but the ambiguous title allows one to imagine how it is possible to fall *in* love *in* Copenhagen, but also fall in love *with* Copenhagen. This title appears in many a tourist pamphlet. Siw Malmquist sings the title song *Forelsket i København* while riding in the Ferris wheel, *Ballongyngen*, in the *Tivoli Gardens*. While the movie has been forgotten, the song, composed by the famous Danish composer Bent Fabricius-Bjerre, has become part of Danish vernacular.

4. Mexican workers maintain the Danish idyll behind the scenes, and people of increasingly remote Danish descent run the many shops, which offer a variety of more or less Danish items to the tourists. The Mexican presence constitutes a paradox. Very often they commute into Solvang, since Solvang has no affordable housing. Solvang citizens do not particularly like the Mexicans; they are needed and hence tolerated. Their work is cheap, and because of current immigration laws it is not as easy as it was in the past to get cheap Danish workers as *au pair* girls or teenagers taking a sabbatical. One hotel owner speaks for many when relating that he wants the Mexican workers in the background, in the kitchen, or cleaning the rooms. But behind the reception desk and in other visible positions he wants 'white, beautiful people'. Talking to the latter, I found that they came from everywhere. Some were Eastern European immigrants, possibly employed as cheaply as the Mexicans, but white (Larsen, 2006). In the ethnic hierarchy of Solvang, therefore, the Mexican comes in third, after the Danish minority and others of European descent who sympathise with the Danes and hence blend into the harmonic all-white illusion (Linde-Laursen, 1998).

5. The *Danish Mafia* is an exclusive group of old Danes who stick together and run Solvang. In Solvang, once you are in, you pay your dues to the *mobocracy*, and will be cared for. The *Danish Mafia* of Solvang lacks the criminal aspect of the mobster business, but a sense of national pride is the driving force. The term *Danish Mafia* is applied by non-Danes in a derogatory way as a reference to the old local, conservative Danes that resists all change. Used by members of the *Danish Mafia* themselves, the term is used with pride and accompanied by a big smile. Of course that kind of heritage hegemony is problematic. Who decides who is the most Danish or Danish enough to become a member of the *Danish Mafia*? Heritage is a powerful force and in Solvang it is strongly articulated in the landscape and silently enforced in the local pecking order (Larsen, 2006).

6. Leo Mathiasen, 23 February 2005.

7. Leo Mathiasen, 23 February 2005; David Goldstein, 22 February 2005.

8. Prior to 1911 when the Danes settled, the Chumash Indians, then the Spanish, had settled the Santa Ynez Valley. The Danes, the Mexicans and the Chumash share the valley in which Solvang is situated. Each group has its own theme. The Chumas run a Casino not far from Solvang. The Hispanic (now mainly Mexican) population has the mission, and the Danes created Solvang.

9. Although Earl Petersen always declined to be formally interviewed, his work was mentioned by many other Solvang informants. His activities in Leavenworth, Washington, have been documented elsewhere (Price & Miller, 1997: 51, 56–61, 63–64, 66, 71, 75, 101, 182).

10. Karen Logue, 26 January 2005.

SECTION THREE
RE-WRITING AND RE-MEDIATING AUTHENTICITY

Chapter 8
Travel and Testimony: The Rhetoric of Authenticity

DAN RINGGAARD

Introduction

In what follows, I shall describe the rhetoric of the authentic place in three recent Danish travel books that are all seeking out what we would generally understand as authentic meetings with historically significant places. I shall try to understand the rhetoric of authenticity in the travel books by comparing it to what is perhaps the most authentic rhetoric imaginable: the rhetoric of testimony. On the one hand the three travellers all want to become witnesses by testifying to a genuine, personal and unrepeatable experience of place, on the other they are challenged by their roles as tourists. They want to avoid the reproduction of tourism, reproduction being the hallmark of the inauthentic. Etymologically, authenticity means what comes from yourself, implying something that you have done with your own hands. Authenticity in this sense is exactly what Walter Benjamin in *The Work of Art in the Age of Mechanical Reproduction* calls aura and opposes to reproduction (Jay, 2006: 17–19).

In each case I shall pay particular attention to the failures of the rhetoric of authenticity, thus not only scrutinising the workings of this rhetoric but also exposing its unavoidable tangling with the inauthentic. Authenticity as well as the authentic experience of place are regarded as something that is not given but relational, subjective and represented, and as something that is unavoidably tied to its opposite. The primary scope of the paper is descriptive and hermeneutic. It traces a certain way of dealing with place in contemporary travel literature, and uses the concepts of authenticity and testimony to do so. Hopefully it can contribute to a more general rhetoric of authenticity.

Authentic Encounters with Place

The modern traveller does not discover new places, he seeks out places where others, like him, have been before, places that have already been seen and narrated to an extent and in a variety of presence-producing media that is unprecedented. An almost unending number of places have already been chosen by the guidebooks: they are sights, places to be seen, and part of a global circulation of tourism. They are sights because they – for some reason – are considered worth seeing. The traveller encounters the unique under common conditions. The challenge, for some, is to make the place talk, to come to terms with it. The task is to rediscover or even recover the place.

This may be more obvious when it comes to places of great significance. There are places that exercise a certain power because of the events that have taken place there. On places like these, the trees, the buildings, the air, all seem to be standing there as silent witnesses of what might have been horrendous historical events, perhaps intermediated by museums, guides etc. These places will demand of the traveller that he somehow relives the events, and, if the traveller is a writer, puts his words to the service of the testimony and thus carries it on. In this sense, the traveller must become a witness to the place. Not a witness to the events, but to the place where they took place. A second hand witness, if you like.

This kind of witness, the witness that heeds the call of the place and gives testimony, claims, like any witness, authenticity. Or, to put it more precisely, he claims an authentic encounter with place. Authenticity demands a relation, whether it is with an essence (my true self, the spirit of place) or with the past (my roots, the history of the place). There are of course other kinds of travellers. There are those who step into the 'contact zone' (Pratt, 1992) – the place of encounter and interpretation between the traveller and the locals – only to see themselves as foreigners (e.g. people in exile), those who merely drift through on their global wandering (e.g. people in transit), those who wish to know the society and its people thoroughly (e.g. people in an 'encyclopaedic mode'), those who are only there for pleasure (e.g. people in recreation), or those who seek out another and perhaps less ambitious kind of presence than that of authenticity. Travel literature, as well as tourism, has many typologies (Cohen, 1996; Jansson, 2002; Melberg, 2005).

Authenticity demands a relation, and so does place. Place is by definition a relation. Following Tim Cresswell (2004), this relation appears when the physical shape of a place is permeated by the sense of it: the entire load of meanings attached to a place by the culture and the individual in question. Or, as Casey states (2001), this relation occurs in between the body and the landscape, which are both always already imprinted by culture. So, place is always produced between a location and a sub-jectivity. As it is the case for place, authenticity too cannot be something that is already there: it is not a certain trait of place, but something created through an encounter. Of course a location can signal authenticity (for instance by looking 'historical' or being peaceful in a pastoral sense) and the encounter can be somehow predestined to produce authenticity (when enticed by memories or as scripted in guidebooks for instance), but location cannot be authentic. It follows that the experience of authenticity can take place at apparently inauthentic locations. If the traveller has an inclination for 'artificial locations', then these may provide the setting for authentic encounters. This is a result of what David Brown has seen as a dialectics between 'the quest for the authentic Other and for the authentic Self' (Brown, 1996: 39).

The authenticity that is generated in the encounter is doubled in the literature that at the same time creates it and tells about it. In travel literature the authenticity of place has its own paradoxical rhetoric. It is often a rhetoric of groundbreaking epiphanies and ricocheting apostrophes. It defies all pretence and yet persuades us and clearly stages itself as authentic. Like witness literature it wants to overcome literature and tell the plain truth, but it can't without the help of literature (Engdahl, 2002; Melberg, 2005). The impulse of this rhetoric of authenticity often seems to be a reaction against the inauthentic, as if authenticity first showed itself because of a lack of it. This is, according to Martin Jay, what Walter Benjamin realised in *The Work of Art in the Age of Mechanical Reproduction*: the claim for genuineness in art occurred with the mechanical reproduction of the artwork (Jay, 2006: 17–19).

In what follows, I shall try to describe the rhetoric of the authentic place in three recent Danish travel books that are all seeking out authentic meetings with historically significant places.

Reaching Out for the Far East

The two most common rhetorical devices in Carsten Jensen's travelogues *I Have Seen the World Begin* (1996, in part translated in English in 2002) and *I Have Heard a Falling Star* (1997) are allegory and epiphany. Jensen (born in 1952) started out as a literary critic and cultural journalist, and reached a broad audience with these two books. I refer to allegory here in the sense that in his travelogues, this author does not simply describe a place, but interprets it, making it into a general figure of meaning. As in the following passage, when Jensen writes about Saigon:

> Each evening I had a beer at the end of Nguyen Hue Boulevard while contemplating the traffic on the river and the play of colours that the sunset released across the sky and the water. Small ferries carried

pedestrians and cyclists across the Saigon River while they, in the strong current, perpetually seemed to be just about to turn around themselves and, like runaway tops, disappear down stream. On the opposite bank a forest of advertising boards rose on a background of dilapidated warehouses, mildewed cement walls and ramshackle, rusty iron chimneys. Toshiba, Fuji Film, Sony, Philips, the signs said, distant satellites in circuit around the Earth, not signals to the consumers who were not there anyway, but rather invocations and calls from a country that longed to be freed of its isolation. (Jensen, 2003: 343. All translations are my own)

The Western traveller sits in slight seclusion at a café overlooking the local crowds by the compulsory Far East river. The description is unavoidable but turns into allegory the moment Jensen insists on interpreting the advertising boards as expressions of the nation's innermost longings (Andersen, 1998). Throughout the book we can find these persistent acts of interpretation, which often seem like projections of the writer's own cultural heritage. On the reverse side of the unanswered apostrophe of the advertising boards, we can hear Jensen's own short-circuited apostrophe: an invocation of the foreign world that his allegorical doings tend to distance him from.

Throughout these books that describe a journey around the world, rings nevertheless the claim of a mutual humanity. This is especially staged in epiphanies of places. At Angor Wat, the acclaimed cradle of Cambodian civilisation, Jensen is facing the silence of the magnificent, but long ago abandoned place: 'Angor Wat turned me into a tourist in a different, more basic manner, not a foreign guest, but a survived witness to an apocalypse' (Jensen, 2003: 223). There is 'the full silence of nature', but also 'another, yet greater silence [...] The silence that history leaves behind when it has ceased, and man has disappeared after having filled the world with traces' (Jensen, 2003: 223). Confronted with such historically charged place, the tourist is no longer just a tourist, he is a 'witness' to history. In the double silence, among the traces of time past, history is present, but significantly as an absence. The tourist that seeks out place and tries to identify with it, and with what might have been going on there, succeeds for a brief moment. The place seems to open itself to 'another, yet greater silence', although not in a way that makes him feel as if he was there at the time of history; instead he feels such time as an acute absence, a deep, deep silence.

The epiphany consists in breaking with the part of the tourist and becoming a witness to history: not a witness to the event, but to its disappearance. Thus, it appears that historically charged places have an ability to testify, although silently. And some travellers seem to have to heed this call and, as writers, testify. The events may vanish along with the architecture in which they took place, but the place remains. The place is what is left; it is the material link to history. It is tempting to speak here of the call of the place, a call that some feel obliged to answer. By doing that, they are transformed from tourists into witnesses.

A witness is someone who was there. The witness says, 'I was there, I saw it, I can tell people!' – as Horace Engdahl puts it in his essay (Engdahl, 2002: 3). We may say the same about the kind of traveller I have been describing. But while the witness gives voice to what would otherwise remain unsaid, the modern traveller seems to move about in a world where everything has already been seen and said. If this person is to be considered or interpreted as a witness, we must see him as someone who breaks through to something that goes on at an otherwise remote frequency. The traveller as witness articulates the overlooked and the shocking. This traveller – who may be the ideal of many travellers – stands out by interrupting what he sees as the indifferent range of programmes attached to tourism, by establishing a highly individual relation to place. Unlike the witness, he seeks out this experience on purpose.

The turning point of Jensen's two books takes place in the Thien Mu-pagoda in Hue in Vietnam. Here Jensen finds a kind of essential happiness that points beyond his travel, beyond his coming to terms with himself and his quest for humanity:

> I had this sense of redemption. Now I can walk no further. This is the farthest out, the last landscape. I have never seen it in my dreams, because my dreams are not deep enough. To me landscape means longing. I don't really see the landscape I see its horizon. In the monastery garden behind the Thien Mu-pagoda I found the land-scape where the longing ceased. I was behind the horizon. No questions were answered. All were silenced. (Jensen, 2003: 442)

Silence again. The landscape is interpreted as the unacknowledged purpose of the travel. The 'force of belonging' (Jensen, 2003: 440) that takes hold of him there is created by a correspondence to an imagined place from his childhood memories. The chapter describes a strong sense of place, as for the incident at Angkor Wat, an equally important and powerful sensation of another more intimate place that resonates within the place where he is. The childhood memory is of a day when from his hospital bed he saw a hare on a field outside the window. The hare seemed to carry some kind of omen, and took his thoughts to a place that was absolutely foreign to his imagination:

> Where the hare came from: The answer focused on the hare sitting on a frozen, snow-covered field under a sky as grey as lead whose horizon smouldered white and pale red as the low winter sun fought to push its way through. It was a cold and deserted place, not a place for a child, rather a place where a child would feel abandoned, and still all my longing to get away from the ward found itself concentrated in this idea of the hare on the winter-red field. If I were to explain where I have been, as I stood in the monastery garden of the Thien Mu-pagoda and felt that I was in the last landscape, I would have to answer that I have been where the hare comes from. (Jensen, 2003: 443)

The epiphany is created by a correspondence between a foreign holy place and an imagined place from the author's childhood memories – with the (probably) real memory of the hare outside the hospital window as a kind of bridge, or tunnel: 'A connection had been made in my life between then and now, like a subterranean tunnel that suddenly opens between places that are situated on each side of the globe' (Jensen, 2003: 443). The epiphany related to a place resonates in another place and down through a whole life. It is definitely double: not the place itself, but the place as it corresponds with life by way of other places.

Jensen's protagonist provides pathos. He concludes on the epiphany at Angkor Wat in a way that embraces the pathetic as well as the allegorical mode: 'Only the great, forgotten Asian cities can provide the sense of the end of history, this experience that Asians are so familiar with, and Europeans fear more than anything else' (Jensen, 2003: 223). Wonderfully accomplished, while being a complete cliché, this sounds like a sentence out of a realist 19th-century novel, pronounced by a still-living omnipotent narrator. Jensen doesn't just place his allegories and epiphanies on the level of pathos; he leaves them unchallenged. Does one, in this pathetic staging, detect a distance between the narrating traveller and his author? The traveller stands naked before his fellow human beings, bereft of irony and critical afterthought, and at the same time dressed up in the ornate clothing of his rhetorical devices. Opposite the human authenticity that the book claims, stands an empty, stilted individual. It is in this mixture of pretence and vulnerability, self-deception and confession, rhetoric and intimacy that the protagonist of Jensen's travelogues comes into being.

According to Engdahl (2002), witness literature breaks with the literary, meaning the rhetorical conventions of literature. On the other hand, testimony has its own rhetoric, and this rhetoric cannot do without literature. A testimony is never just a testimony, it must seem credible, and its credibility needs arranging. In the essay 'Elaborations of testimony' Kenzaburo Oe (2002) tells about how the witnesses of the Hiroshima bombing and its many consequences that he talked to, changed their testimony again and again working their way towards what they could finally consider a reliable and substantial testimony. Oe sets up a whole rhetoric of testimony based on these conversations, one that is also a rhetoric of authenticity. This is necessary, Engdahl argues (2002), because although the testimony defies literature, it can only become testimony by way of literature. Like testimony, literature leaves things open; it always leaves a trace of the unheard of and the unaccounted for. It is no wonder that Jensen is caught between rhetoric and intimacy when he tries to make himself a witness to the place. While travel literature distances itself from literature, being essentially non-fictional, it must use literary devices in order for instance to be truthful to the experience of place. Thereby, any account of the authenticity of place will have to compose with the interchange of truth and literature, or of authenticity and rhetoric. In Carsten Jensen's travelogues such interchanges appear to be very gaudy.

Cambodian Echoes

Jens-Martin Eriksen (born in 1955) is a novelist. He published his first novel, *Nani*, in 1985. One of his best novels, and one that is relevant to the travelogue that will be discussed here, is *Winter by Dawn*, which contemplates evil in a fictional region akin to the former Jugoslavia. The novel came out in 1997, and has been translated into French (*Anatomie de Bourreau*, 2001) and German (*Winter im Morgengraue*, 2002). From the first page of his untranslated travelogue *The Bridge of the Hours* (2006), set in the Far East, Jens-Martin Eriksen portraits himself as a traveller who wants to – but cannot – enter into contact with the places he travels to, let alone represent them accurately. As he has it, in Cambodia reigns 'an atmosphere of a colossal shock, a strange unarticulated bewilderment, a silence' (Eriksen, 2006: 87). It is a traumatised country that is not ready to give testimony, and whose native tongue has been misused by the regime to an extent that makes it of no use for witnessing. Furthermore, there is no addressee. A witness in Eriksen's book explains how he – who spent many years in a penal colony – had to lead long conversations with himself in the corner of a field because he could not talk to others. The speech that has no addressee must create its own: it must, rhetorically speaking, become apostrophic, it must turn itself to the remote and silent – thus remaining literally unheard.

It is this silence that the travelling writer attempts to break as he writes about places like these. He gives voice to the witness, but first of all he becomes the witness of the place, the one who has been there (afterwards), seen it (as it was afterwards), and now tells about it. Eriksen's book is very much about the difficulties of this kind of testimony. The difficulties derive from the impossibility of giving words to the horror, and the problems of getting rid of the tourist identification in order to become a witness.

Eriksen visits a former Khmer Rouge concentration camp in Phnom Penh. Contemplating the display of the museum he can only conclude that the story of the horror is impossible to tell adequately. It is basically silent. But he adds that the inadequate story is the only possible way to testify about the horror, a horror that becomes visible in the unsuccessful attempt of telling its story. Knowing this is at least something. The travelogue reflects such awareness by staging Eriken's unsuccessful quest for the nature of evil. Time and time again he doesn't manage to enter into the heart of darkness. Evil tends to slip in and out of normal life. Arriving at Pailin, a former Khmer Rouge camp, he once again sees evil slip through his fingers: 'As I apparently have arrived *there*, it seems to me that there is no actual – *"there"*!' (Eriksen, 2006: 131). All there is is another 'Anus Mundi' (Eriksen, 2006: 131), including the former president of the Khmer Rouge, who has a house in Pailin, who according to his neighbour is a pleasant man, but who of course is not in at the time – evil never is, it is always somewhere else. This repeats itself throughout the book, because evil as a metaphysical entity is a religious aberration that nevertheless has a firm grip on the writer, and because its deeds don't lend themselves to representation.

In a key passage Eriksen openly admit failure when it comes to give voice to the stigmatised place:

> I walk into the old French railway station. There is not much activity, actually none at all; the building is empty apart from a man in the corner who lies sleeping on a cart. It is such an incredible sight that it could seem like the emblem of the End of History. The railway station that, like nothing else, has been the pulsating centre of activity, trade and transport, the movement of people, is quiet as a grave. All is dead, it is as if the sleeper on his cart has done his last duties, or for

that matter turned off the light. He is the last man, and this is his job. Here there is no train leaving today, no one comes to or leaves this place. I walk quietly in the building so as not to wake the last man, and arrive at an old fashioned weight on which you once had your luggage weighed. It is of a French make, and on its scale I see that of all the cities, of all the streets in the world, and of all the houses, it comes from a by now long vanished factory located in the same apartment building that I live in at Rue Popincourt in Paris where we lived when my daughter Tatania was born in April 2004. Here, have I travelled around the Earth to find a weight from home on which I can weigh my own failure? In my attempt to find History, which really is an attempt to find the answer to the nature of evil and to what man is and can contain, I shall right here, where all the lights are off and there is no longer any road out of the city or into the city for trade or people, stand like a fool. (Eriksen, 2006: 75–76)

Eriksen, like Jensen, employs allegory and epiphany. He calls the place an emblem, but in a conjunctive mode – just after this passage he speaks of the experience as 'a meaningless coincidence' (Eriksen, 2006: 76). Also the epiphany is questioned as the private world appears in the huge and foreign space of the railway station and of history. It does not make way for a deeper and more real place, as in Jensen. Again we see another place in the place, but this time in an entirely different constellation. The weight creates a correspondence between two remote but contemporary places, not an historical or personal connection downwards in time. The calling of the big silent space does not get an answer from the depth of history, but from another ordinary place on Earth. Eriksen has not entered history, he has not found the answers to the nature of evil or to the secret of mankind, he has instead returned to himself. The testimony found no addressee, the chiming apostrophe of the railway station was just echoes leaving the traveller with a return to sender.

Eriksen fails with open eyes, not just as a knight on a quest for the nature of evil, but also as a tourist. According to Eriksen, who refers to Jean-Didier Urbain's (1993) *L'idiot du Voyage*, the tourist is caught in a miniature world of imitations, circulating among places without ever getting closer to any of them. 'There' is out of reach, also in the world of the tourist. Eriksen's attempts to become a witness are also about breaking through this miniature world of imitations. The traveller as a witness tries to break with the representations of tourism in order to represent the not heard as well as the unheard of, or at least invent new representations of place, which are somehow more truthful or authentic, or at least different.

Ironically, the most successful attempt of Eriksen's to penetrate what he regards as the tourist-miniature world of imitations takes place in an Asian cowboy town, which may be considered the most artificial possible place possible. What would generally be considered an inauthentic locality proves to be the perfect location for an authentic encounter that is commensensically authentic.

The Real Japan

Novelist and journalist Kristian Ditlev Jensen's (born in 1971) first book was the autobiographical testimony of incest *It was Said* (2001). His novel *Favourite Dish* (2004) has been translated into German (*Leibspeise*, 2006). In *Red Cookies and Green Tea* (2002) Jensen tries to come to terms with the 'head-on reality' (Jensen, 2002: 25), which is Japan. Again, it is about breaking through the common cultural ideas, about defying 'Japan the phantasm' (Jensen, 2002: 26) and instead 'see the reality that hit me' (Jensen, 2002: 25) – not just because this is what you must do anywhere, but because the specific Japanese idea of reality, according to Jensen, is characterised by a direct, open-minded and all-inclusive here-and-now related to Buddhism. 'In this fashion Japan *is*. In this fashion Japan *exists* [...] the world *exists*' (Jensen, 2002: 34) – the words in italic being repeated and thus emphasised in the three essays of the book.

However, the encounter with 'the real, the true Japan' (Jensen, 2002: 36), doesn't quite take place until he visits a stigmatised place: Hiroshima. Hiroshima delivers the shock, the tremor that sets everything else that the traveller has seen of the country into perspective. This encounter with the place is supposed to prove that 'the actual actually *is* actual. It is fact. True' (Jensen, 2002: 36). It is to show the real as real and be 'a lesson about the reality of the real' (Jensen, 2002: 36). Truth, reality and authenticity are emphasised again and again because that is what Japan is, clean and direct and as opposed to the bulk of meanings that for instance Europe might be, but also because what we are about to hear is not just any old travel account; it is a testimony: 'It is impossible to imagine how it was. How bad it actually was. But once you've been to Hiroshima you feel obliged to try. You feel obliged to think of the worst thing possible' (Jensen, 2002: 40–41). The traveller heeds the call of the place. This calling obliges him to give witness, and to give witness is to put preconceived notions, prejudices and lies aside and to tell the truth.

It takes identification to do justice to this kind of testimony, and Jensen obeys the call of the place by taking an imaginary walk through Hiroshima at the time of its devastation. At the end he states, just like the witness: 'This was what it was like to be there yourself' (Jensen, 2002: 38). He begins his walk through present day Hiroshima in the centre of the catastrophe, and moves outwards recording the changes in his surroundings: how, to begin with, there is nothing, then a single house, then a rising number of splinters and bits thrown out from the centre of the explosion, and finally the harbour where the buildings stand unharmed. But it is a 'theoretical walk' (Jensen, 2002: 40) because it is without any people. So Jensen takes the walk one more time, this time in the opposite direction, towards the centre of the explosion, while he 'tries to put them [the humans] back into the empty city' (Jensen, 2002: 40).

This strange, uncanny second walk is on the one hand a movement towards truth and reality where the traveller continually imagines and focuses on concrete sensory details as he, with his walking body, absorbs the place; on the other hand it is a blunt staging of this true reality. We see that in three ways. First, the walk is an imaginary one where the writer, like a puppeteer (or like a writer of fiction), places people in the empty city. He makes a list of the inhabitants that are to be called to life, rather like the inhabitants at the castle of the Sleeping Beauty. Secondly, he puts his walk into rhythm as he counts the metres he still has to walk, and measures the suffering by diagnosing the degree of burns on the individuals that run past him. Thirdly, he summons a macabre metaphor and makes it gather the whole text. The description of Hiroshima starts with a shock, quoting an eyewitness account about how some boys had the pattern of their shirts burned into their skin because of the explosion. Later we hear about a picture of a woman whose kimono likewise left its pattern on her skin. Finally an uncanny metaphor is used to pin point the whole experience of Hiroshima: 'Here the real world and the imagination are put together. Here they melt, they burn into one thing. Reality' (Jensen, 2002: 43).

They do that because of an appropriation of place which is imaginary, sensory, bodily and verbal all at the same time, and because of a movement through place where every detail seems to be its own silent witness to pain and reality. But it is also an unheard of and challenging staging of pain and reality. It becomes apparent, beyond all reasonable doubt, that also testimony has its rhetoric, and that it is, in this case, is a peculiar lucid blend of pathos and cynicism.

With his highly choreographed imaginary walk Jensen makes up a cool double to his terrified witness. The effect is highly provocative. One may compare it to a similar use of leitmotif in yet another essay form Engdahl's anthology on witness literature, Hertha Möller's 'When we don't speak, we become unbearable, and when we do, we make fools of ourselves'. Möller (2002) needs to describe an unheard of incident that she witnessed in Rumania during the reign of Ceausescu. She slowly circles around this incident by way of other stories, and connects them with a metaphor of berries that she charges with meaning in a far less demonstrative way than Jensen. Without denying herself a rhetoric of testimony, she, quite contrary to Jensen, tries to diminish the expressiveness of the testimony in order to make it seem more trustworthy.

Jensen ends his essay by siding with reality again. Hiroshima was his breakthrough to the Japanese reality: 'One knows now, in a completely new and fresh way, that it is always the pure existence of the sacred now and here – perhaps the moment and the space that art critics have termed *the aura of the art work*, and what architects has summed up in the concept of *spirit of place* – that is the basic condition for anything [...] to be the most beautiful in the world' (Jensen, 2002: 45). It was an authentic meeting then for Jensen, an experience of the essence of the place. One might ask: how can horrific historical event like Hiroshima point to a sacred presence? And can one really grasp the Buddhist acceptance of reality that – according to the essay – is Japan, through the brutal exception of Hiroshima? That a place so traumatised can pass waves of intensity to the whole of ones experience of the country seems reasonable, but the claim of unconditioned acceptance of a clean swept reality by way of an horrific open wound seem to have more in common with Western religious pathos than with Japanese Buddhism. Here Jensen's traveller misses, if not the point, then the place, and he must acknowledge that the real place, as Eriksen puts it (2006), is always some place else.

Failing Authenticity

The purpose of this paper was to describe the rhetoric of the authentic place through the example of three contemporary Danish traveloques. The three writers all pick out places of great significance, places that have a strong relation to history and thus have the potential of becoming the loci of authentic experiences of place. In order to release this potential authenticity they must relate personally to the locations by way of knowledge, sensibility and – of course – writing. In attempting this they face the problem of creating unique encounters under the common conditions of global tourism, and they have to choose a rhetoric for what is by definition not a matter of rhetoric but of truth.

Carsten Jensen's double bind of projective allegory and border crossing epiphany is the most revealing and the least convincing, essentially because it tells more than it shows. The echoing apostrophes of Jens-Martin Eriksen and the somewhat comical traveller, tracing the untrace-able, stages this kind of travelling as a hopeless one from the start, but nevertheless insists against all odds on the quest for the authentic. The obvious staging of the authentic meeting with place in Kristian Ditlev Jensen's text on Hiroshima has a rhetorical brutality that in a provocative, almost perverse way, corresponds to the things that have taken place there. In all three texts there is a claim for authenticity that is at the same time problematised directly or indirectly. To the travellers these places do call for an authentic meeting, and being the kind of travellers that they are, they must heed that call and give testimony.

The fact that they all fail, that none of them manages to testify convincingly begs the question: Is failing authenticity the only authentic thing to do? Or to put it differently: Can one relate convincingly to the experience of authenticity in any other way than by failing to grasp it? Perhaps one can. But failing authenticity is definitely one way of addressing authenticity, a way in which the inauthentic confirms itself as the inescapable second side of the coin. From this point of view, on this second level of language, none of them fail. They take authenticity to the fore. They scrutinise the concept, desired by so many modern travellers including themselves, and leave it somewhat dangling.

Chapter 9
Cool Kullaberg: The History of a Mediated Tourist Site

KAREN KLITGAARD POVLSEN

Introduction

The peninsula of Kullen has been a visitor site for 250 years. Nowadays the cliff, the hamlets of Mölle and Arild, and the area around them are experiencing a revival. Lars Vilks is a contemporary Swedish artist making his 'ruined' art at Kullen; but nature, the houses, the hotels, and urban planning are restored by architects thus creating a new 'chronotope'[1] that seemingly exists outside of time, but is very time-specific. This is accomplished with historical knowledge and reflection, with contributions from art and artists, and through science pamphlets and exhibitions that inform visitors of the geology, botany, and zoology of the place. The cooperation between art, academia and tourism began several hundred years ago, when tourism was an elitist and not a mass phenomenon. This is one of the reasons that the story of Kullen is still powerful. Scholars and artist may be perceived as trustworthy producers of a story and history that can be understood as authentic and original. From Carl von Linné to Lars Vilks, art and science has been legitimising the outstanding qualities of the place in specific periods. Here I can only discuss the most important turning points. Frequently repeated, artistic and scientific expertise has become an important certificate for authenticity - whatever that is. Every archaeological layer claims to be authentic, but is phantasmagorical because it is constructed and reflexively reconstructed – always referring to a previous original. As a represented 'topos', Kullen is suited to incorporate the visitor's imaginings of authenticity, depending on how much she or he knows about its story. Visitors may know more of it when they leave; the signs in the exhibitions, the pamphlets, all tell part of the story so that the visitor may become 'educated' in ways of seeing and experiencing their more bodily sensations.

How is a place established as an authentic place, and how has this authenticity been formulated through several hundred years, thus creating a convincing tourist tale? Authenticity is here understood as a triangle of objective (physical), constructed (mediated) and existential (bodily) meanings (Wang, 1999). My method is a kind of cultural-archaeological[2] reading of some of the representations of a specific place, the Kullaberg cliff, situated in the south-western border of Sweden, today a popular tourist attraction (see Figure 9.1). Kullaberg has been awarded three stars in the Swedish Michelin guide, and is visited by more than 500,000 people each year, mainly during the summer season, from May to August.

The main attraction is its apparent authenticity of nature; however, it exhibits a constructed and a modernised nature, consisting of vast nature reserve areas, golf-courses, diving spots, hiking paths, climbing and swimming areas, botanical displays and areas designated for family picnics, with bins and grottoes. Today a part of the area of the peninsula of Kullen is the biggest nature park in Sweden, consisting of three different reservation areas, and a belt of marine reserve along the coast. The centre of the area is Kullen cliff, a horst 16 kilometres in length, half a kilometre in breadth wide, the highest spot being Håkull, 187.5 metres above sea level. This does not seem much compared to the heights of

Figure 9.1 Kullen Peninsula: Kullaberg Cliffs

northern Sweden. The cliff is situated between the Skagerrak and the Baltic Sea. It runs very steeply down to the sea, especially to the Skagerrak, so that the views from Kullen are extraordinarily breathtaking. The steepness of the cliff makes it seem higher both seen from above and from below. The horst consists of old granite, compressed to gneiss, and is very weathered by the sea, rain, wind and humans looking for stones and metals. This has created a number of grottoes, mostly along the coast. The cliff thus looks rough and old – very 'wild', compared to the gentle landscapes of the surrounding Skåne, and extreme, compared to the nearby Danish island of Sealand, which is almost always clearly visible from Kullen.

Both zoology and biology of the cliff are heterogeneous; due to the mild and dry climate and even though the cliff features the typical geology of the Scandinavian Peninsula, it is a haven for southern plants. Accordingly, since the 18th century, the place has been metaphorically described as a northern Arcadia (Barton, 1998) or in the 20th century as 'a Swedish Riviera'. 'The Italian road' above the old fishing hamlet of Mölle, nowadays a tourist venue with nostalgically renovated hotels providing gourmet restaurants and wellness centres, reflects the situation on the borderline between North and South. A booklet for tourists predating 1950 (Behrens & Malmberg, no year: 8) pictures the place as follows: 'Sea, plain and forest – boundary territory between the Finnish-Scandinavian Achaean rock and the south of Middle Europe – and between Achaean time and present.' Kullen is thus constructed as a chronotope, a crossing of both time and place in a mythical space situated somewhere in between.

In what follows I will take a closer look at this mediated place as it appears in some chosen examples of travelogues and descriptions, from the medieval scholar Saxo to present days. But before doing so, I will briefly discuss the term 'authenticity'. According to the Old and New Testament, it means the 'genuine' or 'real' thing. Gilmore and Pine (2007: 1–2) contrast 'real' and 'fake', and state that 'nothing kills authenticity like ubiquity', but they also stress that authenticity nowadays is a severe challenge to the experience industry. Authenticity is a constructed experience that does not seem staged – as Disney World does. It is an experience of reality, but this reality is in itself socially constructed (2007: 18). Here I use the term in this broad sense. When dealing with place representations, that is mediated in media, and performed in subjective descriptions of experiences connected with the places, the term is, strictly speaking, a contradiction of itself. Thus, authenticity refers to an imagined or socially constructed authenticity of place and experience.

Authenticity is constructed. But this fact does not make it a 'fake', but a socially constructed experience that functions as an authentic one. Whenever authenticity is at play, an imagined original is also at play, thus the authenticity of the place represents a reconstructed authenticity. In this sense tourist texts are often nostalgic texts. They may present a 'restorative nostalgia' or a 'reflexive nostalgia' (Boym, 2001), indicating the possible porosity inherent to the construction of the authenticity of the place.

Romantic Geographies

The 18th century as an important turning point is my point of departure for investigating how the site was reinvented as a romantic destination for persons of sensibility, as a nature of possible affects. Before the 18th century, Kullen had already been described as an ancient meeting place of man and nature. The place's stunning visual qualities may explain that, from the Middle Ages onwards, Kullen has been described as a place of origin. Around 1200, Saxo Grammaticus refers to Kullen in his history of Denmark, *Gesta Danorum*, as the place where Palnatoke skied. Palnatoke, a Danish pagan hero, who also is mentioned in the Icelandic Sagas of Snorre, was thought to be the founder of skiing outside of Lapland, after being challenged by Harald Bluetooth (950–986 CE) to ski down the steepest north cliff at Kullen, in order to prove that he was the best at this originally Sami tradition. The pagan legend was revived at the height of Danish national romanticism by Adam Oehlenschläger, who published his tragedy *Palnatoke* in 1809. Saxo also presented Kullen as the place in the sound between Denmark and Sweden where the most herring were to be caught – in fact, their abundance was so great, that one could go out into the Øresund and catch herring with one's bare hands and the boats were stuck between the many fish which surrounded them so that the oars could not be used. Thus, from the Middle Ages onwards, Kullen was constructed as the place of origin of sports, and a place of an unbelievable abundance and beauty. Several symbols of the North coincided here – skiing (sports' heroes), the rough, wild cliff as a 'forerunner' of the Nordic North and a sign of prehistory and the astonishing abundance of nature otherwise connected to the southern hemisphere. Once the tale was told, these narrative patterns would be repeated time and again until today.

Carl von Linné (1707–78), the great Swedish botanist, was familiar with the writings of Saxo when he visited Skåne in 1749, after he had made his famous journeys to Lapland and Dalarna in the 1730s. He had widely published on Swedish plants and worked on a system of classification of plants. Many of his works were published in The Netherlands, and he was already a famed European intellectual, when he arrived at the University of Uppsala in 1741. After Linné's arrival, Uppsala became famous all over Europe: students and travellers went to Sweden to visit Linné and the places whose botany and flora he had studied (Hartmann, 2000; Eliasson, 1999). The beaten track for travellers in Sweden in the second half of the 18th century thus followed the footsteps of Carl von Linné. This 'beaten track' became significant as many Europeans published travelogues about their Swedish travels, which lead them to the Sami people and Dalarna – and Kullen. In 1751 Carl von Linné published 17 pages on Kullen in his important *Philosophia botanica*. He described Kullen as a mountain with an extraordinary richness and variety of plants, but he also wrote about the fishing hamlets, the enormous flocks of herring that caused the fishermen's wealth and also provided wealth to the many country manors in the area – again, a picture of wealth and abundance in nature, as well as in human society: The idea of a Nordic paradise. It is difficult not to overestimate Carl von Linné's significance as someone to put Sweden and Swedish nature on the European agenda. He opened people's eyes to Nordic nature, Nordic plants and Nordic history in academic circles, but also among the educated middle classes – people who began to travel to see things for themselves, thus creating the first secular tourist itineraries in Europe.

A few years later, in 1754, Petrus Sundius delivered a doctoral thesis in Latin on Kullen. He documented the cultural history of Kullen with folksongs, sagas etc. Already in the second half of the 16th century, the basis for the romanticism, which would later be connected with Kullen, was established. Not only was the cliff old, people had been there since ancient times, which was legitimised by various myths and archaeo-logical remains: many rock engravings and flint axes etc. were to be found during the next few centuries. The myths of an original hero and athlete, and of untrammelled nature became important in the years before and after 1800, during which the Danish national poet, Adam Oehlenschläger and the minister and author N.F.S. Grundtvig became important exponents of Danish national romanticism – presenting Nordic mythology as a counterpart to the ancient Greek and Roman mythologies (Klitgaard Povlsen, 2007). Sweden had its own national romanticism, with interests in mythology, etc., but Kullen and Skåne appealed to the Danish writers and artists because Skåne had been Danish at a time when Denmark had been a major European power (until 1658). Kullen would become an emblem of the North and a synonym for 'original' Nordic nature for many Danes in the centuries to come.

The idyll, however, was not without horrors. Because Kullen was a dangerous place for passing ships, a lighthouse had to be installed, and the first lighthouse keeper was the famous Danish astronomer Tycho Brahe, who received Kullen as an entailed estate from the Danish King in 1577 (See Figure 9.2). Unfortunately, he did not look after the lighthouse, and many shipwrecks were found on the coasts around the cliff. It is not possible to determine whether this is the reason that the legend says that 'the Kullaman kills the people he can get at', but Tycho Brahe himself contributed to the legend of Kullen as a place for observing the stars and sky. Nevertheless, the legend of the cruel Kullaman still exists, and even with a modern lighthouse, people die every year, often falling down the steep sides of the cliff. The result is that, from early stage onwards, Kullen was associated with this dual imagery of idyll, abundance, and beauty, combined with the horrors of sudden death and cruel nature. In the aesthetic theories of the 18th century, the place itself thus combined beauty with sublime horror (Burke, 1756, 1998); the perfect basis for

Figure 9.2 Lighthouse

following descriptions of the landscape. An ideal location to construct a place of Nordic pre-romanticism as a space for imagined affects and emotions. The years around 1800 were those during which the romanticism of Kullen was constructed – a romanticism that is still very much alive in many tourist publications, for instance the Danish *Nordeuropæiske Badehoteller* (Just, 2007), in which Kullen is portrayed as the only place in Scandinavia with two entries, both of them nostalgic, reflecting the decades around 1900, Kullen's grandest period. But by the 1800s, Kullen had already become a popular attraction.

Kullen around 1800

The concept of the landscape and its depiction changed during the late 18th century. During the Enlightenment, language and paintings were considered transparent media that represented reality, and thus made it accessible to reason and intelligence (Mitchell, 1990: 18). Perception as such was understood as visual, and was often explained through metaphors of looking (Koschorke, 1990: 96). To facilitate perception, some landscapes and examples were regarded better than others; painting or writing were most often thought of in didactic terms, in comparisons, parallels, and analogies. Many artists and writers were looking for suitable examples and themes which would be described according to objective and 'empirical' parameters. Nature was widely interpreted as a reservoir of didactic examples for artists and scientists to choose from. This relation changed fundamentally during the 1780s. The ideal land-scapes of the 17th-century French painters, Claude Lorrain and Charles Poussin, came into fashion in Europe, and in England in 1791, William Gilpin presented his theory of the picturesque landscape – a landscape that looks like a picture. His example was the Scottish Lake District, which he assisted to promote as a 'tourist destination'. It was not the landscape itself as an empirical fact that was the deciding factor for Lorrain's and Poussin's paintings, just as it was not necessarily the land-scape itself that was picturesque. It was the eye of the beholder that was able to perceive the landscape in order to render it picturesque, just as Poussin and Lorrain imagined their ideal landscapes with sheep and Greek temples: these landscapes did not exist in reality, but were nonetheless perceived as authentic pictures of a bygone time that could be reconstructed in paintings, in the traveller's eye, and in the 'natural' gardens that were created in England, Germany, and Denmark in the latter part of the 18th century, complete with sheep, temples and donkeys.

In a similar way, the Nordic landscape became a possible subject for the imaginative eye. In particular, the wildness of the cliffs in Norway and Sweden appealed to the well-educated middle classes. Some of them had made a Grand Tour through the Alps to Italy, others had read travelogues of Grand Tour travels. A certain fascination with the Alps was characteristic for a 'new' bourgeois experience, partly nurtured by Albrecht von Haller's influential poem *Die Alpen* ('The Alps', 1729), which had become extremely popular during the second half of the 18th century. Mountains were not only perceived as terrifying, and sublime, they were also seen as remainders of the past and as a memento of the creator behind time and place, God himself. Not everyone was able to 'see' this, but the imaginative and trained onlooker knew how to look, how to understand the more or less hidden ideal aspects of nature, such as the unknown time-span that had passed since the creation of mountains. Thus, sentimental travellers began to travel to Kullen to see the cliff and to enjoy the sights. Frequently they tried to inscribe themselves in this 'book of nature'. They scratched their names into the cliff, thus memorialising themselves for future and returning travellers. The cliff became a symbol for eternity, and loving couples were especially fond of marking their names, and thereby their love, for eternity. Ernst von Schimmelmann, later to be Danish Prime Minister, went to Kullen in the 1770s with his young and beautiful wife Emilie. Her premature death in 1780, and her husband's mourning, made the cliff appealing to young people in and around Copenhagen. During the summer, small boats crossed Øresund with young couples that wanted to find the names of Ernst and Emilie, and often to inscribe their own names into the rough cliff. Thereby, they indicated that they too experienced a great romantic love-affair, possibly lasting beyond death – as long as the cliff lasted, which was thought to be forever, or until doomsday.

When, in June 1786, the young Friederike Brun (born Münter; 1785–1836) crossed Øresund from Helsingborg together with her husband, her parents, and her small son, she wrote a piece on this excursion which was later published in various periodicals and books, and, published in a German periodical in 1791, became especially popular in Germany and Switzerland. The popular piece was the first of its kind to express a new relation to nature described in prose.

The piece is short, only 20 pages. The author leaves Sealand in the morning at six o'clock, just after mid-summer, on June 26th, 1786. Leaving 'soft' Sealand behind in a very small boat ('a nut shell'), the small party sails on the 'limitless' North sea towards the blue cliff of Kullen. Thus, from the outset, the author creates a picture that might remind us of

Figure 9.3 Kullen Peninsula

the paintings of C.D. Friedrich – the small human being moving away from culture (Sealand) towards a distant, frightening, but also promising, nature. The picture is symmetrical, with the boat between 'culture' and 'nature' – the smallness of it underlined, so that the vastness of nature is also emphasised: Man is small, God's creation is unbounded.

Subsequently, the Swedish town of Helsingborg is a disappointment. The town is not wealthy, not beautiful, only its inhabitants suggests something else, as they seem to be happy, nice, and simple people: healthy, with beautiful teeth, and often with dimples in their cheeks. Thus, they are the picture of happy simplicity and poverty. Here, a wagon is hired that carries the party around and up the cliff that now is now described looking like a Fata Morgana of imagined stormy skies of 'furchtbarer Schöne' – horrendous beauty. Like a Fata Morgana, the cliff comes into sight and disappears time and again. But the group approaches, and at the same time approaches the sea – this time the Baltic Sea – they can see the fishing hamlet of Mölle. They can see some mansions on the one hand (culture) and on the other, the vast ocean (nature) – in-between is the small wagon being lead upwards by some local men. We encounter the same symmetry that was described in the beginning – a construction to be repeated throughout the text. The point is that the observer/writer is placed between settings that contrast the common rules of the central perspective. The narrator does not master, but is mastered, and she does not want to make the reader understand the geography of the landscape, but rather she wants the reader to feel and imagine it. Her 'eye' or view is dynamic, it moves and renders nature dynamic too as it comes into sight and disappears, is sometimes close, sometimes in the distance. There is no logical coherence in the narrative, things are in constant motion. This is a new 'gaze', a new description of a landscape that later recurs in many of Friederike Brun's travelogues (Klitgaard Povlsen, 2007b; Jost, 2005), but this is the first time, and it is also the only one of her writings on a Nordic subject.

The author's intention was to build up emotions, the culmination of the text – right in the middle – being an emotional outburst. The reader only gets a very brief sketch of the view from Kullen's summit, stressing it as a place for contemplation, where the waves are mumbling very low – a place of shadows (Brun, 1799: 188). The shadows allude to her dead baby son, and other beloved dead. The view over the two seas (the North Sea and the Baltic Sea), which mirrors the sky, also becomes a mirror for the longing soul. In the text, the eye of the beholder turns inwards, not outwards. This could be perceived as a stereotypical description today, but it was a novelty in writing on Scandinavia prior to 1800. Descending the cliff, the author looks for the engraved names of her many friends who had visited the place before her. Most names have been eroded by the waves, only those of the poet Stolberg's remain, and Ernst and Emilie von Schimmelmann, the latter had died only six years earlier. The names of the living disappear – except the poet's – but the names of the dead remain a *memento mori*.

The author's imagination, however, goes further back than to the dead known to her. Descending even further, she imagines the mythical 'root' of the cliff – she imagines the god of the sea, Poseidon, sitting on his throne in one of the grottoes below the cliff.

The return to Denmark is pictured as a return to harmony. She describes Sealand and Fredensborg as an idyllic gardent The words she uses are 'beautiful', 'soft', 'picturesque' ('mahlerish') – peaceful. In contrast to rough Swedish nature, Denmark is portrayed as domesticated nature. But this kind of nature is appealing and soothing to the author, after the cruel and emotional effects of Kullen. Again, this motive becomes stereotypical throughout Nordic romanticism: Denmark as the peaceful garden, Sweden with more original, but also cruel, nature.

Friederike Brun was popular: the piece on Kullen appeared in several periodicals and as a chapter in two collections of her travelogues. She had many followers. A number of descriptions of excursions to Kullen were published in the following years – some of them by her close friends. Her closest friend, the Swiss writer Karl Viktor von Bonstetten, travelled with her and her son Carl, and his son Carl, through Sealand to Kullen, in August and September 1798 (published 1799 in the *Neue Teutsche Merkur*). Bonstetten is not impressed in this text. He compares Kullen unfavourably to the Swiss Alps, and thinks the Swedish cliffs are smallish. He is also unimpressed with the Swedish (or the Danish) peasants. According to him they have no gardens whereas Friederike Brun had described their gardens in 1786 and, compared to the Swiss, are poor farmers. Bonstetten's eye is a rational eye. He wonders why the light-house farmer on Kullen does not produce potatoes or vegetables, but only milk? He also describes a tour to the top of Kullen to view the two seas but does not dwell in length on their description. He is, however, highly interested in the formation of the cliff, this 'natural ruin', and in the many granite formations found in Sweden and Denmark, and he develops theories regarding their origins. But what Bonstetten's text reveals is that the Kullagaard, the farm near the top of Kullen, was a rather polished inn for travellers. Bonstetten was astonished that it was so cheap and good, and it is evident that in the years around 1800, a whole system of local guides, wagons etc. could take the travellers around the area, providing them with facts and an introduction to the place.

In the following years and decades, one can follow other travels through literature. Several German, Swedish, and Danish authors write about Kullen: Christian Molbech (1812, 1817), Jonas Carl Linnerhjelm (1803), Ernst Moritz Arndt (1804), Ludwig Haussmann (1806–07), Ulrik Thersner (1819), and Steen Steensen Blicher, in 1839 (Möllefryd, 1978). When the Danish sculptor, Albert Thorvaldsen, returned to Copenhagen from Rome, he too went to Kullen (1839), and from the 1840s on, one could find advertisements in Danish and Swedish newspapers for group excursions to Kullen, for instance in *Helsingborg-Posten* (1841). Kullen had become an attraction.

During the 1860s, *Øresunds-Posten* advertised weekly excursions from Copenhagen to Kullen, and also from places in Sweden. King Oscar and Prince Eugen visited Kullen in 1866, and the Swedish Royal Family made excursions from their castle, Sofiero, to Kullen, during the summertime. In 1880 a shipping company was founded to sail to Mölle during the summertime, as was another shipping company called Kullen-Copenhagen, and in 1885, the Malmö-Mölle company was opened. Ritter's Bureau in Copenhagen sold group excursions en masse: Kullen had become a tourist site. The Swedish King Oscar visited Kullen in 1894, and, like an 18th-century traveller, he inscribed his name in a grotto – from then on called the Oscarsgrotto.

Danish painters were earlier than their Swedish colleagues in discovering Kullen as a picturesque landscape. Already in 1835, F.C. Kierskou stayed in Mölle, and the painters that later went to stay in Skagen, including P.S. Krøyer and Thaulow, Holger Drachmann, Frants Henningsen, and others, who went there in 1872 and later, first went to Arild and Mölle.[3] By 1856, so many Danish artists came to visit the place that a Danish woman opened an inn for them to stay in. They painted fishermen, boats, and nature, reminiscent of the style of the 'Skagen painters', who are famous in Denmark. During the 1880s, Danes dominated the far-too-few inns and pensions. New places were built, as were new ferries, wagons, etc. In 1892, approximately 5000 tourists stayed at Kullen and in 1893 there were already 15,000. Krøyer frequently visited the place in the 1880s and 1890s. He was famous, rich, and reportedly, fun to be with, so many followed him to Sweden and to Skagen. In the 1890s, Kullen was one of the most popular places for painters in Scandinavia (Sørensen, 2004) choosing peasant life, common country folks, and the Nordic light as their motives. The artists became an influential promoter of Kullen among the middle classes, just as the scientists had been an important factor for the 18th-century middle class travellers. Despite its popularity, Kullen was not exclusively perceived as an idyll: the poverty and simplicity of life was frequently stressed by the impressionistic painters, and rightly so, for the herring had disappeared, and dry summers had made farming difficult. Kullen was poor, its inhabitants and cliffs were romantic and 'original', and the tourist industry provided a possible future and substitute for the herring fishing.

1900

Around 1900 Kullen was a well-known tourist spot, with many hotels and pensions. Arild was considered to be the most cultivated hamlet on Kullen, because it was favoured by the artists, but Mölle was the most popular, with Danish, German, and Swedish tourists in abundance. Mölle grew fast, the taxes went up, many new shops were opened and the rate of childbirths rose during this period of optimism. Those were the years in which Kullen acquired the name 'the Swedish Riviera' – a place to spend one's holidays (Löfgren, 1999). The main attraction in the 1880s was the rumour that here men and women could bathe together – and did not have to use separate beaches. Indeed Kullen was the first place in Europe to allow mixed bathing, and this was the best advertisement a place could have. The German Kaiser Wilhelm visited Mölle in 1907, and in 1910 the railways were extended to Mölle, and Kullen thus had a direct line to Berlin. This was the period during which the finest hotels were built: the Grand Hotel and Hotel Kullaberg (Just, 2007) have been restored and reopened in recent years, and represent nostalgic reminders of Kullen's golden era, today the hotels are more luxurious and beautiful than ever before and offer wellness weekends all year. The golden era lasted until 1914 and the First World War. Then it ended. Nevertheless, Kullen remained popular tourist site near Copenhagen where Danish and Swedish academics, artists, and celebrities would have their cottages, and stay for the summer. The number of cottages grew as it began to do in many places in Scandinavia (Löfgren, 1999). The area became desolated during winter time, but during the summer it was a holiday idyll.

A number of tourist guides books, and booklets published during the 1940s and 1950s show that Kullen remained the most important tourist destination in Southern Sweden, even though the boom of the 1910s had ended.

Kullen Today

In 2006 the Republic of Ladonia celebrated its ten-year anniversary. It was founded on 2 June 1996, when the Swedish artist and professor of fine arts, Lars Vilks, sent a letter to the Swedish Prime Minister, declaring one square kilometre on Kullen's north side independent of the Swedish state. This 'independence initiative' dates back to 1980, when Lars Vilks began to construct his monument, 'Nimis', on the northern shore of Kullen, where the cliff is very steep. The beach is difficult to access, and Lars Vilks worked hard to build his monumental sculptures with drift-wood and wood, later also concrete, which he had to carry two kilometres down the cliff (Andersen, 2002). Because the area is designated a natural preserve, the project was illegal. Nevertheless Vilks was able to work for two years without being noticed by the authorities due to the remoteness and difficult accessibility of the place. When the building project was discovered, the local authorities at once demanded it should be removed. They considered it to be a building, not a sculpture. Lars Vilks appealed several times, and when the verdict was pronounced and the Swedish State supported the local authorities, he sold the sculpture to Joseph

Beuys in 1984, and after Beuys death in 1997, to the artists Christo and Jeanne-Claude. The court procedures made Vilks and his work famous in Sweden. Vilks saw the court trials as an important context for the sculptures – as a piece of art in itself. Nimis (Latin: 'too much') consists of at least 80 tonnes of driftwood. Its 12 towers form a labyrinth with a stone wall facing the sea. The other sculpture, 'Arx' (Latin for fortress) is also heavy. It was built of concrete that Lars Vilks had carried down to the beach in his rucksack. Publisher David Stansvik suggested that Arx could be turned into a book project. This project led to the subsequent sale of Arx to over 300 private citizens, each of whom bought a part (a page) of the stone sculpture. The collective parts of Arx were then 'published' as a 'book in concrete' with 352 'pages'. Fifty copies of the 'book' were ordered, but so far, only two copies have been produced at the beach of Kullen, one big and one small. A 'pocket sized' edition is in production, weighing less than the bigger ones of hundreds of kilos. In 1999, a third sculpture was created: 'Omphalos' – named after a small sculpture in Delphi that was believed to mark the centre of the word, also called the navel of Ladonia – is made of stone and concrete, and weights a tonne.

The Gyllenstiernska Krapperup Foundation, formed to promote art and culture, sued Vilks for having built the sculpture illegally. Once again he was drawn into the district court, and again he was ordered to remove it. The same foundation had asked for the removal of Nimis and Arx (1500 tonnes), but as they were located on private property, the Supreme Court ruled against it. Omphalos was bought by the artist Ernst Billgren, but this did not prevent the authorities from ordering the removal of the sculpture, which was damaged in the process and subsequently bought by Moderna Museet in Stockholm. After that, Lars Vilks asked for permission to erect a memorial to Omphalos. His argument was that many tourists asked for the monument. He was allowed to erect a monument no taller than eight centimetres, which he did. The small sculpture was a copy of the original one.

But Nimis still exists (see Figure 9.4). It is not easy to find. Because the sculpture is officially illegal, no signposts or maps refer to its location. One has to reach it by foot, following a path, which is marked by yellow 'N's painted on the trees. The path is steep and rocky, so if you reach Nimis, you have already had an experience of nature and of your own body – too much of it. As the whole dispute surrounding Lars Vilk's struggles with the Swedish Welfare State seems to be. The statues are enormous, and so are the bills for the court proceedings. Nimis is still enormous despite ongoing attempts to destroy the sculpture by burning or cutting the wood with chain saws (Andersen, 2002). Nature with its

Figure 9.4 Nimis

storms, windy weather from the west, rain and snow, also destroys the sculpture, which resembles 'alien' and 'futuristic' elements and equally looks old and worn. The many tourists inscribe their names in the wood, just as visitors around 1800 inscribed theirs in stone. During all the years visitors had to climb up and down the cliff, an experience that today is available also in climbing courses at Kullen. Arx keeps growing and being produced in more copies, and the court proceedings concerning Omphalos concluded that these sculptures may legally remain in place. The statues are situated near Arild – the old painter's hamlet. Thus, this revives the myth of the true artist who is able to 'see' nature as something else, something original. Lars Vilks also stresses the hard physical work he has to do which may be seen as a parallel to the hard walking and climbing contemporary tourists are performing at the cliff – with the bodily experiences as their only goal The sculptures are a kind of land art, but their setting connects them to the golden age of Nordic landscape painting in Denmark and Sweden. The 'ruined' sculptures thus denote a wide time-span – past and future – and their settings are part of the art-work.

Despite their remote location and difficult accessibility, Lars Vilks' sculptures have become an important tourist destination. They reflect the aura of prohibited art as an 'original' art. The artist is known as one who fights against the Nordic bureaucratic welfare state, and the state of Ladonia is a virtual utopia that represents an appealing 'joke'. Posted on the Internet, it has become a success. At first it had no inhabitants – only nomads, but nowadays many thousands are seeking asylum in Ladonia – becoming a citizen of Ladonia is free, you have only to fill in an online form. Ladonia is a monarchy with a queen, Yvonne I Jarl, and a president. It has its own money and all the other symbols of a traditional nation state, however allows free access to everyone. Its borders are marked with red signs, but the borderline is porous and fictive. Ladonia does not exist, but this non-existence has become the paradoxical sign of its existence.

The presumed authenticity or originality of Kullen as a tourist site is thus constructed and reconstructed by scholars and artists who from Saxo until today refer to a previous construction as the original one. This is reflected ironically in Lars Vilks' works. The tourist industry contributes to this construction by providing the logistics and by restoring and presenting the place so that its history and the history of artistic and scientific contributions are visible and repeated for the visitors. Kullen is neither Legoland nor Disney World. It is an authentic place of another origin – and this origin has to be reconstructed continually to convince new visitors of the possibility of an authentic experience. This experience is a construction of effects which are similar to those of the romantic period after 1750 when the modern construction was formed. It is, however, different in the sense that it resembles a reflexive affect which is not only made possible for the educated traveller but for everyone who wishes to participate in climbing, swimming, walking and reading the signs and posters. To get 'educated' or 'sensitised' (Löfgren, 1999) today at Kullen is to have an authentic bodily experience of an original place with a long history that has neither beginning nor ending – an experience of the 'real thing' (Gilmore & Pine, 2007).

Notes

1. I use chronotope to describe a construction of a specific relation of time and place, inspired by Bakhtin's analysis of chronotopes in the 18th-century novel (Bakhtin, 1981: 84–258).
2. I do not use the term in a strict sense *à la* Foucault, but I look into selected material from different periods without any attempt to write a linear cultural history.
3. Arild may be among the first rural artist colonies in Scandinavia, see also N. Lübbren (2001) *Rural Artists' Colonies in Europe 1870–1910* (Manchester: Manchester University Press).

Chapter 10

Crime Scenes as Augmented Reality: Models for Enhancing Places Emotionally by Means of Narratives, Fictions and Virtual Reality

KJETIL SANDVIK

Introduction

Using the concept of augmented reality, this chapter will investigate how places in various ways have become augmented by means of different mediatisation strategies. Augmentation of reality implies an enhancement of the emotional character of the places: a certain mood, atmosphere or narrative surplus of meaning has been implemented. This may take place at different levels, which will be presented and investigated in this chapter and exemplified by some cases from the fields of tourism and computer games.

This chapter suggests that we may use the forensic term *crime scene* in order to understand the concept of *augmented reality*. The crime scene is an encoded place due to certain actions and events which have taken place and which have left various traces which in turn may be read and interpreted: blood, nails, hair are all (DNA) codes to be cracked as are traces of gun powder, shot holes, physical damage: they are all readable and interpretable signs. As augmented reality the crime scene carries a narrative which at first is hidden and must be revealed. Due to the process of investigation and the detective's ability to reason and deduce, the crime scene as place is reconstructed as virtual space which may be (re-)told as part of solving the crime, that is (re-)telling the course of events and thus revealing the murder mystery and finding the murderer.

Introduction: Revisiting Meyrowitz

Ever since Meyrowitz wrote *No Sense of Place* (1985), his ideas about how (at that time) new media influence our perception of time and place have been widely debated within media research. This article would like initially to agree with the points being put forward by Meyrowitz, that 'the evolution in media [...] has changed the logic of the social order by restructuring the relationships between physical place and social place and by altering the ways in which we transmit and receive social information' (1985: 308), but at the same time to point out that today's new media are not just (re)shaping our sense of place but actually producing new types of places and new types of spatial experiences. The new media – and first and foremost digital media – have given us a variety of media generated and mediated environments (various 3D-worlds from *World of Warcraft* to *Second Life*) as arenas for a wide range of social, political and economical activities. But as media research in the 1990's tended to regard these activities and their mediatic environment as of another order than the 'real world' – as an exotic *cyberspace* – the media evolution in the new millennium has made it increasingly clear that the borders between online and offline places and activities are blurred and dissolved and that physical and mediatised places are becoming intertwined (cf. Bolter *et al.*, 2007: 149ff).

I would like to argue that – in the same way as with the relation between online and off-line worlds – the lines between physical, mediated and mediatised places are blurred, that they are all part of the same continuum and that when it comes to our perception all types of places are mediated and mediatised. Following this line of thinking we might claim that we do not just experience, for example, Katmandu in itself; we do so as tourists who have created an image of the Nepalese capital from *Lonely Planet*, travel programmes, romantic notions of Eastern culture and spirituality and from the tales told by other tourists, and thus we are part of a 'mutual process of structural *site sacralisation* and corresponding *ritual attitudes* among tourists' (Jansson, 2006: 28). The actual place is thus transformed into a *touristic space*, which is a space that is 'both socio-material, symbolic and imaginative' (2006: 28–29). Following this line of argument, the experience of places will always be connected to various forms of mediatisation which define and frame the way we experience and how we define ourselves and the roles we play in connection to this experience. As Jansson points out, tourists will 'engage in the representational realms of marketing, popular culture, literature, photography and other sources of socio-spatial information' and use this mediation not only to develop 'a referential framework for the planning of a trip, but also a *script* for how to *perform* and perhaps reconfigure their own identities within the desired setting' (2006: 13–14).

I would like to propose that these and other forms of mediatisation of places which are both connected to mediation of the actual place on the one hand and to the mediatisation of our experience of this place on the other can be seen as a process of *augmentation*; an emotional enhancement of our sense and experience of place by means of mediatisation. As such my understanding of augmented places is in the line of how authentic places are being perceived in this anthology (as displayed in the introductory chapter) as a result of various (technologically, artistically, and economically) mediatisation processes through which places are produced, transformed and appropriated.

Strategies for Augmented Places: The Crime Scene as Model

To elaborate on this process of augmentation I will use the forensic term *crime scene* as a model for understanding augmentation of places.[1] Crime scenes are constituted by a combination of a plot and a place. The crime scene is a place which has been in a certain state of transformation at a certain moment in time, the moment at which the place constituted the scene for some kind of criminal activity. As such the place has been encoded in the way that the certain actions and events which have taken place have left a variety of marks and traces which may be read and interpreted. Traces of blood, nails, hair constitutes DNA codes which can be decrypted and deciphered, in the same way as traces of gun powder, bullet holes, physical damage are signs to be read and interpreted. Thus the place carries a plot (a narrative) which at first is hidden and scattered and has to be revealed and pieced together through a process of investigation and exploration with the aid of different forensic methods, eyewitnesses and so on – through reading and interpretation. During her investigation the detective's ability to make logical reasoning and deductive thinking as well as to make use of her imagination is crucial to how the crime scene is first deconstructed and then reconstructed as a setting for the story (that is the actions of crime). By decoding this reconstructed place the story itself is also reconstructed: the crime is being solved, the murderer revealed.

Using the crime scene as a model for understanding augmented places then implies that we are talking about a place which has acquired a certain surplus of meaning, a certain kind of narrative embedded into it.

Augmentation of actual places – that is the process in which a place is transformed into a 'crime scene' – implies that the characteristics of these places have been enhanced in that a certain mode, atmosphere or story has been added to them as extra layers of meaning. This may happen in at least five different ways.

Narrativisation

Augmentation may take place as a process of *narrativisation* in which the place constitutes a scene for the performance of 'true' stories. This is the case when London's Eastend is functioning as a setting for 'Jack The Ripper tours' which allow tourists to partake in guided city walks following the blood drenched trail laid out in the actual streets of late 1800 London by the first known serial killer in history. As a result of the guide's narration and the navigation through these streets and along historic buildings like Tower of London, the modern, highly illuminated city gives way for an image of dim gas lights and dark alleys where defenceless prostitutes were easy targets for Jack's razor-sharp scalpel.

But this type of augmentation may also happen in a process where an actual place constitutes a setting for new stories. This is what happens with the global art project 'Yellow Arrow'. Here you are invited to put up small yellow stickers at different locations in an actual city and then upload a personal story with connection to the chosen location. The arrow-sticker is provided with a certain SMS number so that others who come across your yellow arrow can use their mobile telephones to read the story, with which you have chosen to augment this certain location.

Augmented places as places which have some narrative embedded into them may be found in different cultures and different historical periods. Native Australians (aborigines) believe that *song-lines* run through the landscape telling the story of their ancestors and how the land came into being, and by following this narrative trail these stories can be retold. The mnemonic method known as *memory theatre* can be traced back to antiquity. Here speeches were memorised by linking the different parts of a speech to well-known and recognisable architectural features of the place in which the speech was to be given. By scanning the variety of statuary, friezes, articulated columns within the hall, the rhetorician skilled in this art (*Ars Memori*) could remember the different aspects of his speech. The augmented place then would provide the order and a frame of reference which could be used over and over again for a complex constellation of constantly changing ideas. Thus the same place could be augmented with many different narratives (cf. Yates, 1966).

In today's popular culture we also find augmentation of place by the means of narrativisation in theme parks. Not unlike the Memory

Theatre, the theme park becomes a memory place whose content must be deciphered:

> The story element is infused into the physical space a guest walks or rides through. It is the physical space that does much of the work of conveying the story the designers are trying to tell. [...] Armed only with their own knowledge of the world, and those visions collected from movies and books, the audience is ripe to be dropped into your adventure. The trick is to play on those memories and expectations to heighten the thrill of venturing into your created universe. (Carson, 2000)

Augmentation of place through means of narrativisation thus implies an element of performativity: the place comes into being through our performance (actions, movement, navigation). As we will see, this performative element implying the active use of the recipient's body as a central part of the reception (and thus construction) of place is present in most of the augmentation strategies presented in this article.

Fictionalisation

Augmentation of places may also happen through *fictionalisation*. Here the actual place is working as a setting for fictions as seen in Henning Mankell's use of Swedish small town Ystad as storyspace for his Wallander books, in Gunnar Staalesen's use of the city of Bergen as a *noir* setting for his tales about private eye Varg Veum, and in the way Liza Marklund constructs a Stockholmian underground as a stage for her protagonist, criminal reporter Annika Bengtzon. For the readers of Mankell, Staalesen and Marklund these actual locations, which are used as crime scenes, have become augmented: Wallander's Ystad is interacting with and blended into 'real life' Ystad and actually changing the identity of the actual small town. Tourists visiting Ystad visit at the same time a real and a fictional town and telling the two apart is quite difficult. As argued by Sandvik and Waade (2008: 8) the *concept* and the imagination of Ystad as a city and physical, geographical location can hardly be distinguished from the crime stories and the popularity of Wallander's Ystad. Here the concept of the crime scene may be regarded as one aspect of Ystad as a location that illustrates this mediated and media specific spatial production. It is not crime scenes containing actual crime acts, but rather crime scenes in crime fiction and crime series about Inspector Wallander, that transform the city into an augmented place and an emotionalised and embodied spatial experiment. When tourists visiting Bergen attend a Varg

Veum tour they are taken on a guided city walk through parts of the actual town but following the trails laid out not by some historical person or chain of historical events (like in the case of Jack the Ripper above) but by fictional characters and their actions and thus the actual places have become augmented as a result of fictionalisation.

An interesting case here would be the small American town of Burkitsville, which was used as a setting for the fictional tale told by the web-campaign and movie *The Blair Witch Project*. *The Blair Witch Project* was fiction presented as reality. The project's website told the story about three film-college students missing in the woods around Brukittsville, Maryland while exploring the myth about the witch from Blair, a town situated where Burkittsville is today and which was allegedly abandoned by its inhabitants after a series of mysterious murders and disappearings which were believed to be caused by a witch's curse. The website reconstructs the story of the city of Blair and the myth about the Blair Witch as well as containing reports on the police investigation of the three missing students, the recovery of diaries and docu-videos (which made up the *Blair Witch Project*-movie which premiered in theatres months after the release of the website) shot by the students as they were hunting the witch (and obviously themselves being hunted). Everything here – apart from Burkittsville itself – is fiction. But this fiction enhanced the actual city of Burkittsville with an aura of mystery which the town itself afterwards has been using as part of its branding strategy.[2] Even though there has never been any witch, missing students or abandoned city, tourists visiting Burkittsville can attend guided 'Witch Tours' in the area where the story about the three missing students takes place (see www.burkittsville.com/).

Demonisation

The ways of augmenting places described above relate to specific places which are emotionally enhanced either by ways of narrativisation or fictionalisation. But augmented places may also be the result of certain *categories* of places being used as settings in books, movies, TV series which may impact on how we later perceive these types of places. American suburbia, small-town communities, the English countryside are examples of categories of places which have been exposed to augmentation in the shape of displacement, estrangement and various strategies of *demonisation*. From David Lynch's *Blue Velvet* to the TV series *Desperate Housewives*, suburbia has been reconstructed not just as a quiet, sleepy outskirt but as a place with a dimension of creepiness added to it, its polished surfaces hiding deranged people and activities. *Twin Peaks* reconstructed the small-town community as a mysterious place where things and people are not what they seem. The English countryside is no longer just idyllic houses, rose gardens, nice inns and so on: augmented by the TV series *Inspector Barnaby* and its fictional Midsummer County, the countryside is also a potential high-crime area with murder rates exceeding most cities, the population taken into account.

Simulation

Broadening the scope of augmenting places by means of narrativisation and fictionalisation we may talk about how places may be simulated. It can be argued that touristic practices such as 'murder walks' in connection to either real or fictitious crime events (as described above) may be seen as simulation of places and spatial experience: the participating tourists are performing navigational operations which simulates those of the murderer (e.g. Jack the Ripper) or the investigating detective (e.g. Wallander). However, in the following I will focus on how computer games are using simulation as spatial augmentation strategy.

Simulation as narrative strategy is well known in crime scene investigations in the performing of reconstructions of how the actual crime may have happened. Here the investigators are playing out the roles of, for example, the potential murderers, helpers, victims, witnesses and so in an attempt to recap the chain of events in time and space.

The reason for talking about simulation here instead of representation is that when it comes to computer game narratives – or playable fictions as they more correctly should be called – these are not represented to a reader or a spectator, they are acted out by a player. The player participates in a simulation of actions and events as if they were real. And this is exactly what the crime scene reconstruction does: in the same way as the player puts herself in the role of the game character (the *avatar*) 'the profiler' puts himself in the role of the criminal (like detective Lacour in Danish TV series *Unit One*, for example).

So, simulation of actions in time and space is what we find in computer games. Here various computer-generated graphical structures and animated objects which can be manipulated by the player allow us to explore and interact with a certain type of narrative spatiality which is constructed – or at least comes into being – by ways of our agency and our integrative and controlling operations.

One of the basic characteristics of crime fiction is that solving the crime is more important than the crime itself. As readers or spectators we are engaged in the detective work of police officers from the homicide divisions and forensic experts of the CSI team. The tension-building in this type of fiction is connected to how this work is done, what challenges and obstacles are encountered along the way, the time pressure and so on. This type of fiction includes an explorative investigation of the crime scene, interrogation of witnesses and suspects which all in all construct a picture of the crime and who might have done it. This plot structure in which exploration and puzzle-solving are major characteristics is found in computer games and especially in the action-adventure genre. So, when computer games remediate crime fiction we are speaking of a medium which already shares some genre features with the crime novel, the crime movie or the crime TV series, but with the important difference that in the computer game we are no longer readers or spectators but participating agents in the investigation.

The crime mystery *Dollar* has been written especially for the PC by Liza Marklund using the crime scene settings she uses in the crime series about crime reporter Annika Bengtzon. In the computer game though you do not get to play the famous reporter, but become a part of Stockholm police as the chief of investigation in a case about a millionaire heiress who has been killed at one of Stockholm's fashionable hotels. In order to fulfil this task you must comb various parts of the Swedish capital and interrogate several more or less suspicious people. By doing so, you start to reconstruct the story about the victim who was a well-known person in Swedish high society as she was to inherit a large business empire. She was a person with many enemies and whom many would like to get rid of. And as is the case with any murder story by Marklund, the crime is intertwined in a complex web of political and financial conspiracies, games of power and shady activities like trafficking and prostitution. Many of the suspects and others you encounter throughout your investigations have plenty of reasons to keep information from you.

Even though *Dollar* may be compared to an adventure game like *Myst*, for example, where the main game-play is based on exploring the game world and solving puzzles and thereby constructing the story of the game, in this game you don't get to perform the adventurous tasks yourself. You are dependent on your CSI assistants to perform forensic work and interrogating suspects, eyewitnesses and so on. It is your task to decide what these assistants should do by collecting and analysing the different information they provide and then trying to piece together the over all picture. This is achieved by reconstructing the movements and actions of the victim and potential murderers through the use of different maps, reconstruction models, diagrams displaying how different people

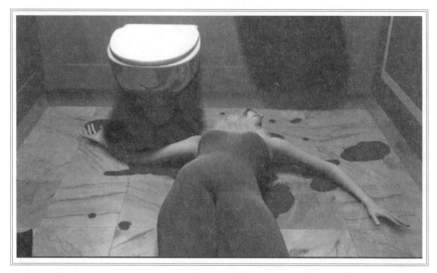

Figure 10.1 Screenshots from *Dollar.*

Figure 10.2 Screenshots from *Dollar.*

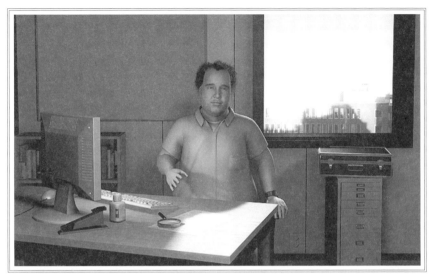

Figure 10.3 Screenshots from *Dollar*.

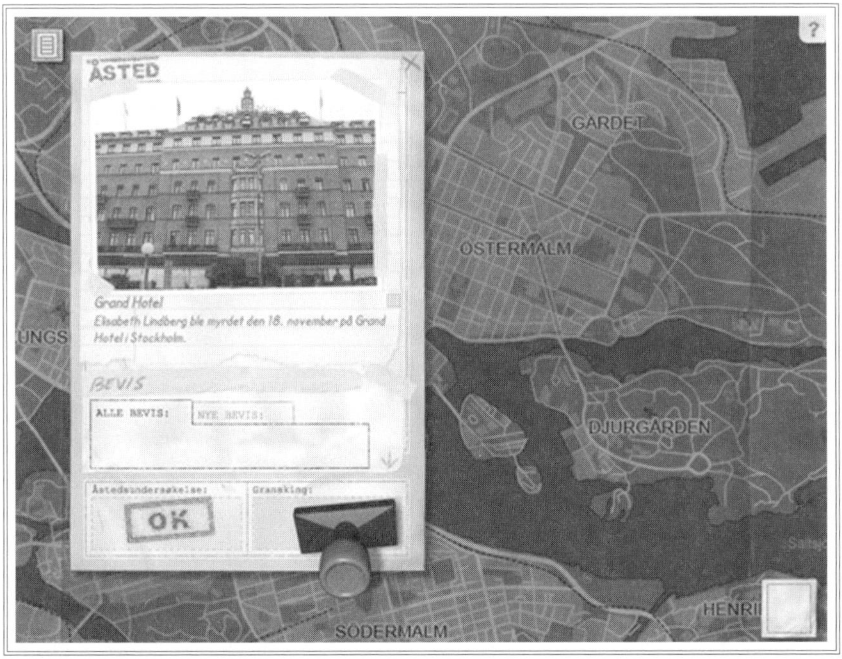

Figure 10.4 Screenshots from *Dollar*.

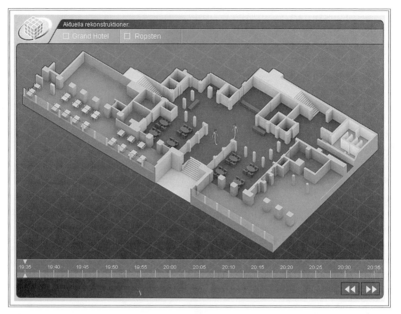

Figure 10.5 Screenshots from *Dollar*.

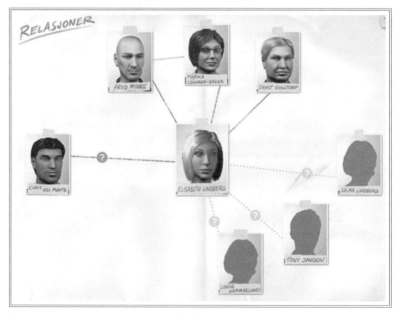

Figure 10.6 Screenshots from *Dollar*.

involved are connected to each other, and so on. The plot laid out by Marklund is complex, labyrinthine, using a variety of different locations and containing blind alleys, false scents and misleading information. Your choices are crucial to how your investigation develops and to whether you will succeed at solving the crime.

This is the core logic of the interactive and play-centric setup found in computer games: the story has to be performed by you instead of narrated or shown to you, and a vital element in this performative story is that your performance not only (re)constructs the story, but also (re)-constructs the spatial environment it takes place within. Even though you do not get to move around to the different locations in Markslund's *Dollar*, you use your assistants to do so and you may also use the different tools mentioned above, like a computer program to model and thus reconstruct the hotel in which the murder took place, for example. This is how you – by making choices, selecting and analysing information, reconstructing locations and patterns of action and movement – make the crime plot as well as its setting unfold as a result of your partly spatial performance.

Palimpsest

Finally, augmentation of places may happen in the form of the *palimpsest*, that is the over-layering of an actual place with some kind of fictional universe creating a sort of *mixed reality* in which the place has a status both as an actual location in the physical world and as a story space. Here we find cultural phenomena like different kinds of role-playing games in which a physical space is being used as a setting for the game itself. But unlike the stage set in the theatre or the film set in movie productions, the place itself has not been constructed, altered or manipulated.

Augmentation as palimpsest implies that the actual places (the specific town quarter, the specific street, the specific café) as well as non-participating people just happening to be present at the time of the game are included as a setting for the game. Thus, to the participating players the chosen quarter, street or café is more than just a location in the physical world, it is embedded with a certain meaning (narrative, emotion etc.) and thus part of the game fiction being played out. The use of costumes and props is also part of this augmentation. This is the case with so-called 'in-crowd' role-playing games which typically take place in urban areas like *Vampire Live*, which is played out once a month in the centre of

Danish town Aarhus, using, for example, cafés as locations: 'The "plot" unfolds over a period of several hours in the basement around a table tennis-board and some ordinary café tables and different role-players come and go' (Knudsen, 2006: 320).

Another example of these types of augmented places which are constituted by a kind of mixed reality are so-called pervasive games in which actual places are symbiotically fused with information- and communication technology such as mobile telephones containing instant messaging, camera, GPS (global positioning systems) and internet. An example of a game in which both game universe and game-play have become ubiquitous and embedded in the player's physical surroundings could be Electronic Arts's adventure game *Majestic* (2001). Here the game-play and the way in which the game story is constructed include receiving mysterious phone calls in the middle of the night, getting anonymous emails and attending fake websites. *Majestic* was promoted as the game which 'will take over your life' and was aiming at producing a game experience in lines of what is experienced by Michael Douglas's character in David Fincher's *The Game* (1997). And even though the game actually flopped and was taken off the market not long after its release, *Majestic* forecasted the trend within game design which today is known *pervasive gaming*.

Pervasive games derive from a trend within computer design which seeks to develop computer systems whose processes are not just defined to the mediated space of the computer, its screen and interface, but which are transgressing 'the box' and become embedded in the physical environment in the shape of intelligent rooms, intelligent kitchenware, intelligent lighting systems, intelligent clothes and so on. Here physical reality and computer-mediated reality become mixed. The same type of mixed reality is what we find in pervasive games, which may be defined as 'game spaces that seek to integrate the virtual and physical elements within a comprehensibly experienced perceptual game world' (Walther, 2005: 489). In a game like Alive Mobile Games's *Botfighters* (2001) the game design contains possibilities for using physical places as 'game universe' offering a game-play including a combination of tracking and site-specific interaction between players both online using advanced mobile phones with GPS and off-line battling each others in the streets. In *Botfighters*, the player 'shoots' other gamers located in the same physical area with the help of mobile phones including positioning technology. A downloadable Java client also makes it possible for a radar display and graphical feedback to be shown on the mobile phone.

In these cases the mediated, virtual space is collapsed into the physical, real place (and vice versa). Because the game is pervasive, that is penetrating the physical world, and ubiquitous, that is potentially present everywhere, the fictional game world becomes a part of the player's physical environment. At the same time the physical environment becomes part of different mediated spaces ranging from the GPS's graphical representation of the physical environment and the player's position in this environment to SMS and emails as communication channels for navigational information, as well as websites containing online dimensions of the game universe.

Putting the Body into Place: Some Closing Remarks

As cultural phenomena, computer games and pervasive games are related both to play and games in general and to the performative arts (like theatre). Thus computer games and pervasive games introduce a strong bodily dimension to how they are experienced. As fictions they are not being read or watched, they are played and as such they are dependent on the player's direct and physical actions and this is how computer game fictions in many ways simulate our behaviour in 'real life'. Janet H. Murray has explained that computer game fictions more than anything else present themselves as dynamic, narrative processes which are embodied by the computer and played out as a result of the player's performative agency:

> Whereas novels allow us to explore character and drama allows us to explore action, simulation narrative can allow us to explore process. Because the computer is a procedural medium, it does not just describe or observe behavioral patterns, the way printed text or moving photography does; it embodies and executes them. And as a participatory medium, it allows us to collaborate in the performance. (Murray, 1997: 181)

Thus the experience of plot and place in computer games relates to the human bodily conception of being situated in our surroundings, what Torben Grodal labels our 'first-person experiences' (Grodal, 2003: 42). Here movement in three dimensions is what constitutes our reception of the world and thus also our conceptualisation of the world in which even non-physical events and phenomena are being conceptualised by the use of spatial metaphors (cf. Lakoff & Johnson, 1980). It follows that the way a computer game engages not only the player's cognitive apparatus but also her body is vital as to how plot and place in computer game fictions are experienced:

> Computer games and some types of virtual reality are the most perfect media for total simulation of our basic first-person story experiences, because these media allow a full PECMA [perception, emotion, cognition, motor action]-flow by connecting perceptions, reasoning and emotions. Motor and pre-motor cortex and feedback from our muscles focus our audiovisual attention and enhances the experience with a 'muscular' reality which produces 'immersion' in the player. (1980: 38)

Engagement of the player's body takes place on several levels in computer games, ranging from the virtual physicality inherent in the player's *immersion* in the game universe and her presence by sub-stitute (*telepresence*) which is found in the player's control over the game character and game story to the tactility in encountering and operating the games interface. This emphasis on the body is also articulated in various forms of transgressions of the computer mediated world into the physical place which can be seen in how many computer games have surround sound. Such features expand the fictional universe compared to what is shown on the computer screen, together with new types of inter-faces which with the use of cameras and other censor technology includes the player's body as a navigational tool. Similar transgression may be found in so-called 'out-of-the-box' games (pervasive games) as described earlier in which the game universe not only appears as computer made and mediated but also as embedded in the physical environment, in which the player's body becomes a part of this game universe. Thus playing a game becomes a performance constituted by role-play and choreography.

As such computer games (in line with the other categories of aug-mented places presented in this chapter) may be regarded not just as a spatial turn in today's media studies (cf. Falkenheimer & Jansson, 2006: 15ff) but also as part of a certain *performative turn* (see Jones, 1998) in our culture as such which – in opposition to the *linguistic turn* (cf. Rorty, 1967) which regards the world as text and the *visual turn* (cf. Mitchell, 1994) which regards the world as picture – regards the world as a stage for our actions and bodily investments (cf. Knudsen, 2006). Computer games therefore become a certain way of representing – or rather simulating – the world which may be described as a *performative realism* (*ibid.*) which also may be found in the spatial practices of augmentation through narrativisation, fictionalisation, demonisation, simulation and over-layering described in this article, and in which there are no recipients in the traditional sense, only participants whose bodies have been inscribed in the action and events in time and in space.

So, with regard to Meyrowitz, what is at stake here is not so much that mediated places are changing our sense of place or making our sense of place collapse altogether, but that mediatised places, that is places which are augmented by uses of media, provide new spatial experiences. We understand places through media (e.g. *Lonely Planet*, *Google Earth*, travel literature and so on), we use media to construct places (using cameras, mobile telephones, GPS, manoeuvering through 3D structures by means of an interface and some kind of *avatar* in a computer game etc.), and media shape our experience of places through different augmentation strategies as explained in this chapter.

Notes

1. This line of thought has earlier been unfolded in collaboration with Anne Marit Waade (cf. Sandvik & Waade, 2008)
2. It may be argued that place branding should represent yet another strategy of augmenting places somewhere between narrativisation and fictionalisation, but to me there is more to place branding than just augmenting. Place branding is about changing the very characteristics and story of an actual place. As pointed out by André Jansson in his paper 'Filling the Void: Urban Renewal, the Transitional Gaze, and the Discourse of Fatefulness' (p. 2) at the Nord-Media 07 Conference (Helsinki, 16–19 August 2007) place branding 'must be understood as more general, abstract processes of mediation through which spatial phantasmagoria are channelled' and is due to 'an interplay between emotional-representational dimensions': on the one hand (with reference to Goffman) 'an experience of standing at a crossroad with significance for one's life biography' and on the other hand 'a mode of spatial interpretation, creation and appropriation, through which the transitional potential of a certain place is accentuated' and which is 'tied to the tropes of futurity and progress, articulating what a space *might become*'.

Chapter 11
Murder Walks in Ystad

CARINA SJÖHOLM

Introduction

In a brochure issued by the Tourist Office of Ystad, Sweden, we can learn that 'Inspector Kurt Wallander of Ystad police is the main character in a series of ten detective novels by Henning Mankell. A few years after the first Wallander book was published, curious tourists started to appear in Ystad. That was ten years ago, and today Kurt Wallander is more popular than ever.'

In Ystad Studios the production company Yellow Bird has in fact produced 13 films, three for cinema and 10 for television and DVD release, between 2004–2005, based on the character Chief Inspector Kurt Wallander of the Ystad Police Department. A new series of films is already on its way, and in the summer of 2008 three British films based on this character were shot in Ystad by the BBC and Yellow Bird with Kenneth Branagh in the lead role.

The popularity of the novels by Henning Mankell, as well as the filmic adaptations of them, has given rise to a vast public interest in the character Wallander and his whereabouts in Ystad, where there are now guided tours around the studio premises. There is a special Wallander studio where parts of the films were made. In the studio, which is now a part of a designated tourist attraction, you can find the apartment where Kurt Wallander lives, as well as parts of the police station and a forensics laboratory. In the brochure 'In the footsteps of Wallander – A guide to Ystad and the surrounding area for fans of criminal inspector Kurt Wallander' one can read that a tour at Cineteket – the public part of the film studio – is 'a must for any film fan. Well-informed guides talk about the studio's background and share anecdotes from film sets and shoots'.

Ystad is a small town (around 17,200 inhabitants in the city proper) situated on the southeast coast of Skåne in Southern Sweden. Ystad is an old harbour, and a former garrison town, which has recently turned into a centre for film production in southern Sweden, due to national and regional funding. Hitherto, the most successful product has been the films with Chief Inspector Wallander. The local tourist office together with several other agents are now marketing Wallander in order to establish a new kind of tourism, centred around experiences connected to fiction and film.

The Sense of Ystad

In this case study I will present how the marketing of Wallander is organised, and deal with issues concerning *authenticity* and *sense of place*. The study is part of a current research project, 'Travels in the tracks of novels, films and writers: a cultural analysis of literary tourism'. My presentation relies on field observations, participation in several guided tours and interviews made in Ystad with people connected to the Wallander endeavour in different ways. For some years I have also participated in and been able to study several types of guided tours, connected to other novels and films. As a source I have also used tourist brochures, as well as other forms of public information. The source for some of my more general statements is primarily a quantitative survey with about 130 written answers from municipal tourist agencies from all over Sweden, concerned with different types of literary tourism. I have mainly studied tourism focused on crime novels and crime writers, but have in some field studies also collected facts around some other Swedish literary genres.

I will analyse the various products that have been created around the fictional character Kurt Wallander, as he appears not only in the novels and the films, but also in the guided studio tours and in the murder walk, the latter of which is based on a map with specific instructions. My aim is to show how subjective feelings for a place, the sense of place, interact with the physical location, and how it is possible to understand these both materially and symbolically. These places develop new local meanings, where social relationships can be created, maintained, and enacted. Place is thus, in this context, something which continues, a process.

Fiction and concepts of authenticity interact within the limits of a specific cultural genre, *the murder walk*. During these murder walks, the concept of authenticity is revised, since fictitious characters and places are mixed with 'real' ones. The participants in the walks embody the geography; they place themselves inside the fiction, and thereby transgress the traditional border between fantasy and reality, otherwise upheld in crime stories and movies. Only through this walk is the embodiment – and thus the rethinking – possible to achieve.

One could ask if these places are imaginary or real. They have at least created a sense of place in the reader or the moviegoer, and do exist according to this mediated experience. 'Wallanderland' is here an example of how a place can be created and fictionalised through economic and commercial conditions. The fictitious Wallander has helped to establish Ystad as a destination for tourists. 'It is impossible to value how much we earn due to Kurt', according to one of the guides of the Wallander tours.

With the novels, the films, guided tours and a brochure of how to follow in Wallander's foot steps I want to give some examples of synergy effects between literature, film and tourism, which is an expanding market (Frost, 2006; Jones & Smith, 2005; Rodhanthi, 2004).

Murder Walks and Literary Tourism: Creating Products and Spaces

There are over 120 literary societies in Sweden, and many of them take care of buildings, museums and places that in all sorts of ways are connected to writers, and sometimes the fiction that the books deal with. Many tourist projects have been built around events and locations depicted in novels, and their success as attractions has been tremendous at some places.

The crime novels of Henning Mankell and the cinematic adaptations produced in Ystad are some of the vital elements in the specific practice of something between film- and literary tourism: that is, tourism focused on geographic spots and sights that are connected to authors and/or their literary creations. The relationship between tourism, literature and film tends right now to be in a formative moment within the field of research. At the same time it has become a commercially attractive sector within tourist business (Herbert, 1996, 2001; Robinson & Andersen, 2003; Squire, 1994). Increasing numbers of people read and plan their travels based on the concept of following a writer in his/her tracks, alternatively following a route from a novel, or, to experience something they have seen in the cinema (Beeton, 2004; Thompson, 2007). The example of Wallander shows that the combination of 'tourism–novel-writer-film' is a successful product; the market creates the needs, and the service business has found a new concept, a product that is an 'easy business to set up' (Strömberg, 2007).

It is noteworthy that the staff at Cineteket and the personnel within the tourist agency of Ystad when interviewed point out the different strata of visiting tourists. They claim that there is a difference between literary tourists and film tourists; the literary tourists, travelling in the tracks of writer Henning Mankell and his character Wallander, seem to be a bit embarrassed by their own interest, and find it important to show that they are also interested in other cultural events and traditions in the region. Film tourists are however much clearer in their ambitions, they often have very precise questions connected to the locations. 'Sometimes film tourists enter and seem quite astonished to find that there are also novels about Inspector Wallander', says the guide, and 'the films help the books to find new readers'.

A touristic site like this is constantly recharged with meaning, dependent upon who you are, when you travel and how. You can be a reader of novels, you can be a movie-goer, you can just look for some rest or distraction, or you can more actively seek experiences. And when you return to this place you have new expectations. Literary and film tourism is primarily a way of searching for the things you have read about or seen in other representations. Often it is the reading of fiction or what you have seen on the screen that motivates travel in this kind of tourism. You have been there already, almost. But when you arrive at the actual site, other things may be of greater importance than what you have read ...

Our diverse experiences, mediated as well as others, have a great importance for our interpretation of a place. Place is something that not only exists *a priori*, it *becomes*, and when – as in this case – the places are made into products and commercialised through fiction and film, they also develop a strategic meaning (Urry, 1995). Place is created through use. You can be interested in the stories of the novels, the filmic adaptations or of the writer as a biographic person. You can be interested in the writer's experiences of his writing in more general terms or his interpretation of a certain location or even attracted by stories told by other visitors.

There are thus different motivations for tourists to visit literary areas (Busby & Klug, 2001). Some tourists visit a literary place because of its connection to their own childhood memories; some don't even know that it was a literary spot before they were there (Busby & George, 2004). Several tourists travel to gain more knowledge about the writer and the books, and some visit the place since they had read about it in novels, and thereafter wanted to get to know the literary landscape.

It is possible to speak in terms of how places are made into products, and to ask if there are strategies to turn a place into a touristic attraction. Locally represented practices are increasingly important, due to the expansion of this kind of tourism, which Sandvik and Wade (2007) describe as a *media-scape*. One can note that guided tours in the tracks of diverse media narratives are disconnected from their first source of inspiration, and do lead to a kind of experience travel in which the tourists become characters in a role play. In order to fictionalise a place, you have to have a certain amount of 'fantasy', a way of 'seeing' the place according to the reader's experiences.

Films produced regionally are seen as an important factor for economic growth. They generate income at a regional level, and they also promote the region when they expose the landscape and surroundings of Ystad. But when they finally attract tourists they are also part of the industry of experiences (Löfgren, 2003). The promotion of the films leads to the promotion of the landscape that in turn leads to the promotion of other products, mostly experiences and services.

In the Tracks of Wallander

Ystad Tourist office has published a brochure, 'In the tracks of Wallander: A guide over Ystad and surroundings for those who like the fictional character Kurt Wallander, Chief Inspector at Ystad Police Department'. In the brochure Henning Mankell as well as his creations Kurt Wallander and Linda Wallander (Wallander's daughter) are presented, but above all there is a map with 32 Ystad sights, mentioned or used in the novels and the films. This brochure is free and around 30,000 copies are printed each year. The latest issue (2007) also has a list with 20 locations where the films were shot. Besides statistical information about the books, their selling rates, and translations, there are also some biographical facts, for example that Henning Mankell, married to theatre director Eva Bergman (daughter to Ingmar Bergman), lives partly outside Ystad, partly in Mozambique, where he is artistic adviser for Teatro Avenida, and you will also be informed about his engagement in the struggle against AIDS. Here I will use this brochure to show how it is possible to follow the character Kurt Wallander in his footsteps through Ystad.

When entering Ystad Tourist Office you will see portrait pictures of actor Krister Henriksson as Kurt Wallander. Mankell's novels are also for sale in several languages, Wallander postcards, the book *Wallanders Ystad* (Ambrius, 2004), published by the local newspaper *Ystad Allehanda*, and featuring texts in Swedish, English and German, making it evident that Ystad and Wallander are connected with each other. You are also handed the brochure with the intention that you will read this brochure and then travel around Ystad on your own. During the summertime it is also possible to go on different Wallander tours, arranged by the Volunteer Fire Corps, with their vintage fire squad car. 'The ride starts at

Stortorget (The Market Square), and takes in the famous (and not so famous) sites and locations from the books and films'. The Fire Corps is a part of the Ystad community that is not directly involved in the Wallander universe but has a lot to gain through the affiliation.

> You can also enjoy a guided tour in the studio where parts of the films were shot, and you can buy a Wallander package: dinner at one of Wallander's favourite restaurants, accommodation at the hotel where he used to eat lunch, and coffee at Fridolf's konditori, labelled as Wallander's favourite coffeshop, where he often either drinks coffee or beer and orders a herring sandwich, typical of the region.

The Wallander package also includes a 'Wallander pastry'. It is a blue-coloured fancy cake with marzipan and a taste of arrack. The story is worth telling: in the café there is a certificate, attesting to the fact that the confectioner has the approval of the Wallander family to use the name for the pastry; for immaterial, correct reasons the pastry *does not* – officially – allude to Chief Inspector Wallander – the copyright holders of the character name 'Wallander' denied this licence – but to a family, who happened to have the same name, who came to the assistance of the confectioner when they read the story in the papers. The story of the pastry is now a part of a web of storytelling together with other contextual stories, like the fact that Henning Mankell is politically and socially engaged. The stories help to maintain each other, and create new layers of meanings.

All this, from the Fire Squad car to the blue pastry, builds the experience of Wallanderland. But each part individually can also function either as an element in Wallander tourism, or as an isolated experience. There is a possibility for a visitor to come to Ystad and have the blue pastry without connecting it to the writer Mankell or his character Wallander. The experience industry, designed to promote Wallander, can also function as conventional tourism. The old can be a vessel for the new, and vice versa.

What kind of places do we see then, if we follow the maps and lists in the brochure? It all starts with the Police Department, which is described as the second home of Kurt Wallander. Then you go to Mariagatan no. 10, the home address of Wallander in the books. But in the brochure there is no mention of the fact that this house in not the actual location which is used in the films. This often causes confusion among the tourists. In the films, there is another house at Mariagatan which is used for the exterior shots, and which has been rebuilt in the studio for the interior shots. The text in the brochure tries to make this place concrete, sensual: 'The street lamp spreads a yellow light, the car is parked in the street. Often you can hear opera arias from the apartment. Mabasha was abducted from this place in *The White Lioness*, and murderers have been sneaking around here when trying to get Wallander.' It is easy for the crime reader to be transported to the books and the films by the presentation, which makes the scenes visible.

Further on in the tour, sketched out by the brochure, Kurt Wallander has been transformed into 'Kurt'; the relationship to the main character is now of a personal nature. An important element in the narrative, novels and films (and especially the earlier ones) is the bad health of Wallander. He tries to get help at the Ystad municipal hospital (also marked on the map) to handle his stress symptoms, but also to cure his diabetes. This is sometimes used as an explanation of the popularity of this fictional character; he has an anti-heroic stature – he is an ordinary man.

The tour in the brochure continues to locations connected to other characters in the novels and films, and includes locations where crimes have been committed and where murderers live. The distances between the places or sights start to increase and, consequently, you cannot walk between them, you have to use a bike or go by car. A certain order, a certain walk from point to point, is proposed in the brochure, but you are very free to choose.

The guided film studio walk is of a more traditionally preconditioned kind; you follow a route ordained by the guide. The film studio is located at the former garrison, and has a public part, called Cineteket, where there also are expositions on filmmaking more generally, and a presentation of the Ystad film environment. The guide tells about the two versions of Wallander; one acted by Rolf Lassgård in an earlier series of films, produced in Trollhättan in Western Sweden, in a 'fake Skåne', and the other one, acted by Krister Henriksson, produced in Ystad. The latter one is, the guide points out, a more international figure, fit for the 21st century: slimmer, healthier, and with a better relationship with his daughter. Several times it is mentioned that 26 million copies of the Wallander books have been sold. Now there is a third Wallander, Kenneth Branagh ...

When entering the studio the guide greets us, saying that it is time to 'visit Kurt and Nyberg' (Nyberg is the chief medical examiner at the police department). The question about the two addresses at Mariagatan no. 10 and no. 11 is raised. Furthermore, the guide carefully points out which scenes were shot in studio, and which scenes were shot on location.

We are told that the work begins when 'Henning' (the author) presents a story outline, later to be developed by several co-writers. 'Henning thought it was a good idea to make films with his Kurt', says the guide, and implies the personal relationship to the writer by using the given name. This is a common device in guided writers' tours (Kaijser, 2002; Meurling, 2006). Another way of showing how close one is to the famous author is demonstrated when the guide tells us that Mankell has a cottage near Ystad, but she has promised him not to disclose exactly *where* ...

In the studio apartment when we enter Kurt's living room, the guide turns on the CD and plays some opera music as a means of creating the right atmosphere. The guide ends the tour by asking us to 'stroll around in Kurt's apartment and see how he lives'. She hopes that we have had some 'insights in the world of film', and that we realise that much of it 'is fake'.

Fact and Fiction

The art of the moving picture is of great importance for our way of looking at landscapes. Regional developers and tourist businesses alike are ready to manage this as a new form of 'branding culture' where place-specific qualities are marketed and sold. Many of the new crime novels represent a specific place and a recognisable geography, which is of importance for those who read them, but also for the adaptation possibilities. It often creates a somewhat confused interchange between filmic representation, literary text, and geographical facts. Few things pique the imagination as much as a well-known geography.

But what happens with an actual place when it is marketed through a fictional text? The motivations for the different agents when they market their region are different. Some think in terms of marketing, and others about educating or mediating. And different novels relate to factual conditions in different ways. Some crime novelists point out that all places mentioned in their books are factual, and recreated after thorough research, while others feel free to blend facts and fiction. The reception of the stories by the audience depends on several factors, e.g. how the fictional stories are related to reality, who is conveying the stories and whose stories are told. One can wonder what happens when a surrounding, a writer and a work of art together constitute a tourist attraction.

A tourist attraction is a social construction, and in this process there are many factors involved: it is a matter of not only practical and economic considerations, but also the expectations of the visitors. The visitors are influenced by diverse kinds of former experiences of the actual place. For example, if you have read the book which the promoted writer has written, or if you know *anything at all* about the writer, if you know anything about the fictional characters, if you have seen an adaptation or read about other people's experiences of the place, the books or the writer.

It is intriguing to reflect on what it is that local authorities and business find possible to develop these days when tourism is promoted as a saviour for local problems. Cultural tourism has become more and more important in the global tourist business but also at a local level. When a place has had some success, it will inspire others. It is usual within the Swedish tourist business to copy successful enterprises, rather than to take the risk of developing your own. It is quite clear in my survey that several tourist agencies in Sweden have tried to duplicate the Ystad model of literary tourism, of course with other names and characters than the ones we find in Wallanderland. And when the Wallander concept is discussed in Ystad a new layer of fiction tends to merge with the others, i.e. the metafictional level where the story of the touristic enterprise becomes a part of the touristic attraction.

An ethical question worth consideration concerns who uses whom in this local game. Who benefits? Is it the writer, the fiction or the place that is at stake? Or is it a matter of exploitation? Is it even possible – or necessary – to discuss the processes at work here in terms of the wearing out of a place?

Multisensationalism and Situated Travels

The marketing of writers and their works is a phenomenon that has been around for a long time in Sweden. Celebrations of authors as well as guided walks have a long tradition, something which finally has reached the tourist business.

A basic assumption is that the visitor can make the connection between a writer's biography and his/her works. This biographical aspect in reading is very popular and highly feasible within the tourist business – in spite of scholarly research in literature and literary theory that for decades has tried to turn away from the biographical writer and instead explore the text and the encounter between text and reader. The common interest in personal history is great, and in my interviews it is clearly stated by tourist business representatives that this personal history is what the tourist wants to hear.

A significant trait in our time is new fusions and hybrids (Löfgren, 2003; Willim, 2005). Of the research that has been conducted upon the experience industry, a great deal has focused on additive factors: many experiences are meant to give customers components that they can blend and compose themselves, according to the situation and context (O'Dell, 2001). In that way consumers are turned into producers of their own experiences. In classical cultural analysis it is the processual element of the experience that is accentuated, and not only when it comes to the more exceptional experiences – those that we approach in a clear and visible way. Sometimes a visitor can find that he or she has been involved in a process, which afterwards is possible to define as an experience. Transposed into the travels of the kind we are discussing here, it is obvious that experiences are organised around a row of discrete units, which seen individually are rather trivial. But in this context they appear as symbolic bridges, connecting the different parts of the experience, and making it all into something extraordinary.

In this context it is possible to speak of 'multi-sensationalism': diverse kinds of sensual experiences are added in order to gain the complete experience (see Sjöholm, 2003). It can be wise to distinguish between the kind of experiences that are sensual, emotional or connected to a certain place and time, and those experiences that are of a more transcendent nature, conscious, cognitive, something which makes you wiser in a cumulative process (O'Dell, 2002). The economy of experience pre-supposes a great deal of reflexivity; you have to judge the experience in order to be able to retell it or dream about another one.

The Importance of Being Authentic

For a sight to be worth seeing several things are required. There are many who travel, trying to find out how a real person (for example a writer) could have been living, but there are also those who travel in the tracks of fictitious persons. A fictive event can also turn a place into an attraction. The paradox is that the tourist can find the fictitious as the most authentic; the reality needs an aesthetic form in order to appear real.

In the touristic arena the souvenir is a material artefact that is often judged on its level of authenticity and the *unicity* is a central criterion when tourists value authenticity (Löfgren, 1999). The evaluation of the authenticity is not only connected to the thing itself; it has also to do with the person who has produced it. Local handicraft is often seen as a guarantee for authenticity. Another quality here is the *situation* during which the artefact is acquired. The material artefacts or souvenirs that are treated in the realm of literary tourism are often the books and the films, and maybe maps and the kind of documentation made by the tourist; photographs, notes, diaries.

Are these medial places imaginary? Obviously they have created a sense of place for those who have read the books or seen the films; thus, *they exist*. Here, I do not discriminate between the places that a novel reader wants to see, and the ones that a cinema spectator wants to see *again*, even if we know that the guides of Ystad studios claim that there are differences between the literary tourist and the film tourist. Independent of the source of inspiration, the landscape is interpreted through the novels you have read or the films you have seen. The landscape is re-created through this new context. As well as a literary text is able to describe an existing place with great exactitude; a reader is able to transform the place into an imaginary place, with the help of imagination and experience. In the imagination of the reader, the diverse dimensions of the reading are mixed with certain visual and corporeal impressions. Many elements in the reading are important in the experience of the actual place; the writer's ability to describe the place as well as the mood of the actual reader. The mixture of real and imaginary landscape provides space for the imagination.

The true power of concepts and views obtained from literary texts is their ability to get the reader to confirm them, argue Krolikowski and Chappel (2004). As time passes, notions of a place are so internalised that a great deal of effort is required if one is to see something else. Literary images can thus dominate and make it difficult to see something of 'one's own'. But a literary text can also function as a gate to a landscape that does not exist in reality, but is possible to reach through the fiction. And the same goes for 'real' historical events. Some archaeologists describe how they at times try to understand a place by imagining its original features. The place is in this way interpreted through knowledge or acquaintance.

Literary tourism deals to a great extent with the staging of experiences. Everyone has to make his/her own composition. The balance between public representation and individual experience is crucial. It gives way to a cultural process where a new public sphere is created when the writer and the literary work are the condition for literary tourism, for example a guided tour (Squire, 1994). In this process, literary landscapes are commodified, and oscillate between being public images and individual arenas. And by individual we can mean both the writer's and the reader's visions.

To be in a place where you have never been before, but at the same time feel that you have experienced that place – and also in a physical sense – is of great importance. There is in a way a consumption of the landscape, a game of sorts. Sometimes it is more important to *have been there* than *to be there*.

The local has gained more importance as this kind of tourism is growing when certain places are promoted, packaged and marketed (Hansen & Wilber, 2006). Ystad is a village that has attracted German tourists for quite some time now. But through the creation of Wallanderland a new Ystad has been born, which is reinforced by commercial and cultural values. Mankell and Wallander have together secured Ystad as a tourist destination.

There is a geographical aspect to authenticity. Travels to certain places are supposed to be more authentic than others (Sheller & Urry, 2004). This has partly to do with the established historiography of the location; the way one travels to and through it, and the level of consumption taking place there. What is thought of as an original setting has a certain value, and another important factor is *selection*. Several scholars, for example within tourism research on sociological origin, have emphasised the subjectivity of the authentic (see Andersson-Cederholm, 2007; Cohen, 1988; Taylor, 2001; Wang, 1999). Authenticity is not a singular entity, but is often layered. That which is true for me does not have to be true for you! This does not automatically mean that authenticity is an illusion, lost in subjectivity and thereby impossible to grasp. However, truth is always negotiated.

In artists' and writers' homes there are often several kinds of activities being staged, such as expositions. Often it is claimed that these activities are conducted 'in the spirit' of the writer or the artist or even the fictitious character. When the Cineteket guide asks us to sit in Kurt's chair and be photographed, the concept of authenticity becomes a tool that is used and mobilised to charge the setting with a particular aura of 'authenticity' and thereby – which may be a paradox – make the location, the films and the books more sellable.

The Performative and the Tourism of Experience

In today's tourism the enactment of feelings is accentuated (Frykman & Löfgren, 2004). The performative dimension and the presence of the different senses have become increasingly important in the tourism and experience industry. In tourism research you can note that the highlight of the tourist gaze – to see what the tourist sees – has been augmented by the production and creation of experiences through the involvement of the tourist in different activities. It is, for example, obvious in the kind of walks that I have mentioned above, and which are essential elements in something I would like to label crime tourism or mystery tourism. You are guided as before, but you are also expected to interact.

Guided tours are actually a genre in their own right, a performance of sorts. Of course there are as many aspects and stories as there are guides. And there is also space for a dialogue between the guide and the visitor, an interaction, as well as a transfer between different guides and even different generations of guides.

The concept of authenticity produces values, meaning and coherence for the audience, the visitors or participants. It functions as a tool for social categorisation and positioning, and creates and maintains identities and styles. It becomes a means of distinguishing between 'us' and 'them' – 'we who like this' apart from 'you who like that'. As French sociologist Pierre Bourdieu would say, the place is charged with *cultural capital*. This all takes place in a complex interaction with several agents: journalists, travel agencies, museums, and audiences. The evaluation of experiences and the thoughts around authenticity and non-authenticity is an interplay that creates meanings and new values, where we compare our own experiences with those of others. To discuss what we were engaged in becomes a way of prolonging the pleasure and re-creating the experience.

There are many interacting factors behind the success that has characterised guided tours of this kind. There is a Museum pedagogy that cherishes 'learning by doing' and has chosen not to *expose* the cultural heritage but to *enact* it. This has become part of a marketing strategy. The Cineteket guide notes, for example, that it is always a success to show the studio and ask the visitors to touch things, and use the furniture. Tactility is a kernel in the staging of experiences.

Regional politics is another factor, with its need for the district's ability to compete and develop a brand, and with employment effects and attractivity for the service sector. The mission of today's museums has less to do with lifelong learning than with regional development. Nowadays the public sector is expected to work in a self-sustaining manner, which in turn demands a certain amount of creativity.

Within the tourism industry today it is commonly understood that many tourists expect to participate in the attractions they visit. But what is it all about? What is a true experience? The guide is a mediator and a guarantor for the truth of the message. In spite of that, there are obvious fictitious traits in all guided tours, and it can as a matter of fact be a part of the sport to find blots and errors. In most visitor groups you will find the Expert: the one who knows the streets best, the district, the books, the films, the technology ...

You are what you experience. In order to be seen as a whole human being there are certain things that you have to have been through. Often it is the story itself that is the point of it all, not just the fact that you travelled at all, but also that you return and can tell stories (Löfgren, 1999; O'Dell, 2001). The experience of travel has as much meaning as the products. To be on holiday and travel is not just to be off duty – it is also and always a question of larger ideological discourses: social class, cultural capital, economic limits and national identity all work to delineate boundaries and create possibilities. As a tourist you perform according to these patterns, and there is a complex and meaningful connection between these socio-cultural conditions and the way you tell and retell your experiences as stories. You will find what you are looking for, something which several of my informants confirm in their stories.

Conclusion

With a broad approach it is possible to see the importance of the many parts in the whole, and to grasp the cultural situations that surround reading in combination with travel. Interaction and co-production are of great importance. Fiction influences reality, which in turn influences the fiction, which in turn ... and so on. Fiction can function as an optical lens for reality. The difference between fiction and reality creates dynamics. To distinguish between the two worlds is almost impossible – and maybe not the most important task. Literary tourism deals with the staging of people's experiences, some real, some fictitious.

It is a question of a consumption of the place, often in a playful form: To be somewhere you have never been before, yet to be able to recognise the place, to *feel* the place and its corporeal qualities. Emotion and emotionality are resources to be affirmed (Bærenholdt *et al.*, 2004; Crouch, 1999).

In this study I have tried to give some examples of how fiction in diverse forms has been used in order to create locations and spaces – both with respect to incoming tourists and the local inhabitants. You do not have to come from afar to experience Ystad as exotic – if you accept the fictionalised reading of it.

What happens then with the inhabitants in a town, marketed with imaginary geographies? Do they see it as a potential or as a colonising threat? Probably both, depending upon how strong the attraction is and how it is developed ('what if everyone goes by car?'). *Something* is due to happen with a village or a city that becomes mediated through the tourist business and the experience industry. Evidently Wallander is used for branding and marketing Ystad – because nowadays every place with some self-respect must find its identity, something significant, and a representative face. You have to have a value on the experience market.

The body is a hazardous term, possible to connect both to the corpse in the murder mystery and the actual body of the tourist, the receiver of sensations and empirical data. The space term is no less complex; it covers the actual place – such as Mariagatan in Ystad – as well as the theoretical relations that occur or are possible to interpret between the actual place and the fictitious events. In the crossroad of body and space the walking tourist embodies the detective, the victim or the murderer and is still someone – or something – else. That *something else* is the core of the murder walk.

Chapter 12
Negotiating Authenticity at Rosslyn Chapel

MARIA MÅNSSON

Introduction

Media and tourism are two industries that feed off each other in an intricate network, where the entertainment industry influences the tourism industry and vice versa. Popular cultural media products like *The Da Vinci Code* by Dan Brown (2003) function not only as novels in themselves but also as books and films which are part of a global entertainment sector where film production companies co-operate with destination marketing organisations as a means of gaining awareness among tourists. Thus, tourism is going through a mediatisation process where tourism and media consumption are becoming increasingly linked to one another: the tourist gaze becomes intertwined with the general consumption of media images as tourists consume mediated representations of places (cf. Crouch *et al.*, 2005; Crouch & Lübbren, 2003; Jansson, 2002; Riley *et al.*, 1998).

Meanwhile, media and communication studies have arrived at an inflection point where the interrelationship between media and space is in focus (cf. Couldry & McCarthy, 2004; Falkheimer & Jansson, 2006). This emerging field of research – communication geography – is concerned with the issue of how communication produces space and how space, in turn, produces communication. Media influence people's sense of space, and the boundaries between imaginary, symbolic and material spaces are therefore dissolving (Jansson & Falkheimer, 2006). In this context, space is seen as something negotiable and volatile. Thus, space has no fixed meaning as it is dependent on whom and in which circumstance it is observed. This means that people create their own imaginary spaces from a multitude of influences and media have a prominent role in this process (cf. Beeton, 2005; Busby & Klug, 2001; Kim & Richardson, 2003). Take, for instance, a tourist's journey to a destination. It is preceded by talking to friends, reading novels and guidebooks, watching television programmes or films and so on, which contribute to the emergence of an imaginary landscape that guide tourists' anticipation of a destination prior to visit (Franklin & Crang, 2001).

When media, tourism and space intermingle, 'authenticity' is a relevant perspective to address. It is a concept that has been present in tourism studies ever since MacCannell's discussion about staged authenticity in *The Tourist*, originally published in 1976 (1999). Since then, there have been many different studies dealing with this concept (for a longer discussion of authenticity in tourism see Reisinger & Steiner, 2005 and Wang, 1999). The perspective in this chapter, in line with Cohen (1988), is to view authenticity as something fluid and negotiable. Thus, 'tourists' ideas of authenticity set the standard for what is authentic for them and what is not. What tourists think is authentic becomes authentic for them' (Reisinger & Steiner, 2005: 75). A tourist's perception of an authentic tourist site can, therefore, be influenced by historical sources as well as by fictional media products like film and literature. Consequently, real and fictional narratives can interweave in tourists' construction of the authentic tourist site.

Hence, the aim of this chapter is to explore authenticity in connection with media, physical spaces and imaginary spaces as they converge in tourists' experience of visitor attractions. This is exemplified at the site of Rosslyn Chapel in Scotland, and the way it is depicted in fiction – *The Da Vinci Code* novel and film. My intention is to portray the negotiation process between consumed media images and tourists' embodied experience of Rosslyn Chapel. Further, this chapter also addresses the question of contested authenticity. Tourists' experience of Rosslyn Chapel creates a plurality of representations and these views challenge the notion of an authentic Rosslyn Chapel. This study raises, therefore, the following questions. How do the tourists interact with the chapel and media products? How do the physical, imaginary, literary and filmic spaces merge? Focus is also applied to competing views and possible conflicts in relation to defining the authentic Rosslyn Chapel.

A combination of different methodological techniques are required for this endeavour, such as auto ethnography, observations, interviews with visitors and management at Rosslyn Chapel as well as textual analyses of the novel and the film.

The Da Vinci Code

One of the top selling novels in recent years is *The Da Vinci Code* (2003) by Dan Brown. The novel is a global success, having sold an estimated

60.5 million copies by 2006 and being translated into 44 languages. The novel is a mystery/detective story with Robert Langdon, a professor in religious iconology, as the main character. He gets involved in a murder mystery with religious connotations that bring him and his newly-found female assistant to various locations like the Louvre Museum in Paris, Temple Church and Westminster Abbey in London and to the final location of Rosslyn Chapel in Scotland. Since 2003, when the novel was first published, a whole economy has arisen around *The Da Vinci Code*. It has generated several spin-off books like *Cracking the Da Vinci Code* (Cox, 2004) as well as the Columbia Pictures film production *The Da Vinci Code* (2006) directed by Ron Howard and released in May 2006 (Grazer *et al.*, 2006). A further initiative was the joint tourism marketing project with VisitScotland, Maison De La France and VisitBritain who cooperated in a global marketing campaign with the film distribution company, Sony Pictures, and its global partner Eurostar to show locations, destinations and attractions associated with the film and the novel (VisitScotland, 2006). Many of the sites mentioned in the novel have experienced a boom in visitor numbers, especially Rosslyn Chapel. Hence, *The Da Vinci Code* and Rosslyn Chapel is an ideal case to exemplify authenticity and negotiating processes.

Rosslyn Chapel: An Arena for Contested Authenticity

Rosslyn Chapel – often called the Cathedral of Codes – stands seven miles south of Edinburgh, on the site of an ancient Mithraic temple. Built by the Knights Templar in 1446, the chapel is engraved with a mind-boggling array of symbols from the Jewish, Christian, Egyptian, Masonic and pagan traditions (Brown, 2003: 564).

The Da Vinci Code novel introduces Rosslyn Chapel for the reader in this dense, factual and almost guidebook-inspired manner. It is depicted as a site with historic roots, connected to various religious symbols and myths. In fact, the Knights Templar did not build the Chapel as it was founded by Sir William St Clair (History of Rosslyn Chapel). The site is associated with many stories like the Holy Grail, Knights Templar and Freemasonry, which might have been the reason why Brown chose to feature it in his novel. Rosslyn Chapel has, therefore, a special role with great importance for the storyline. It is here that the narrative's turning point occurs, although the length of the story set at Rosslyn only spans 24 pages out of the total 593, as many of the mysteries in the story resolve and secrets unfold. *The Da Vinci Code* has had an enormous influence on visitor numbers. Rosslyn Chapel had annually 10,000 visitors before the release of *The Da Vinci Code* in 2003 (Scotsman, 2006) however since then, the number of visitors has multiplied several times. In 2006 the Chapel received 170,000 visitors, which turned the site into one of Scotland's top 20 visitor attractions (VisitScotland, 2007). Thus, the growing influx of visitors started following the publication of the novel but it was not until the release of the film that a great number of people began to visit.

The growing tourist interest in Rosslyn Chapel was exploited commercially by different organisations like VisitScotland as well as the local bus company. Lothian Buses marketed their bus service to the village of Roslin with 'Break the Da Vinci Code. Visit Rosslyn Chapel on Service 15 A' (2006). However, other actors like The Rosslyn Chapel Trust – which manages the site – try instead to downplay the connection between Rosslyn Chapel and *The Da Vinci Code* (Interview Rosslyn Chapel Trust manager, 13 August 2007). The manager of the Trust raises several issues concerning the growing influx of visitors. Firstly, he stated that it is not an ideal situation when the number of visitors is too high to be accommodated by the site. The Trust welcomes all visitors, but the manager stated it should not be a 'visitor attraction for everybody', as the main work of the Trust is about 'preservation of the Chapel for the next 500 years to come'. Consequently, the Trust wants to receive only half the present number of visitors in coming years. The influx of visitors is a dilemma for many sites associated to popular media products and there is, therefore, a growing body of research that deals with the negative impacts of mediatised tourism (cf. Beeton, 2005; Mordue, 2001). Secondly, today's visitors might come for the 'wrong reasons' (Interview Rosslyn Chapel Trust manager, 13 August 2007). The wrong reasons were exemplified in relation to a Visitor Questionnaire that was handed out. The Trust was interested in visitors that ticked the box 'Church visit' and/or 'History' at the following question: 'What interests brought you here to the chapel today?' The other options, that were less important, were: 'Free Masonry, Knights Templar, Paganism, Spirituality, Grail Mystery, and *Da Vinci Code*' (Interview Rosslyn Chapel Trust manager, 13 August 2007). Thus, the preferred visitor should be interested in a church visit or the history of the Chapel and not the circulating myths associated with *The Da Vinci Code*. This is stressed to all employees to such an extent that the guided tour that I listened to in August 2007 even ended with a plea to appreciate the history of the chapel instead of just the myths. However, all interviewees did actually mention *The Da Vinci Code*. Though, for some visitors it was mentioned in order to prove that *The Da Vinci Code* had nothing to do with their visit whereas for others it was, indeed, the key motivator for their visit. It is, therefore, interesting that visitors' fascination in myths – like The Holy Grail – associated with the Chapel are neglected by the Trust, given that the reason for its popularity – *The Da Vinci Code* – is very much connected to these myths. Due to this neglect, there are no visible Da Vinci Code signs to be found upon a visit to the Chapel besides some books in the gift shop (August, 2007). Clearly, The Rosslyn Chapel Trust guards their interpretation of the authentic Rosslyn Chapel, which is rooted in history. This is in line with Fawcett and Cormack (2001) who researched three different literary sites in Canada. They concluded that although tourists are prime agents in the authenticity process, other actors are involved, like the Trust. Such actors are called guardians of authenticity and they are the legitimate body to interpret the site. As a result these actors are occupied with attempts to direct and influence tourists' perceptions of the actual tourist site. In this case, the Trust is trying to emphasise the historical aspects and downplay the mythical (e.g. Holy Grail) and fictional aspects (e.g. *The Da Vinci Code*) of the site.

Consequently, it becomes evident that there are contests as regards the preferred understanding of Rosslyn Chapel where the Trust claims that it has the power to decide the accurate history of Rosslyn Chapel. In other words, the Trust therefore has an objective view of authenticity (cf. Reisinger & Steiner, 2005) where Rosslyn Chapel is perceived to be inscribed with an authentic and true history ready for visitors to take part in. However, as will be seen in the next section, tourists might have an alternative perception of the authentic Rosslyn Chapel. Therefore, competing views seeking to define the authentic tourist site are common. Hence, 'Tourist sites function as contemporary sites of struggle and negotiation between stories attempting to construct and appeal to parti-cular identities' (Cohen-Hattab & Kerber, 2004: 61). The Trust guards their perception of the authentic Rosslyn Chapel and wants to receive visitors with a particular view although tourist themselves might have other influences. *The Da Vinci Code* and other media products might for instance be part of visitors' imaginary space but at a physical visit this notion is supplemented with other dimensions and facets to a new bricolage of the authentic Rosslyn Chapel. I will, therefore, in the next section discuss how tourists, through their embodied experiences, renegotiate their view of the authentic Rosslyn Chapel.

Embodying Rosslyn Chapel

In order to analyse how tourists negotiate authenticity, focus turns towards their embodied experiences at Rosslyn Chapel. The embodied perspective, promoted by for example, Veijola and Jokinen (1994) and Perkins and Thorns (2001), is particularly suitable to describe how tourists engage physically, using all their senses while visiting a tourist site like Rosslyn Chapel. As Crouch and his colleagues note: 'Tourist sites, destinations, cultures and places are (at least in part) made significant through the way we encounter them, and the encounter happens in an embodied way' (Crouch *et al.*, 2001: 259). Thus, the body is engaged actively in the creation of space and in following negotiations of authenticity. Consequently, my own mediatised impression of the space and embodiment of Rosslyn Chapel is part of the analysis. The empirical material was collected during four weeks at Rosslyn Chapel in August 2006 and 2007.

I started my journey to Rosslyn Chapel with the bus timetable, which proclaimed 'Break the Da Vinci Code', in my hand. Fresh in my memory was *The Da Vinci Code* novel and film, as I read and viewed them shortly before my journey in August 2006. My imaginary Rosslyn Chapel was a remote chapel located on a hilltop with a surrounding lush deciduous forest. To a large extent this image was visually based on the introducing aerial shot of Rosslyn Chapel in the film. Further, I imagined a place of remoteness and solitude – in reality I walked on a fairly flat straight road with 20-odd other people, all in the same direction. We all entered the service building and queued up in order to pay the entrance fee. While I moved along, I could follow a timeline with information signs of the history of Rosslyn Chapel. I had an expectation of finding some references to *The Da Vinci Code* at the end of the timeline. However, no such symbols or signs were visible. My mind had to adjust to this new information, thus my renegotiating process of the authentic Rosslyn had started even before I fully entered the site. Even if I knew the novel and the film were fictional they still had created a sense of the place, a mediatised sense of Rosslyn Chapel. Hence, the authentic Rosslyn Chapel was based on several Da Vinci Code signs and symbols and now this perception was challenged by a physical encounter as new impressions were supplemented.

After payment of the entry fee it was time for me to enter the site, time to encounter Rosslyn Chapel in person. The first thing that struck me was the physical location as I presumed it to be somewhat different as the descriptions in the novel still lingered in my mind.

The sanctuary was empty except for a handful of visitors listening to a young man giving the day's last tour. He was leading them in a single-file line along a well-known route on the floor – an invisible pathway linking six key architectural points within the sanctuary. Generations of visitors had walked these straight lines, connecting the points, and their countless footsteps had engraved an enormous symbol on the floor, 'The Star of David' (Brown, 2003: 568).

In reality there were people everywhere when I entered, looking around in the chapel. The sheer number of visitors came as a surprise since I had imagined it with far less people. During my visit I had also expected to come across certain signs and symbols since the novel had detailed depictions of the site's history as well as the physical interior, e.g. 'The Star of David'. However, it was difficult to get an immediate recognition of my imaginary Rosslyn Chapel. 'The Star of David' was, for instance, a product of pure fiction and therefore not traceable. Though in other cases, the detailed descriptions and the physical interior connected. 'Every surface in the chapel had been carved with symbols – Christian cruciforms, Jewish stars, Masonic seals, Templar crosses, cornucopias, pyramids, astrological signs, plants, vegetables, pentacles and roses' (Brown, 2004: 567). These detailed descriptions of Rosslyn Chapel and other places in the novel had also been noticed by other visitors.

Interviewer:	What was it in the book that made you want to see this place in reality?
Stefan:[1]	Well, I don't really know how to answer the question because there are many places described in the book as Paris and you would not notice at first glance the importance of the history behind those places and they are described very …
Anja:	… precisely.
Stefan:	Very precisely, so you can imagine very well what it is and all of them are of course in the mythical area, atmosphere that makes you interested to see them for yourself.

The visitors were helped by the detailed descriptions in the novel to understand the space they encountered. In other words, this is an illustration of how media products influence the embodied experience of a physical space. However, this works both ways as physical sites may also influence the media experience. The next quote illustrates that previous visits to places depicted in a novel may give new insights during reading.

Interviewer:	When you read the book had you been to Paris and London?
Jane:	Yeah. I have been to the Louvre before so yeah. It was weird thinking about the Louvre, the triangle bit in the middle. God, I have been there, seen that. […] So I think

when you read something it makes it more real because you have experienced it and you have been there. And you know what somebody is writing about. [...] I have always been interested in literature and history, so the both together it's quite a good interest for me. [...] English history, I know quite a lot about and a lot of the book is based in facts. But then he [refers to the author Dan Brown] just embellishes, which is good. I like embellishment so I don't read a book and think that must be what it is but it is just something Dan Brown wrote that made me realise this is how I felt about religion myself and about how it is portrayed.

This woman stressed that places depicted in the book became 'more real' when she could frame them in previous physical experiences. Further, her accumulated knowledge in history made her distinguish between the writer's embellishments and the facts of the story. This shows that there is a high level of intertextuality between different signs and images and 'when we read a text, consciously or unconsciously, we place it in wider frames of reference of language and knowledge, cross-fertilising a particular reading with other discourses drawn from our own socially, culturally and historically situated experiences' (O'Donohoe, 1997: 235). Thus, tourists' imaginary understanding of tourist spaces are assembled and strengthened from, for instance, the depictions of places in novels and films combined with any other experience.

Tourists' experiences of Rosslyn are a negotiation between the imaginary and the physical space with media being highly influential in this process. Hence, instead of referring to the tourist gaze (Urry, 1990), it is relevant to talk about the mediatised gaze, since tourists encounter places or sites in connection to former media experiences (Lagerkvist, 2004). This is expected to be enhanced 'as the spread of the entertainment industry continues unabated across the globe, as entire regions are being turned into giant theme parks, as the world becomes a complex web of intertexts and hypertexts, reality, media and tourism are more and more closely intertwined' (Davin, 2005: 178). Tourism experiences include mediated, physical and imaginary facets (Waade, 2006), and these aspects, therefore, influence a tourist's perception of authenticity. A tourist might have a mediated imaginary sense of a space and this sense will be negotiated in the physical contact. For that reason, the next section analyses how tourists negotiate authenticity at a physical visit through their embodiment of the site.

In my field study I met a woman – sitting in the grass outside the chapel – reading a book. It was a copy of *The Da Vinci Code*; she admitted having already read the novel some years ago. Nevertheless, she wanted to refresh her memory and check up some of the details since it was this novel that made her interested to come to Rosslyn Chapel on a visit.

Interviewer: Well, you have read it and now you are here. Is this how you thought it would look like?

Angela: Well, I had, it's entirely different than I pictured it when I read the book and I am trying to get my memory and the reality together but it's a [...] I had envisioned, first of all it's much larger, much more finished, somehow much more pristine not as, I mean I knew it was old but I didn't kind of realise I thought about it as having been deteriorated and worn away for some reason when I read the book. [...] It's truly an old, it's a wonderful building, but I was just expecting it to be somewhat bigger. I pictured it as larger. Having reread the book I readapt my memory back. I thought it was a large place. [...] I was a little bit disappointed at first and also I thought it would have been interesting to have some kind of brochure for, or maybe perhaps not the guide, not the woman who gave a little tour before, but just some handout [...] to have something in which you know it said events occurring in *The Da Vinci Code* [...] a little guide to the connection between *The Da Vinci Code* and this place.

This interview was conducted during her visit to Rosslyn Chapel, while she still struggled to get her imaginary space to connect with her physical experience, and it shows that something happens in a tourist's embodied experience of a mediatised tourist site. It is noteworthy that she even brought a copy of the book with her in order to look up some of the details to get a full understanding of the site. The novel confirmed her imaginary space as the authentic space by both the mediatised and the sensed senses. However, the descriptions in the novel and the story itself were not that easily traceable for her at the physical site. She asked, therefore, for something that would guide her during her visit, a handout of some kind that would connect the imaginary world from *The Da Vinci Code* to the present site of Rosslyn Chapel. Her case resembles my own, previously mentioned, experiences. *The Da Vinci Code* becomes the original and authentic space which the physical site is compared to, in things such as physical attributes.

Further, even if visitors, initially, were unaware of the connection between *The Da Vinci Code* and Rosslyn Chapel the realisation could enrich their embodied experience as well as activate a renegotiating process. The excerpt below is from an interview with a woman who was surprised by the amount of visitors.

Interviewer: Obviously there is a book and this place has become very popular through that.

Claire: Yeah, *The Da Vinci Code.* I did read *The Da Vinci Code* and this church is in it, isn't it? [...] I couldn't remember if it was this church. Is it right in the end?

Interviewer: Yes.

Claire: Yeah, that's what I thought but I wasn't 100% sure. Yeah, right. That makes it a bit more interesting. So I probably do know more about it. I just wasn't sure because I actually thought that the church was down in England. I remember that they go to the church but I didn't realise that it was in Scotland. [...] I was quite interested in *The Da Vinci Code* like the places when I was reading it. You know there are certain places in London that I want to go to at some stage because I was interested in the historical side but yeah this name was familiar. [...] I didn't realise it was in Scotland. [...] So why is it so popular now? That must be it. I didn't understand. It all makes sense now. Oh, when I was reading those signs in the church talking about the Knight Templar and stuff I was just thinking it's possibly the church from the book but still I thought it was somewhere in the countryside near London. I didn't recall that they went all the way to Edinburgh.

She was initially not aware of *The Da Vinci Code's* association with Rosslyn Chapel but when a book was mentioned, albeit without a title, she made a connection. The site became transformed for her with this newly acquired information, it became 'more interesting'. Thus, the Chapel altered from being any old chapel outside of Edinburgh to *The Chapel* from *The Da Vinci Code*. The media product enriched her embodied visit to Rosslyn Chapel as it inscribed the site with an added dimension. In this case the space became mediatised retroactively but it is the same renegotiation of authenticity process, as seen in the previous cases, which takes place. Hence, for tourists, *The Da Vinci Code* is an organic part of Rosslyn Chapel's story. There is, therefore, no distinction between historical and fictional authenticity as they intermingle through tourists embodied visits. The unclear boundaries between physical and fictional space has also been noted elsewhere and previous studies have shown that the authentic space might be the mediatised space influenced by for instance literature (Herbert, 2001) or TV programmes (Couldry, 2005). Like in Couldry's (2005) study of the *Coronation Street* set, the set was perceived as a real place where fictional events were filmed. Further, Sydney-Smith (2006) also emphasises, in her study of crime movies in England, that tourists' expectations of authenticity had nothing to do with the physical location. Rather, it was the filmic location that was the real place and the actual physical setting became imbued with the characteristics of the media production. Imaginary worlds are therefore not seen as fictional, as they are real to the beholder. This is similar to the discussion addressed in this chapter. However as seen with the Rosslyn Chapel case, a physical setting can also influence an imaginary space. This brings us to the last section that discusses tourists' interrelations to media, authenticity and space through embodiment.

Negotiating Authenticity

As discussed in this chapter, media products are interwoven with tourists' imaginations as well as embodied spaces. The embodiment perspective is relevant because people's bodies transform the spaces they occupy through the way they occupy them (Crouch *et al.*, 2001). Thus, tourists' physical interaction with space will, therefore, change their perception of the authenticity of the site visited. A tourist might have a mediatised sense before a visit – nonetheless, this sense can be altered during a visit, as mediated experiences are entwined with lived experiences – fiction and fact, lived and imagined (Lagerkvist, 2006). Further, there is a fear that mediatised tourism will alter the perception of spaces and replace physical travels when fiction and fact intermingle (Tzanelli, 2004). However, tourists are highly media literate individuals who can easily separate reality from fiction because they reinterpret the material and spaces they encounter (Davin, 2005). Edensor (2001) concluded for instance, when he studied the *Braveheart* film and the Wallace myth, that the film had – besides increasing interest in the Wallace myth – created a more reflexive and contested search for information among visitors. Lagerkvist (2004) also showed, in her study of Swedish visitors' travelogues to America, that visitors renegotiated their previously held beliefs while being in America as other perspectives were searched and experienced. Tourists might change their formerly held views of the authenticity of a site through media but mediatised tourism will not replace physical travelling - on the contrary, it triggers an interest in first-hand experiences (Jansson, 2002) just like in the case of Rosslyn Chapel and *The Da Vinci Code*.

In conclusion, a common view in tourism research is that tourism turns things and places into commodities and thereby they will lose their authenticity (Cole, 2007). However, authenticity has no objective quality, as it is socially constructed and negotiable as seen in this chapter, exemplified through tourists' mediatised senses and embodiment of sites. The tourist site, in this case Rosslyn Chapel, has no innate authenticity that can be lost when it gets mediated by popular cultural media products like *The Da Vinci Code*. Consequently, Rosslyn Chapel is more than just the physical site in itself, as tourists will create their own imaginary spaces from, for example books, newspapers, web pages and films. Thus, media, imaginary and physical spaces are interwoven in an ongoing negotiation process, which will continue as new media products are added to people's previously held experiences as well as new physical visits to tourist sites. When media, space and tourism mix in this manner, perceptions of authenticity among visitors will be affected. There will, therefore, not be a single authentic Rosslyn Chapel for the Rosslyn Chapel Trust to protect, as mediatised tourism gives rise to a plurality of authenticities.

Note

1. Note that names of the interviewed visitors are fictional.

SECTION FOUR
RE-EMPOWERING AUTHENTICITY

Chapter 13

Making Pictures Talk: The Re-opening of a 'Dead City' through Vernacular Photography as a Catalyst for the Performance of Memories

METTE SANDBYE

Introduction

This text is dedicated to the artist Pia Arke (1958–2007). She was one of the few Danish artists who managed to bring the post-colonial perspective into a Danish context in a coherent, intelligent and artistically innovative way. Denmark is a country with an extensive colonial past, but this is an almost repressed aspect of Danish history and contemporary Danish culture. Pia Arke made it her main subject and managed to shed important light on previously unarticulated, displaced aspects of the Danish colonial past. In her work, especially the art book *Scoresbysund-historier* (*Scoresbysund Stories* -- see Figure 13.1), she appropriates already existing photographs and relates them to oral culture and personal memory. Discussing Arke's work inspired by human geography, non-representional theory and by visual anthropology, this chapter highlights how she hereby manages to reformulate traditionally linked notions of authenticity, rationality, truth and objectivity related to: firstly the medium of photography, and secondly the scientific field of geography; that is to what 'place' is.

The Town With No Future

'Close the town with no future.' That was the headline of a feature article in a Greenlandic-Danish newspaper, which the Greenlandic-Danish artist Pia Arke read in 1996.[1] The town in question is Scoresbysund in Greenland – Denmark's most northern post, populated by 600 people. Few Danes know about this town, and it has hitherto played no important role in the history of either Denmark or Greenland. It is a town with no

Figure 13.1 Pia Arke: *Scoresbysundhistorier*

'collective memory', an almost invisible town. The author of the article was the Danish district doctor in charge of the area who described Scoresbysund as a town spoilt by violence and alcoholism; an image that is not unfamiliar to the Greenlandic or Danish reader.

This chapter became the starting point for an artistic project carried about by Pia Arke, which resulted in the book *Scoresbysundhistorier* (*Scoresbysund Stories*) in 2003.[2] In the following I will analyse how the artist – through an elaborate use of discovered photographs, as well as her own photographs and texts – manages to 're-open' the city as well as its collective memory and to turn the town into a locus of active, recognised memory and emotions. And I will describe how she manages to re-articulate the question of authenticity so closely related to the medium of photography.

The Most Authentic Medium?

Traditionally, the medium of photography has been closely associated with ideas of 'authenticity' and 'truth'; however, this conception has been heavily challenged by poststructuralist theory since the late 1970s. My main argument is that Pia Arke shows how this notion of 'the photographic authenticity/truth' can be re-invented or re-directed, mainly by connecting the medium to memory and to oral culture. In that sense her work has implications for the theoretical understanding of the medium, and it appeals to re-thinking the analysis and theory of photography.

With *Scoresbysund Stories* Pia Arke manages to transform the hitherto almost non-existing Greenlandic town Scoresbysund into an 'authentic place' by combining vernacular photography and oral memory culture in an articulation of 'space as process' (Crang & Thrift, 2000: 3) as opposed to 'space' as a rationally defined 'thing in the world' (Cresswell, 2004: 11). In her work, Pia Arke also shows that these vernacular forms can be used as a personal, creative and performative counterweight to the objectifying and stereotyping of identity that individuals experience in public life, and that the oral aspect of photography is crucial. But it is an aspect that has been hitherto neglected in most photography and cultural studies.

In the now 'classical' disciplines of photographic history and theory, photography has been overemphasised as an 'art form' and as a language of semiotically interpretative signs. But where does this leave all the vernacular forms of photography that do not necessarily fit into aesthetic theory and history? In studies of family photography Pierre Bourdieu's seminal book *Photography: A Middle-Brow Art* from 1965 is still among the most referenced works. More recent accounts in the fields of visual studies and visual anthropology, however, have challenged well-established theories and historiographies of photography (Pink, 2007; Pinney, 1997; Batchen, 2001, 2004).

In popular accounts of photography family photographs are fused with a particular emotional authenticity. We carry them in our purse, keep them in albums or hang them on walls, as authentic proof of the existence of our beloved. We regard the photograph as 'a mirror' to the world, as already the American physician and poet Oliver Wendell Holmes described the medium in 1859 (Holmes, 1859/1980: 73). However, in the tradition of Bourdieu, amateur and family photographs have been regarded as ritualised, conservative and stereotypical images. But it is time to focus on the use of these images as oral interlocutors (Edwards, 2004, 2006; Langford, 2001) between people, experience and historical knowledge. Inspired by scholars such as Elizabeth Edwards and Martha Langford, I want to advocate for a post-semiotic way of analysing photographs, that is to consider them both as objects and ways of creating a certain consciousness – photographs as visual constructions of the *social as process*. Photographs are not only determined by or mirroring social relations, they can themselves *create* social relations as well as history. Instead of asking *what is* photography, I will suggest that we start talking about what we *do with* photography. And instead of asking whether photographs are 'mirrors', 'real' and 'authentic', questions that have been crucial in discussing the medium since its invention, we need to ask how they can create and communicate our understanding of the real and the authentic.

Representing the Arctic

Photography has traditionally played an important role in representing 'the other'. It has been a powerful tool in the hands of Western anthropologists, scientists, explorers, governments and the media – especially in the process of colonisation. This has been a subject of study in academic work since the 1980s, but to a much lesser extent it has been dealt with in the work of contemporary artists.

The question of the representation of 'the Arctic experience' is an issue that has received less attention in international cultural discussions than, for example, the Indian post-colonial question. The colonisation of Greenland by Denmark began with Hans Egede's landing in Godthaab (now Nuuk) in 1721 and, although it obtained its own home government in 1979, Greenland remains a part of the Kingdom of Denmark. So far, only a few Danish artists have taken up this colonial situation in a critical and analytical way.

Arctic culture and experience has not really been a central issue within contemporary Western art institutions. This is both sad and odd given the fact that Greenland *is* a part of Denmark and Canada has a major Inuit population. Conventional artistic representations of Arctic culture aesthtically worship the exotic by mediating the idea of an 'Ultima Thule', a sublime wilderness on the fringes of Western civilisation, sparsely populated by 'primitive' or 'authentic' people. The same imagery has been transmitted by history books. Looking back to my Danish childhood education, I hardly remember anything about Greenland's history and culture, except from the images of a wasteland of ice and sealers dressed in polar bear and seal skin. In the city squares of Copenhagen I could meet seemingly homeless or inebriated Greenlanders, but nothing in my cultural upbringing taught me to connect the two images.

Very few Danes have actually visited Greenland. Our knowledge stems mostly from representations, and here photography has played an important role – still very little has been written about the photographic representation of Greenland. In the *History of Danish Photography* (2004), Birna Kleivan wrote a chapter on the photographic representation of Greenland, focussing on the late 19th and early 20th century. Most of these images follow the stereotypical anthropological depictions of natives that we know from mainstream global, colonial historiography. Odd examples can be found, such as the photographs taken on the expeditions of American polar explorer Robert Peary during the 1880s and 90s. On several images Peary and his male crew appear dressed in fur coats and mentioned by name, whereas the native women on the images, posing naked in the cold climate, remain anonymous and are referred to as 'The mistress of the tupik [tent MS]' or 'An Arctic Bronze'.[3] At that time, photography was understood within a largely unmediated, unquestioned realist frame as these photographs reflect seemingly neutral and unproblematic records of field data. Nevertheless, it was the predominant photographic gaze through which Danes learned about Greenland. It was certainly an instrumental gaze fused with an ideological and political discourse.

In her work, Pia Arke investigates the story of the Danish colonisation of Greenland and its consequences for today. Being a half-native Green-lander who has lived in Denmark since the age of twelve, her work also represents a form of self-therapy or autobiography. Balancing the different identities and backgrounds is characteristic for her art. The *Scoresbysund Stories* represents the culmination of her work, yet she has followed the same issues throughout her career gradually combining photography with a variety of other material and with text. One could call her collected works a kind of mapping of the post-colonial Greenlandic experience. Pia Arke herself calls it 'ethno-aesthetics', a concept to which I will return later. She shows how the colonial past causes a culturally fragmented subject and how the very act of remembrance can create new positions for being a subject connected to a certain history and a certain place. A lot of her work consists of montages made of appropriated photographs, both private family photographs and images taken from books by polar explorers, for example.

Pia Arke draws inspiration from anthropological methods. She also looks for places outside Greenland that contain knowledge, such as Danish museums and archives, in order to unfold the story that was told by the colonisers and other outsiders.

Scoresbysund/Ittoqqortoormit

Today, Pia Arke's native town Scoresbysund (Ittoqqortoormit being the Greenlandic name) is populated by 600 people. The town is geographically so remote and isolated that only twice a year food and material are shipped there. The town was artificially constructed in 1925 when 87 Inuit from 10 different families in Angmagssalik – including Pia Arke's grandparents – were transported 1000 kilometers north to form a Danish post in Northeastern Greenland before the Norwegians claimed the area. They didn't know where they were going and why. The official story is that the Danish government moved the people to prevent an over-population in Angmagssalik, where they came from. The truth is, that the settlement was planned due to a borderline fight between the Danish and the Norwegian government both claiming territory in the unpopulated Northeastern Greenland. Therefore it was important for the Danish government to colonise and claim Scoresbysund. The place was colonised in August 1924 by 21 people from Denmark, representing the so-called 'Scoresbysund Committee'. On 4 September 1925 the ship with the 87 Inuit settlers arrived. The borderline conflict about the right to the Eastern coast ended in 1933 when the International Court of Justice in Haag settled the issue in favour of Denmark.

Today this isolated town suffers from heavy problems with including alcoholism, unemployment, a high suicide rate and even murder. The story of the foundation of Scoresbysund is little known by both Danes and locals. They don't speak about it just as they don't speak about the social problems occurring there. It is a town with no collective memory.

Arke's mother was born and raised in the town, and Arke herself was born and lived there until the age of three.

The Book

Pia Arke wanted to make the history of this town visible and recognised. She begins her book: 'Scoresbysund is a collection of local stories, woven by the threads of other stories, partly personal and familiar, partly much larger colonial and global stories. The private, the aesthetic and the geopolitical merge here in the middle of nowhere' (Arke, 2003: 9).

She continues to comment on the fact that photography has been a central medium in the process of colonisation, recording and documenting how civilisation has 'pushed forward to the most distant fringes on earth [...] Photography depicts this inevitable process, but it does something more: It helps conquering, reclaiming the territory, possessing it' (2003: 9).

The book (164 pages) consists of photographs from the 1920s and 30s, most of them taken by the members of the Danish colony committee (See Figures 13.2 and 13.3). In addition, the book includes her own photographs of people she met when travelling there, her text and a collection of the first maps of the place as well as a text written by the Swedish author Stefan Jonsson who analyses the construction of these maps in a larger historical and geopolitical context. His more academic and general analysis represents an adequate frame for the artist's more personal narrative. Her text includes archive material and interviews conducted with locals from Scoresbysund and Danes who once visited the town as well as descendants of members of the Committee.

She interviewed both young and old people in the town, re-photographed collections of family photographs, appropriated material from Danish archives, and sorted out the private stories of the nameless people of the many archive photographs. She also photographed the children of the first population of the town today, many of whom she found at the town's small residential home. Being artistic and not anthropological, her work represents less a recovery of authenticity rather than a complex imaginary inventory. By circling around the same stories over years, she manages to articulate general considerations about post-colonial experiences and equally uncovers specific local stories that have never been told.

She recounts personal narratives such as the story of her own half-brother, the mother's first-born ('a mixed child of my mother and a Danish telegrapher that had left the town', Arke, 2003: 132), who as a little child

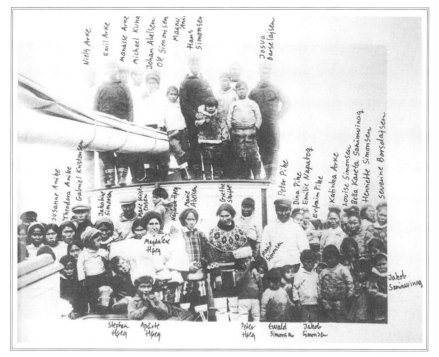

Figure 13.2 Family photograph

in 1955 was killed and eaten by a dog team on the first day in spring with the light and 'the sky was completely orange' (2003: 132). She had never seen a photograph of him until she found one in a private Danish album that belonged to the widow of a former colony manager. Elsewhere, she recounts how a man named Aage disappeared on his boat in the fog, leaving behind his worried wife and eight children. In yet another section, she tells the story about how her grandfather's brother Emil died from an accidental gun shot in 1928, and how the other brother Manasse drowned when he broke through the ice in 1941, leaving behind a wife and many children, who their only brother had to take care of. She recounts how the original 10 families were each given a house built from turf, measuring 12 square metres in floor space. Because mosk oxes were protected from being hunted by Danish law, the town was also suffering from famine only a few years after it had been founded. Since only the coast was claimed by Denmark, and not the wild and isolated inland, the Danes could go mosk ox hunting on the countryside where the law was no

Figure 13.3 Photograph: Justine and Gerda

longer in force. Until 1925 the natives had never experienced such juridical restrictions, but since the area was claimed by the Kingdom of Denmark, they suddenly came under Danish law.

One can describe Arke's work as a 'place-making activity' (Cresswell, 2004: 5). In his book *Place. A Short Introduction* the British geographer Tim Cresswell describes the field of 'human geography' as 'the study of places' (2004: 1), but place seen rather as an activity than a static, rationally defined 'space'. Place is 'a way of understanding [...] To think of an area of the world as a rich and complicated interplay of people and the environment – as a place – is to free us from thinking of it as facts and figures,' Cresswell writes (2004: 11), and he underlines that place 'is as much about epistemology as it is about ontology' (2004: 12). Likewise, Pia Arke's use of photography points to an understanding of the medium as related to epistemology, to the way we understand ourselves in the world.

Piece by piece she collects the story of this almost non-existing town without a history almost like putting together a gigantic puzzle. Arke's representational strategy is to 'invent' the town as a concrete place with a concrete history. This is achieved by a process of making visible the faces and identifying orally the individual stories of these old photographs that she had found in archives in Denmark and elsewhere and saved them from archival oblivion. Naming the people in the old photographs and linking them and the stories they represent to the actual town and its inhabitants can be considered as an act of authentication very different from the referential 'mirror-authentification' traditionally and ontologically attached to photography. She constructs the place of Scoresbysund as an ongoing, mental process, and in her book she maps out an embodied and emotional geography of that place. The town is thus rendered into a concrete place on a map and likewise a representation with a history that exceeds its actual physical appearance. Until then Scoresbysund had been experienced as an almost invisible town, even by its small number of citizens. Through the identification and actual naming of its past, she brings its emotional geography into life: she makes Scoresbysund *an authentic place*, 'a meaningful location' (Cresswell, 2004: 7).

Non-Representational Theory

In his recent book *Non-Representational Theory. Space, Politics, Affect* (2008) the British social scientist Nigel Thrift addresses 'non-representational theory' that he and fellow researchers in the fields of social science and geography have developed over the recent years. One aspect of this theory – also researched by Tim Cresswell – is to complement traditional geographical thought with ideas that consider place not merely as 'concrete location' but as 'mental space' and are inspired not only from social sciences but also from the performing arts.

This approach also tries to bridge hitherto separate academic fields such as anthropology, archaeology, social sciences, geography, architecture and performance studies, and interprets space as something thoroughly latent and relative: 'it is indicative of the substance of the new era of the inhabitable map in which space has more active qualities designed into its becoming' (Thrift, 2008: 16). To Thrift, place is never finished, but is constantly being performed.

Tim Cresswell's way of developing the field of human geography is inspired by Thrift: 'The kind of place at the center of much of humanistic geography is very much a place of rootedness and authenticity', he writes (Cresswell, 2004: 39). But the whole idea of 'place as a center of meaning connected to a rooted and "authentic" sense of identity' (13) must also be criticised or relativised. Identity must be considered in more processual ways 'in the face of the forces of global processes and movements' (13). Instead:

> Thinking of place as performed and practised can help us think of place in radically open and non-essentialised ways where place is constantly struggled over and reimagined in practical ways. Place is the raw material for the creative production of identity rather than an a priori label of identity. Place provides the conditions of possibility for creative social practice. Place in this sense becomes an event rather than a secure ontological thing rooted in notions of the authentic. Place as an event is marked by openness and change rather than boundedness and permanence. (39)

In this quote one could replace the word 'place' with the word 'photography' and the quote would represent the new and much more performative ways of conceptualising photography represented by people like Edwards, Pinney, Langford and Batchen, to whom I'll briefly return.

Another important aspect of 'non-representational theory' is an interest in addressing new everyday forms of democracy and even resistance, to find new ways to avoid 'powerlessness' (Thrift, 2008: 3) through new performative practices of everyday life. Everyday culture is seen as a place 'of hope', as Thrift calls it, a place to articulate other forms of political agency and a call for a new ethics based on the recognition of the other. In order to develop this 'speculative topography' further Thrift calls for new, interdisciplinary working methods and procedures of writing which shed light on this everyday experience of both resistance and affect and articulate 'a poetics of the spaces of dreams and improvisations [...] to listen to articulations that escape traditional discourse such as science, law etc. [...] what established systems discounted as noise' and thereby fostering 'a politics of ordinary moments' (2008: 19, 20). He advocates for 'the construction of new counterpublics through the assembling of more performative political ecologies' (22) with 'affect as a key element of a politics that will supplement the ordinary' (25). In many ways I think Pia Arke's book is a clever answer to his demands: an artistic response to this theoretical encircling of a 'non-representational theory' based on everyday life experience and at the same time to Cresswell's ideas of place as event and process.

Most of the photographic material from the 1920s and '30s that is shown in the book was found in Denmark, either in public archives or obtained from the descendants of the members of the first colony committee, who were contacted by the artist and would let her replicate the old private albums. She then travelled to Scoresbysund taking with her a thousand photographs with the help of which she would identify the people and used them to build up a local archive. This working process is described in the text. She describes how she looks up an old woman Maaria at the residential home. Via an interpreter (Pia Arke only speaks Danish) she wants her to tell her story but before they can even start Maaria tells the interpreter that a few years ago she was hospitalised unconscious. When she woke up a month later she had forgotten her past completely. The interpreter, a local girl, tells the artist that it is the first time she has ever heard that story, suggesting that it might be something Maaria invents for the occasion.

But with the help of other people at the residential home, and in the end with the help of Maaria as well, she manages to identify most of the people portrayed on the old photographs writing their names on the picture and, in doing so, giving the more symbolical act of 'naming' the city a very literal representation. 'The strange thing is that no one ever thanked the Greenlanders. After all they were the ones who did the colonisers a favour by moving the long way from Angmagssalik to Scoresbysund. I have looked in vain in the archives for a recognition of their heroic effort. But the only thing I have managed to find is a telegram from the map maker Lauge Koch to the Scoresbysund Committee saying "Thank you for Scoresbysund!"' (Arke, 2003: 44).

Re-thinking Authenticity Through Naming

In the book Pia Arke quotes diaries as well as official documents from the colonial committee and also newspaper articles found in various Danish archives, most of them at the Arctic Institute in Copenhagen. When the committee claimed the land in 1924 seven Danes were left to live in Scoresbysund to prepare for the arrival of the native Greenlanders the year after. The quotes from the diaries of the seven original committee settlers as well as later Danish members of city authorities are 'matched' with photographs that actually show what the dairies reveal: polar bear hunting, the meeting with the natives, making them pose for the camera etc.

Most of the early Danish settlers are now dead, and in Scoresbysund no one knows today why they are there. The place has never been performed as a self-confident process. Her answer to the newspaper headline 'Close the town with no future' is to give it a past – primarily through oral naming of the individuals pictured on the old photographs. Like Pia Arke, many descendants of the first generation of native settlers have left the town. Yet, she manages to find many of them in Denmark or in Greenland as well as relatives of the Danish Scoresbysund authorities, asking them to help her identifying the people on the photographs and inquiring the stories related to them.

In a chapter called 'The Forgotten' she finds a photograph of a poor, dirty, miserable-looking 6- or 7-year-old boy whom she has problems to identify. 'The photograph is an evidence of the fact that he *was* there,' she begins the chapter, indirectly quoting Roland Barthes's famous phenomenological analysis of the medium in *Camera Lucida* (Arke, 2003: 95). She shows the image to several people and each of them contributes with his or her own reading which often differs from the previous interpretation. One calls him 'a little cheeky devil', another finds that 'he looks like a boy who has been beaten up and thrown in a puddle'. 'A woman in Scoresbysund thought that he served his apprenticeship with a necromancer. She couldn't say why. Furthermore she noticed that the boy had two thumbs on his left hand, which made her husband reprove her: "But we have never heard of someone in Ittoqqortoormiit [Scoresbysund, MS] with two thumbs!" Meaning that if someone would have had that, everyone would have known him' (2003). Finally her own mother leads her on the right track: it is Jaariussi whose father died of tuberculosis, and who fell in a naturally made so-called ice-well and died at the age of 12. Finally she can state that 'he was born April the 17th 1929 in Angmagssalik, and he was six years old, when he and his family moved to the settlement Kap Hope at Scoresbysund in 1935. He died on July 3rd 1941, 12 years old' (Arke, 2003: 96). This statement, the photograph and the various interpretations related to it contribute to an emotional and symbolical authentication process as well as clarifying the discrepancies between the oral and the visual, memory, facts and imagination. The book is full of such traumatic and tragic images, along with stories of families separated by disease, death or adoption, all of them conveyed with the directness that only oral narration can give.

Recently, as I have already mentioned, research in vernacular photography, such as family and amateur photography, has developed around an interdisciplinary combination of art history, cultural studies and visual anthropology, and with seminal contributions by scholars such as Geoffrey Batchen (2001, 2004), Christopher Pinney (1997, 2003), Elisabeth Edwards (2004, 2006) and Martha Langford (2001), to name just a few. They have redirected well-established controversies over the authenticity question in photography ('photography as a mirror') towards a consideration of issues such as emotions, affect and flux of meaning in relation to what people *do* with photography. Both Batchen and Edwards stress the performative and communicative aspects of photographs and the fact that their meaning is never fixed but always dynamic. Photographs are not only passive and willing objects subject to discourse and ideology – the main point of much post-structuralist photography theory of the 1980s. Photographs are also 'interlocutors', as Edwards calls them: they *create* social relations and rites themselves through a dynamic exchange between people. 'Our photographic memories are nested in a performative oral tradition', Martha Langford says (Langford, 2001: preface). 'Photographs must be "listened to", not "read"' (2001: 42). In her book on family photography, *Suspended Conversations* (2001), she is inspired by Walter Ong's theories on the meaning and potential of sound and voice in cultural analysis. Also Edwards underlines the importance of touching and talking about photographs, regarding them as an important part of an oral culture of everyday life. She calls family photographs 'interactive' because they make things happen – stories are told and emotions appear that otherwise would not have been articulated had the photographs not existed.

'We need to invent a mode of photographic history that matches this object's complexity, and that can articulate its intelligibility both for the past and for our own time,' says Geoffrey Batchen (Batchen, 2004: 44). He advocates for 'an empathetic, phenomenological style of historical writing that can bridge the temporal and emotional gap between us and it' (2004).

I think this is exactly what Pia Arke did. At the same time as it evaluates the notion of 'place', her work underlines that we need to extend the theory and understanding of photography beyond the dominant semiotic, linguistic and instrumental models to an approach inspired by a phenomenology where material and oral aspects play a predominant role.

Martha Langford's book is focusing on the photograph album: 'I will suggest that rather than changing our ways of remembering, the organisation of photographs in albums has been one way of preserving the structures of oral tradition for new uses in the present [...] Our mimetic photographic memories need a mnemonic framework to keep them accessible and alive. The album reflects that need...' (Langford, 2001: 21). The problem in Scoresbysund has been that the photographs of family- and everyday life were not taken by native Greenlanders and that they were dispersed in various private Danish albums. It was not until the 1960s that a few of the locals started photographing themselves. In this sense, the artist becomes a composer of a collective family photograph album 'for new uses in the present'.[4]

A Third Place

In continuation of the tradition of 'visual ethnography' represented especially by the anthropologist John Collier from the 1950s and onwards, the British social anthropologist Sarah Pink has focused on visual methodologies and the relationship between applied and academic anthropology. As she writes in the introduction to her book *Doing Visual Anthropology* (2001/2007), in the late 1980s, as a result of the ' "postmodern turn" in ethnography' (Pink, 2001/2007: 10) 'anthropology experienced a "crisis" through which positivist arguments and realist approaches to knowledge, truth and objectivity were challenged' (1). Pink advocates for various ways of including photography in anthropological research, for instance by photographing during field work and including comments on the actual photographs by her informers: 'by paying attention to images in ethnographic research and representation we are developing new ways of understanding individuals, social relationships, material cultures and ethnographic knowledge itself' (17). In developing new ways of doing visual anthropology, Pink experienced 'exciting connections between ethnography and arts practice' (4), in working methods and in a common 'departure from the realist paradigm' (5): 'The relationship between arts practice and visual ethnography is a two-way process, while visual ethnographic practices can inform photographic representations, the visual practices of documentary artists also provide new and inspiring examples for visual ethnographers' (2). In the approach to the idea of mapping local history and giving voice to the un-told, to oral history and to cultural history and memory there are similarities between Arke's artistic practice and that of visual anthropologists such as Pink and Collier. Academic researchers can be inspired by art projects like Scorebysund Stories and vice versa, but as for the differences let me just point out that Arke's work is much more subjective, poetic and personal than a typical academic work and it is built on principles of montage as opposed to a more coherently structured text.

In various formats, but especially in a small booklet that was published in 1995, Pia Arke has used the term 'ethno-aesthetics' to describe her own artistic practice as a position from where identity can be created. She prefers this term to the term 'post-colonial': 'I prefer the word ethno-aesthetics because it is a messy term, inspiring additional work. It is, as I have suggested, a mixture of two groups of disciplines: on one hand ethnology, ethnography, anthropology; on the other artistic practice, art theory, aesthetics' (Arke, 1995: 11). She criticises the term post-colonialism 'because it suggests that colonialism is over' (Arke, 1995: 28), and she describes how she, as a person being neither the ethnographic object nor the subject, needs to find 'a third place' – a place she has found through being an artist and addressing her own background as an artist.

In an interview made in an early phase of the project, in 1998, she describes how she uses photography to articulate what is situated between 'the spoken and the un-spoken'. And she describes the Scoresbysund-project this way: 'It is about the role of the individual subject in relation to the power structure you live in. I relate to that in a visual way with my history project from Scoresbysund. I investigate how you can form your own identity from a knowledge of who you are, what you can claim, and what you can influence. These things lag behind many places in Greenland' (Rasmussen, 1998: 177, my translation).

Because of the remoteness of Scoresbysund I have not been able to make a thorough investigation into the reception of the book by the 600 inhabitants of the town.[5] I have talked to Arke's brother Ole Brønlund and to her cousin Theresia Pedersen, who both live in the town. Theresia underlines that the book has been very important to the community of Scoresbysund, and that many people have shown great interest and own the book. 'It is full of images that I have never seen before,' she says. For many people just seeing the images of themselves and their ancestors has been important, but Ole mentions that it is a problem that the text is in Danish, and many Greenlanders are not able to read Danish. So locally the texts have mostly been appreciated by the Danish inhabitants and by tourists visiting Greenland.[6]

In order to justify Danish colonial history, Scoresbysund has been reduced to a name on a map as well as an actual town with heavy social problems and no mental past, no memory. Pia Arke authenticates memory via the indexical qualities inherent in the photograph. To conclude, what I find interesting in *Scoresbysund Stories* is the way Pia Arke manages to fuse emotional, affective, performative, phenomenological uses of photography with text in order to create the town as a place of longing and belonging, at the same time carrying out a constructivist critique of political and ideological place production related to colonial history.

Illustrations

Scoresbysund Stories, p. 50. This photograph showing Pia Arke's grandparents Niels and Katinka was shown in *The Times*, 1932, accompanied by the text: 'Eskimos met by the expedition on their way to the base'. Pia Arke names the un-named subjects in old achival photographs from Scoresbysund, giving them an identity, a place, and inscribing them in history.

Scoresbysund Stories, p. 94: 'The Forgotten'. 'The photograph is an evidence of the fact that he *was* there,' the text begins.

Scoresbysund Stories, p. 159. August 1925, the ship from Angmagssalik. Pia Arke names the first native settlers in Scoresbysund.

Notes

1. Pia Arke was born in Greenland. Her mother is Greenlandic, her father was a Danish telegrapher working in Greenland.
2. The text is in Danish, but in this essay the book is called *Scoresbysund Stories*. All quotes are translated by Mette Sandbye. The book was a culmination of more than ten years of work researching in archives and private memories about the history of Greenland. Previous related works are for example *Telegraphy, Nature Morte, Tupilakosaurus, Arctic Hysteria* and *Legend I–V*.
3. These images were used by Pia Arke in her work *Arctic Hysteria* from 1997.
4. On her many research visits to Scoresbysund she also gave lectures about the photographs and the stories for the children at the local school, who took an enormous interest in the material.
5. Telephone conversation, conducted 16 December 2008. I thank Ole and Theresia for their willingness to share their thoughts and information with me.
6. The Pia Arke Association is trying to raise money for an English edition of the book, esteemed to appear in 2009.

Chapter 14

Globe 1: A Place of Integration or an 'Ethnic Oasis'?

SINE AGERGAARD

Introduction

This chapter describes the ways in which a specific place – set up as part of a political initiative to promote integration – is transformed into an 'ethnic oasis', a place of recreation for ethnic minorities. It is shown how political investment in a geographical area and the identification of a specific location in this area as an authentic place for integrating the minority and majority populations, is transformed into another form of authenticity based on shared embodied experiences among ethnic minorities living on the outskirts of a Danish provincial city.

The discussion of Globe1, the sports centre set up to promote integration, is split into three parts. These are based around the different methods of data collection which have been employed while carrying out fieldwork in preparation for a larger research project on integration and sports in the western part of Aarhus (Agergaard, 2007). The data collection methods used were:

(1) Discourse analysis of the official documents of Globe1: this helps describe the political investment in the area and the ways in which the sports centre is politically constructed as a place for cultural exchange and integration.
(2) Interviews with employees in Globe1: these interviews provide a more complex picture of the problems the staff members have encountered during their first working year.
(3) Observations of daily activities in the sports centre: these observations help describe ways in which the users of Globe1 have turned the sports centre into a place for spare time activities for people from ethnic minorities.

Consideration of these data firstly leads to a theoretical discussion in which a phenomenological approach is adopted to understand the nature of this particular place as an 'oasis' for ethnic minorities living in an area of a Danish provincial city with many social problems. Secondly, the article addresses theories of authenticity in order to compare the ethnic minorities' emotional experiences of authenticity through engagement in sports activities with the political construction of the sports centre as an authentic place for integration.

Political Investment in the So-called 'Urban Area'

In 2000, the Municipality of Aarhus applied for and gained support from the European Union to develop and regenerate three neighbourhoods in the western part of Aarhus: Gellerup, Hasle and Herredsvang. More or less arbitrarily, but in line with the instructions from the European Union, the three neighbourhoods were joined together in a new geographical construction called the 'Urban Area.' The area is also a lived social reality in which the inhabitants share common living conditions.[1] It consists of some of Denmark's poorest neighbourhoods. For instance, four out of five residents live in concrete social housing built in the 1960s and 1970s. Also, more than half of the inhabitants of the area are refugees and their descendants (Urbanprogram, 2004).

Having received 40 million Danish kroner (DKK), the equivalent of £3,750,000 in support from the European Union, the Municipality of Aarhus had to raise a similar amount of money in order to begin the regeneration of the three neighbourhoods. The project eventually ran from 2002–2007 with the overall aim to achieve economic and social sustainability in the western part of Aarhus. It has been set up in such a way that outside agents and institutions can apply for funding for projects that they feel fit the programme's remit.

One area of interest for the Urban Programme is 'spare time and culture as integration-promoting activity.'[2] It was with this theme in mind that Globe1 was established in 2005. The project was given 6.75 million DKK from the Urban funds, the Municipality of Aarhus provided a further 12.5 million DKK of funding, while a local housing association and a national fund each donated 5 million. The resulting centre consists of a main sports hall, an enclosed room for martial arts and exercise activity for women who do not want to be seen by the public, a playroom for children, a café, workshops and places for handiwork, as well as meeting rooms and offices.

Method

Deciding which methods should be applied in order to analyse the complex ways in which a specific place (in this case a sports centre) is mediated and lived poses several challenges which, in this instance, included the question of how to address both the way in which the place is presented in political discourse, and the way the staff and users of the place negotiate and change such political visions in their everyday practice. To investigate these various aspects, discourse analysis, interviews with the staff, as well as observations of daily practices in the sports centre are employed.

Discourse analysis can be useful when investigating the underlying political principles of a given place. In this respect, Foucault's inaugural lecture at Collège de France entitled *L'ordre du discours* (Foucault, 1971/ 2001) may prove helpful. His understanding was that the discourse of a social institution (or a specific place) orders or affects its users – students, prisoners, employees, etc. Bearing Foucault's structuralist heritage in mind, the concept of 'order of discourse' describes how members of institutions are framed in their verbal expressions and acts.

In what follows, discourse analysis focuses on written statements as they appear in recommendations and the memorandum concerning the establishment of a sports centre, as well as on the presentation of Globe1 on the municipality of Aarhus' website. Therefore, in this particular context discourse analysis does not inquire into the ways in which the discourse about Globe1 is acted out in informal politics, instead it focuses on the ways in which the political vision of the place is formally defined.

Foucault has emphasised several times that, 'there are no relations of power without resistance' (Foucault, 1980: 142; Foucault, 1976/98). Therefore, following Foucault, the challenge is also to address the ways in which individuals' practices differ from, and actively resist a dominant discourse. As the anthropologist Susan Whyte has pointed out:

> The problem[3] is to find a way of describing a dominant pattern while showing how people to a high degree ignore or actively resist it. (Whyte, 1994: 65, author's translation)

This sort of problem will be addressed here by describing not only the dominant order of discourse through analysis of the official political documents of Globe1, but also the experiences of the staff and users of the sports centre who, as the main actors, demonstrate through their practice that they resist, even if not directly, the dominant discourse, and at the very least they appear to ignore it in various ways.

Interviews were conducted with the staff of Globe1 in August 2006, one season after the establishment of the centre. The interviewees included the director, who is the representative of the Municipality of Aarhus and of the political vision at the place, as well as the employee who is responsible for the activities in the centre. The latter also works as a coach, so is well acquainted with the everyday activities in Globe1.

In addition, Globe1's booking plan for autumn 2006 and 2007 provided details of the groups using the centre. This information could be used to identify the kinds of users who visited Globe1, and it provided a starting point for raising questions about the users' age, ethnicity and geographical affiliation. Also, it was possible to ask whether the users were school children, youngsters in clubs, adults engaged in projects, and whether the users mainly belonged to ethnic minorities or was there mixing with the Danish majority? Do the users, for instance, live in neighbourhoods on the western or eastern side of Globe1, that are known to be mainly inhabited by ethnic minorities and ethnic Danes, respectively? Moreover, during the autumn of 2006, a series of observations were made of the so-called 'associationless youngsters' – a primary target group for the integration planned to take place in the centre.

The Discursive Construction of a 'Place of Integration'

The specific political documents concerning the establishment of Globe1 outline bridge building between so-called 'associationless youngsters'[4] and local club-based spare time activities as one of the main purposes of the centre. In other words, the idea was to provide access to physical activities (by way of open house arrangements) for youngsters from ethnic minorities, and, in the long run, integrate them into sports clubs.[5]

In other political documents, another purpose of the multi sports centre is presented, and that is Globe1's function as a place for integration. According to the politicians, the activities that take place in Globe1, as well as its location, should have a broad appeal to the citizens of Aarhus.[6] Thus, a second aim of establishing Globe1 is to attract citizens from other areas of the city, which, it was hoped, would help strengthen the Urban area.

As a site for integration, the location of Globe1 is considered crucial, since it is placed on the border between a lower class suburb (to the West), inhabited mainly by ethnic minorities, and a middle class, dominantly white suburb to the East. On the western side of Globe1 you find Gellerup and Brabrand, and on the eastern side, Aabyhøj; two areas of the city inhabited by distinct sections of the population. Immigrants and their descendants make up almost half of the population of Brabrand and Gjellerup, while only 9% of the population in Aabyhøj belong to this category. The construction of Globe1 as a place for integration, bringing together different parts of the city and different sections of the population, is also expressed on the map which can be found on the municipality of Aarhus's website.[7]

Arrows have been added to the map shown in Figure 14.1. The horizontal arrows indicate the ways in which Globe1 connects different parts of the city (Brabrand and Aabyhøj). The vertical arrows indicate that Globe1 is placed in connection with other recreational areas in the western part of Aarhus (Hasle Bakkelandskab, and Brabrandsøen). In addition smaller horizontal arrows show that Globe1 can be easily accessed from the poor housing area called Gellerupparken.

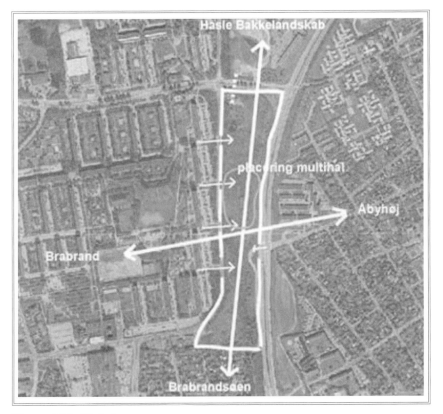

Figure 14.1 Globe1

In the cartographic perspective presented on the map above the proposed site for Globe1 is at the centre. A centre that could be described as mediating between different dichotomies: between black and white (ethnic minority and Danish majority), culture and nature, city and countryside, work and recreational life.

In his classical analysis of the Kabyle house, Pierre Bourdieu describes a number of binary structures in space such as up-down, east-west, spring-harvest, humid-dry (Bourdieu, 1996a: 22). Furthermore, Bourdieu distinguishes between the physical space – the specific place where our bodies are located – and the social space that is constructed through our social relations (Bourdieu, 1996b). Bourdieu points out that the physical space is always ranked and structured in diverse forms of spatial oppositions. In other words, power is expressed in the ways in which we are positioned - for instance inside or outside of a specific place – and in the ways in which places are located in relation to each other – for instance as recreational and living areas. In the case considered here, local policy is expressed in the constitution of Globe1 as a meeting place. A place located so that it can welcome people of different ethnicities inside, and mediate between the city and semi-rural lifestyles being lived on the outside.

However, in another of his works Bourdieu also stresses the dialectics of objectification and incorporation (Bourdieu, 1977: 88). There is a dialectical relationship between the social structures that are objectified in space and the body that moves in and between specific places. Thus we must not take the political vision – in this case the vision of the sports centre as a place for integration – for granted, or as something that can be translated into practice with ease. Instead, we must inquire further into the users' everyday experiences and practices at the specific place.

The Complexity of the Political Project

The two aims – integrating the 'associationless' and attracting citizens from other parts of the city – appear less easy to put into practice after talking to the employees of Globe1. In this respect, interviews with the director and with the person responsible for the activities at the sports centre point out the complexity of the task of integration.

Just after the establishment of the centre, the employees began organising a number of open house arrangements in line with the political vision. However, such arrangements had very little pedagogical success. The person responsible for the activities in the centre describes how Globe1 became a 'drop-in centre', and the employees lost control of what was going on. For instance, the employees were threatened by some of the youngsters. Moreover, the employees did not succeed in establishing contact with girls from ethnic minorities, who are very seldom members of sports clubs. It also proved much more difficult to integrate the 'associationless youngsters' than the discursive construction of Globe1 as a place of integration suggested.

After one season, the employees of Globe1 changed their strategy. Instead of making open house arrangements for 'associationless youngsters', they outsourced most of the available hours in the centre to institutions and clubs. Only two hours a week are now reserved for projects attempting to attract the 'associationless youngsters'. According to the director, the centre has decided to cooperate with the established clubs and hope that some of the 'associationless' will join these associations. This is described as 'the leading hand pedagogy'. The director now considers Globe1 as a centre dedicated to working with issues of integration with a number of staff available for specific tasks rather than working to integrate the so-called 'associationless youngsters'. In other words, the tasks dealt with in Globe1 have developed in a less straightforward way than was expected by the politicians.

The employees have also had little success in regards to the second aim of Globe1: namely to attract citizens from other parts of the city. Both interviewed employees emphasise that for integration to occur, the Danes need to participate as well as the ethnic minorities. But, initially, the Danes from the eastern side of Globe1 were reluctant to enter the multi sports centre. According to the employees, many of them simply did not bother to get involved.

In the next section, observations of the present activities in the centre are analysed. Over the years in which Globe1 has existed, more Danes have begun to enter the centre as part of institutions or clubs, but it is still questionable whether integration is taking place between Danes and members of ethnic minority groups.

Everyday Activity

When looking at the booking plan (for autumn 2007), the general picture is that the time and space available in the centre is used partly by institutions (public schools, kindergartens, and after-school care) and partly by sports clubs. Out of these institutions and clubs, about 70% are from the western side of Globe1 and represent mainly children and youngsters from ethnic minorities, while the number of institutions and clubs from the eastern side has now grown to 30%. For instance,

Globe1 is frequented weekly by children from a private Muslim school and from the public schools in the urban area with the highest percentage of children from ethnic minorities (Nordgårdskolen, Sødalskolen and Tovshøjskolen). However, the centre is also frequented by children from schools in which the pupils are mainly Danes (Gammelgårdskolen and Åby skole).

According to Anthony Giddens, social integration is the reciprocity that develops through interaction when there is physical co-presence between people (Giddens, 1979, 1984; Ottesen, 1998: 98). Following this understanding, it is debatable whether the fact that children from ethnic minorities and ethnic Danish children – separately – use Globe1's facilities leads to integration. The employees of Globe1 experience increasing success in attracting Danes to the centre, but these Danes are mainly children who come to participate in school sports, and there is not necessarily any interaction taking place between children from the western and eastern side.

Some children from ethnic minorities have showed interest in joining the football and basketball clubs of children from the eastern side, but many teams from these sports clubs are already fully booked, and the clubs are reluctant to start new teams. An explanation for this is that the coaches of such teams are volunteers, and it cannot be expected that these volunteers engage in integration work. Also, aside from the few Danish clubs, many of the sports clubs that use the facilities in Globe1 can be considered ethnic minority clubs since their members are mainly from a specific ethnic minority (e.g. Somalis, Turks, Palestinians etc.). In other words, it is also questionable whether integration is taking place between the different ethnic minority groups that use Globe1.

As part of their vision of integration, the employees of Globe1 have tried to introduce new sports disciplines to the people coming from the western part of Aarhus. For instance, they have given professional handball and basketball players training hours in the centre, and made arrangements so that these professional (ethnically Danish mainly) players come to train children from the area. However, very few people have shown interest in such endeavours, and the sports clubs in the area continue organising the same activities, primarily football.

A day in Globe1 is characterised by certain routines. Children from ethnic minorities and ethnic Danish children enter the centre in turn in the morning to participate in school sports. Also in the morning, one can find women from ethnic minorities in Globe1, participating in different kinds of educational or physical activities organised for the unemployed. Later in the afternoon, the club activities start and, at this time, mainly boys and men from specific ethnic minorities enter the centre. Thus, it appears that the users in Globe1 enter in groups that are not necessarily mixed in terms of age, ethnicity or gender. This leads us to a discussion of the ways in which Globe1 can be characterised.

A 'Place of Integration' or an 'Ethnic Oasis'?

As discussed above, the reality of the political construction of Globe1 as a place of integration has been questioned. The argument brought forward here is that Globe1, instead, has become an 'ethnic oasis'. 'Ethnic' – following the commonsensical connotation given to the term – in that it is mainly used by children from ethnic minorities in the Urban area and by specific groups from different ethnic minorities, while 'oasis' refers to the fact that Globe1 is a place of recreation for people who are living on the outskirts of a Danish provincial city.

The Urban area is far too complex to be compared with a non-fertile desert, and Globe1 cannot literally be called a fertile area. Still, an analogy with an oasis is worth a try. According to public opinion, the Urban area (particularly the neighbourhood Gellerup) is considered a 'problem area' (Roland, 1998). This stigmatisation also contributes to the isolation of the people in the area. Recently, the Urban area has been categorised as a ghetto (Regeringen, 2004; Programbestyrelsen, 2005). As Bauman puts it, a ghetto area is not only a 'no go in area,' but also a 'no go out area' (Bauman, 1998: 26). Stigmatisation does not only keep outsiders away from the area, the inhabitants are also less likely to leave the area (Diken, 1998). For instance, youngsters from ethnic minorities are less likely to travel out of the area than Danes of the same age living in the same area (Agergaard, 2008). The social and geographical mobility of the inhabitants in a ghetto area is often limited to staying on the outskirts of the city where they feel at home.

The function of Globe1 as an 'ethnic oasis' in the Urban area, can be supported by the expression employed by one of its employees, who describes the ways in which the centre has become '*the* house of the area.' It is used for sports by specific ethnic minority groups, but they also use the facility for cultural arrangements ranging from prayers and parties after the Ramadan, to discussion meetings, etc. In an area where vandalism, arson fires, and burglary are widespread problems, it is remarkable that very little vandalism and only one burglary has taken place in Globe1 since 2005. As an oasis, Globe1 has the privilege of being a place that is thought of as a site of recreation and calm compared to the at times chaotic conditions of the surrounding area.

The Place as Lived

To understand the ways in which ethnic minorities make use of Globe1 as an oasis, we may draw on the approaches of phenomenology. The phenomenology of perception developed by Maurice Merleau-Ponty is also a phenomenology of space. Thus, theories of the human being as a mental subject or physiological object are criticised and replaced with a phenomenology that focuses on the body as a sensing being that is always located in space. Merleau-Ponty stresses that there is no opposition between the body and space, between ideas and the material. The body is not in space to conceive it. Rather, the body belongs to space (Merleau-Ponty, 1962: 40).

In other words, bodies are not present in space in order to acknowledge, for instance, political ideas of integration. On the contrary, the bodily presence in space is meaningful in itself. This embodied presence is important to understand the ways in which the everyday use of Globe1 differs from the political vision of the place. For users, Globe1 is an experienced reality that does not necessarily require mental reflections.

The specific nature of Globe1 as a sports centre also makes it necessary for us to acknowledge the embodied experience of the place. Athletes enter many different spaces without necessarily reflecting on the purpose of the places (Agergaard, 2006).[8] So, what kind of meaning does being present in the sports centre acquire for the population of the western part of Aarhus? To elaborate on this embodied meaning, we shall turn our attention to theories of authenticity, as discussed by Wang (1999). Indeed, these theories can help us distinguish between different perceptions of a specific place. Phenomenological emphasis on the embodied presence in space can lead to inadequate analysis of the politically constructed vision of a place. Therefore, in what follows our focus should be both on constructed as well as on embodied feelings of authenticity.

Constructed and Embodied Authenticity

Theories of authenticity are employed to research tourists' motivation for going to certain places, and to account for their experience at these places. The term authenticity originates from museums, where it is used to evaluate whether objects are what they appear to be. However, the word authenticity has also come to refer to an existential condition of being, that modern society destroys (Wang, 1999: 350; Olsen, 2002: 160).[9] Thus, authenticity can be an object-related as well as activity-related sense of meaning that is unspoiled by the surrounding society.

What we are interested in here is conceptualising the sense of meaning aroused through people's engagement in sports activities in Globe1 and how their experiences differ from the political construction of the meaning of Globe1 as an object – in this case a place of integration. We are dealing here with a recently built sports centre – rather than tourist sites which you have to travel far to reach and are characterised by an historical or other sort of extraordinary nature. Still, the characterisation of tourism as a simpler, freer, more spontaneous, or less serious, less utilitarian and romantic lifestyle which enables people to keep a distance from or transcend their daily lives can also apply to sports and in particular resonates with my observations of the ways in which sports activities work for the ethnic minorities, whose everyday lives are filled with socio-economic problems. In other words, theories of authenticity developed in tourist studies can help characterise the ways in which the users' embodied engagement in a sports centre is distant from the political position and construction of the facilities.

Wang (1999) has described two conventional meanings of authenticity in the literature: objective and constructive authenticity. Wang also suggests a third – existential authenticity – which is inspired by phenomenology.[10] First of all, objective authenticity is when specific objects are recognised as authentic (e.g. a tourist location is authentic, for instance, due to its historical nature). Here authenticity has not to do with the tourists' or athletes' experiences but with an absolute criterion of an object as authentic. Secondly, constructive authenticity is the result of social construction. In other words, a tourist location (or other kind of recreational location) is not inherently authentic, but constructed as such. For this construction to take place, specific views, beliefs, perspectives, or powers are put to use. The third meaning Wang suggests is that of existential authenticity, which 'involves personal or intersubjective feelings activated by the liminal process of tourist activities' (Wang, 1999: 350). In other words, it is due to the activity that you engage in as a tourist (or athlete in our case) that you personally and socially experience things as authentic and in a more general sense meaningful. Wang writes that existential authenticity is a feeling developed through participating, rather than spectating (e.g. at a sports activity).

Consideration of this overview of theories of authenticity, as outlined by Wang, suggests that there are different ways of attaching meaning to a specific place (and experiences therein). So, with reference to the current discussion, Globe1 can be seen as authentic in terms of it being an object. Particularly, the location of the centre as an object between two distinct neighbourhoods provides this place with an inherent form of meaning as a meeting point. Secondly, there is the political construction of Globe1, which seeks to give the centre authenticity as a place of integration. This form of meaning is constructed through the use of political power and from specific perspectives (for example, that of a local politician or of the director of Globe1). Then there is the sense of meaning that the users experience when engaging in activities at Globe1. Wang points out, that existential authenticity involves bodily feelings and contributes to the building of self-identity, strengthens family ties and social community. In a similar way, it is my impression that the strong embodied engagement in activities in Globe1 shows the importance of these activities for the athletes' personal identity as well as for the ethnic minority groups. The activities seem to arouse a bodily sense of meaning that is different from the everyday lives of ethnic minority groups in the western part of Aarhus with its socio-economic problems, which are constantly being addressed by political initiatives such as Globe1, schemes to bus children to schools outside the area and so on.

It is worth mentioning that debates continue over whether the establishment of self-identity for ethnic minority groups is a temporary phase in the process of integration, or a potential route to segregation and perhaps even reverse discrimination (Elling *et al.*, 2001). It is beyond the scope of this article to discuss these issues further, and instead for the purposes of this discussion, it is accepted that sport can have an integrative or socialising effect. However the issue of integration is not necessarily important for the users of the place, far more important is the bodily sense of meaning that members of the ethnic minority groups may gain from participating in the activities at Globe1.

Conclusion

This chapter has described first of all the huge political investment in a suburb of a Danish provincial city, and the political construction of one of the supported projects in the area (a sports centre) as a place of integration. Through discourse analysis of policy documents concerning the sports centre, two political aims have been identified: the aim of integrating 'associationless youngsters' from ethnic minorities, and the aim of attracting citizens from other parts of the city to an area mainly inhabited by people from ethnic minorities. Secondly, interviews with employees of the sports centre have revealed some of the difficulties in orchestrating these political ideas of integration, and how the employees' modified such aims for instance by outsourcing the task of integrating 'associationless youngsters' from ethnic minorities to local clubs. Thirdly, observations of the everyday activities at the sports centre have shown that Globe1 is mainly used by institutions with a high percentage of children from ethnic minorities, and that the clubs that use the centre often consist of members from the same ethnic minority group.

Accordingly, it is suggested that Globe1 can be characterised as an 'ethnic oasis', since specific ethnic minority groups use this place for recreational activities. Taking into account, Wang's theories of authenticity, we have suggested a distinction between the constructed political meaning of a place, and the embodied meaning that the users can experience through participating in physical activities at the place – an embodied meaning that might contribute to the construction of identity as a person and as part of a social group, but one that we must be cautious not to over interpret.

Further research must be done to investigate more thoroughly the specific experiences that users of the sports centre have, and their conception of this particular place. However, the present chapter has pointed out the nature of a sports centre as a place of recreation, and a place where participation in sports activities takes place without the athletes (as well as users in other kinds of social practices) being necessarily interested in the political vision of the place.

Notes

1. Epinion (2005: 39ff) collected statistical information showing that the average income in the Urban area is 147,779 Danish kroner (DKK), compared to 216,134 DKK in the rest of the Municipality of Aarhus. Also in this area, the unemployment rate is higher (11.9% compared to 6.1% in the rest of the Municipality), and the level of education lower (37% of people living in the Urban area have only basic education from public school, while only 19% of residents in the rest of the Municipality of Aarhus don't go on to further study).

2. See www.aarhuskommune.dk/portal/borger/flygtninge_indvandrere/urban?_page=urbanprogrammet. Retrieved 25 June 2007.

3. In her inaugural lecture as professor of anthropology at University of Copenhagen, Whyte defines problems as ambiguities that need methodical exploration: 'They are a way of orienting ourselves in order to proceed' (Whyte, 1998: 8).

4. The discursive construct 'Association-less' is a direct translation of the Danish word 'Foreningsløse.' This is a term that has become widely used in public debate, statistical research, and sports policy to categorise a group considered to be on the margins of Danish society and democratic organisational structure (Anderson, 2002: 141). The concept is, therefore, used together with

the assumption that the 'association-less' must be integrated, in this case, into Danish sports clubs.

5. See www.aarhuskommune.dk/portal/borger/flygtning_indvandrer/urban_ bydel?_page=projekter.emne/indsatsomraade_3.1.emne/multihal_i_ urbanomraadet.htm. Retrieved 25 June 2007.

6. Aarhus kommune, Sport og Fritid (2006).

7. See www.aarhuskommune.dk/portal/erhverv/det_professionelle_kulturliv/ kulturomraader?_page=kulturhuse.emne/Globe1.emne. Retrieved 25 June 2007.

8. This is not unique for athletes but is also the case for instance for workers in a garage (cf. Agergaard, 2006). The political vision of a place is not necessarily important for the ones who engage in everyday practice.

9. Olsen criticises the tendency in tourist research to oppose modernity, the copy and tourist with the traditional, the original and the other. In this way the tourist role becomes opposed to authenticity (Olsen, 2002: 176). In other words, the concept of authenticity has to be defined in more details to be able to continue talking about different aspects of authenticity.

10. Wang's inspiration from phenomenology is expressed in particular in his definition of existential authenticity as: '... an existential state of Being activated by certain tourist activities' (Wang, 1999: 358).

Chapter 15

Online Tourism: Just like Being There?

JAKOB LINAA JENSEN

Introduction

New media, particularly the internet, change as well as accelerate practices of tourism. Today everybody can become their own travel agent and book tickets, hotels and trips online. Travellers can obtain virtual representations of their destinations before actually going there and afterwards they can present their travel activities through text, photography and video. The internet adds social dimensions to the activity of travelling since tourists on their travels can communicate with those back home or maintain contact with fellow travellers even after the journey.

Online tourism re-actualises debates among internet researchers and theorists concerning the social potential of online communication. What happens to sociality online when interactions are closely linked to experiences of travel and tourism in real life? Further, online tourism also highlights the ongoing discussion concerning the spatial status of the internet because tourism as a social phenomenon is about space: about the appropriation, the construction and the distinctions of space (Urry, 1990; Rojek, 1997).

I will address those issues by discussing two prime examples of online tourism, the online community of Virtual Tourist (www.virtualtourist. com) and the application Google Earth.

I show that besides social and informational benefits of using Virtual Tourist and Google Earth there are also corporeal and emotional dimensions of the experience. The core users participate in processes of embodiment and emotion-sharing, both through their self-presentation and through the way physical places are constantly referred to. I discuss how the users' presentations of travel stories and photographs contribute to their identity formation in a local as well as a global context. Even more importantly, the users form informational and often emotional community networks, which might not otherwise have been facilitated. I end

213

up concluding that use of the internet facilitates and strengthens the tourism experience, which I will refer to as augmented tourism.

Authenticity, Spatiality and Community

Tourism has been on a steady rise for decades and so has the body of scholarly literature within the field. For instance, tourism has been regarded anthropologically as an important form of social interaction (Chambers, 2000) and sociologically as paradigmatic for the condition of the post-modern human being (Urry, 1990; Löfgren, 1999). For Dean MacCannell (1999: 2) modern tourism is a way of searching authenticity which is thought to be elsewhere; in other historical periods or cultures or in purer, simpler lifestyles. Tourism is a quest for the unspoiled, original experience. However, the majority of tourists get a *staged* authenticity which simulates an authentic experience (1999: 98–99).

Authentic experiences might be even harder to obtain in an online setting, raising the question whether authenticity matters any more or maybe needs to be redefined. Wang (1999: 351–52) questions traditional notions of authenticity within tourism research and argues that there are at least three types of authenticity in tourist experiences:

Firstly, there is the objective authenticity referring to the authenticity of the originals. For example: is this a real tool used by real natives? Is this a real, traditional village etc.? Objective authenticity links with Walter Benjamin's concept of the 'aura' of the original work. Secondly, there is the constructive authenticity referring to the authenticity projected onto objects or phenomena, either by tourism producers or by tourists themselves. It might also be referred to as symbolic authenticity.

Whereas both these concepts attach authenticity to the object or phenomenon, either real or symbolic, the third type of authenticity, existential authenticity is about the experience within the mind of the tourist. Existential authenticity is the state of mind achieved by tourist activities but is not necessarily dependent on the authenticity of the object or the phenomenon itself. It is a much more subjective, lived type of authenticity. We need to readdress the limits of authenticity as online tourism experiences might be authentic, either in a constructive or in an existential sense.

Another relevant question addresses the spatial ambiguity of online experiences. For early internet scholars like Turkle (1995) the internet was portrayed as something 'out there', a virtual world or an alternative space with new norms and rules where it is possible to realise a post-modern dream of leaving the body behind and creating new identities. Later scholars have shown, however, that the social dynamics of the internet are to be found in a dualism between online and offline experiences, that the internet is a part of everyday social practices (Wellman & Gulia, 1999; Kollock, 2000). Many online communities are closely linked to the physical world and foster virtual as well as physical social relations. Mentally, it is possible to move seamlessly through texts and images. Physically, the user moves from website to website, transported at the speed of light among different hosts situated in the entire physical world. While 'surfing' the internet in front of a computer, we are physically as well as metaphorically moving around; we are stationary, but our activity is highly mobile (Parks, 2004).

Within the field of tourism such dynamics between virtual and the real experiences is not new. As Orvar Löfgren (1999: 14ff) has argued, tourism as a concept is based on a constant interplay between physical and virtual destinations, between landscape and mindscape. The tourist imagines a destination before going there, compares the actual and the expected experiences, and subsequently constructs a memory of the destination. Some have claimed that online interactions are incommensurable with true social interaction and sense of community (Sproull & Faraj, 1995). However, time has shown that the internet has become a forum for informal as well as intimate communication, in online discussion groups, in patient support communities and in a variety of other cases. Online interaction is not necessarily second-class communication and intimate relations might be formed online as well as offline. Tourism is a particularly salient example as mediated tourist experiences go hand in hand with mental images of distant destinations and the experience of actually going there (Linaa & Waade, 2009).

Further, it is becoming increasingly difficult to distinguish between actual and mediated experiences. An example is the death of Princess Diana. Even though most people had never seen the Princess except on TV, millions felt so emotionally attached to the media icon that they burst into tears in public at the news of her death (Couldry, 2003: 68–69). Media no longer only reproduce reality; they fundamentally alter the conditions for social action and produce events of their own. They no longer only mediate – they 'mediatise' (Jansson, 2002).

The Cases: Virtual Tourist and Google Earth

There are two reasons for case selection. First, they are selected based on a 'most different case-strategy' (Yin, 2002). Technically, Virtual Tourist is a 'traditional' web-based community dedicated to presentation of travel experiences and exchange of travel-related information. Google Earth, on the contrary, is an application which needs to be downloaded and installed separately. From the outset Virtual Tourist is a textual community where the spatial dimensions have developed over time. Google Earth, however, is a spatially based application where the community dimension has been added later.

Secondly, they are emblematic cases of the constant dualism between virtual and real space which is characteristic for online tourism. Even more importantly, they demonstrate how online tourism is no longer only a question of buying tickets and searching for information but also about forming new relations, maintaining friendships and presenting oneself as a traveller and a human being. Online tourism becomes part of the post-modern identity project.

Virtual Tourist is by far the world's largest online tourist community. The homepage www.virtualtourist.com is the starting point for reading members' profiles, searching information on destinations and accessing the online discussion forums. In total, it has 1,076,726 members around the world (Virtual Tourist, December 2008). Like many online communities, there is a high percentage of 'lurkers', people who just sign up but do not contribute actively to the community (Nonnecke & Preece, 2000). However, there is substantial activity at Virtual Tourist as the members altogether have posted 1,682,124 travel tips and reviews and 3,348,453 photos (December 2008). No less than 2.2 million locations are described or referred to. The community is based on the users' profiles, where they present themselves and their travels and write 'virtual mini guides' on the destinations visited. Further, users exchange information about destinations, accommodation, food and entertainment through various discussion boards.

Google Earth is created by the California-based Google Corporation, inventors of Google which is today the world's leading internet search engine. The application is a part of the company's strategy of making the internet's vast amount of information searchable in easy and intuitive ways. Contrary to Google itself where searches are performed by typing keywords, Google Earth presents a geographical interface based on an exact model of the physical world. The application is built upon several different technologies: for example Google's well-known search engine, various visualisation techniques and satellite images from NASA. It is possible for the users to interact with the map by putting virtual 'needles' on the planet, thereby providing information, pictures or travelogues on certain destinations. Further, they can talk to and form relations with other users through the adherent 'Google Earth Community'. Thus, Google Earth is an application as well as an online community.

The Interfaces: Aesthetics, Embodiment and Space

Virtual Tourist combines features of self-presentation and networking. The basic component is that each member creates a profile containing personal information and an overview of travel activities. The latter is both graphic and textual as each user is requested to highlight countries visited on a 'World Map'. Further, users are requested to provide information, photos, stories, tips and tricks on the relevant destinations, altogether turning Virtual Tourist into a giant hub of information, a global online travel guide book. The slogan of Virtual Tourist is 'real travellers, real info'. It is strongly emphasised that the main part of the information available is provided by real travellers, 'just like you'.

The web design is quite traditionally based on a heading and three columns, each providing different information and links (see Figure 15.1). The aim of providing accurate member-generated information on certain

Figure 15.1 The interface of Virtual Tourist

places is emphasised by a clickable world map along with textual links to certain destinations around the world. Further, the quality and quantity of the site is emphasised through live updates on the number of members and travel tips available.

Google Earth, on the other hand, is an application which needs to be downloaded to a personal computer in order to work. Opening the application, one encounters a representation of planet Earth floating freely among the stars of the universe. The image of the sky is modelled on true star constellations. In a cartographic sense, Google Earth represents a move from two-dimensional atlases and maps, which have been dominant for centuries, to a three-dimensional representation aimed at giving the impression of actually navigating through a landscape. Google Earth is constantly updated with new features and satellite photos in order to provide an exact representation of planet Earth (see Figure 15.2).

While using Google Earth it is possible to navigate up and down, right and left, and back and forth in every possible direction, thereby giving the user ultimate control of the views and routes across the planet. Google Earth simulates the familiar feeling of a physical globe. By dragging the mouse it is possible to tilt or twist the globe and to spin it around, as

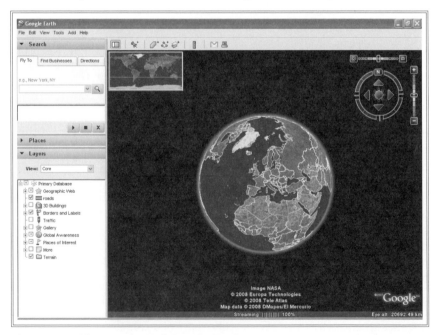

Figure 15.2 The interface of Google Earth

though it was a globe in the living-room. The bodily sensations are similar to the armchair traveller in the sense of 'having the whole world in his hand'. On the other hand the users might have a certain feeling of embodiment, some kind of the feeling of 'just like being there'.

Community Dimensions of Online tourism: Information, Self-presentation and Identity

Members present themselves through their profiles, describe their trips and provide images and advice for fellow travellers. Virtual Tourist as a corporate actor capitalises on members travelogues as the information, photos and tips provided are included in an advanced information system making everything readily searchable and available. Thus the individual profiles developed by the members are turned into a vast body of information available to all other members and visitors.

Members identify and position themselves within the community by the personal text and pictures within the member profile. Many members start by inserting a slogan or a picture of themselves, often both. The text is often used as a kind of statement of the way one prefers to travel. Examples are:

Live well, laugh often, love much – Rhiondaj, USA.
Veni – vidi – and took lots of pictures ... – Michael, Austria.
If you are in a hurry, make a detour ... – Sachara, Germany.

Obviously, most pictures show the members in a situation 'on the road', either in front of a beautiful landscape, in the middle of a party somewhere in the world or in a potential 'dangerous' situation, for example on the top of a mountain or with a python snake around the neck. Some, especially those with children, present themselves within a family context, often including pictures of partners and families.

Besides the slogans and pictures there is a shorter or longer introductory text in which the members describe their way of life, their travel or general opinions on life. Often members refer to their most recent journey or plans for those to come. Many members seem to make a huge effort to declare that they are travellers, not tourists. In other words they refer to tourist roles as sketched by Maxine Feifer (1985) who distinguishes between tourists, anti-tourists and post-tourists. Most members of Virtual Tourist regard themselves as anti-tourists or travellers, emphasising that they actually do interact with local people in foreign countries and distance themselves from classical tourist icons such as 'tacky' souvenir shops, 'Pig parties' in Spain and being cheated by touts. Normal 'tourists' are generally ridiculed but post-tourists, travellers having an ironic distance to the other groups, are often present. Commenting on the arrogance of some members, MrJemm from United Kingdom declares in his profile:

> Traveller? Ha! We're all TOURISTS!

Among other discourses on Virtual Tourist, the backpacker discourse is particularly dominant. That is no surprise as backpacker tourists are generally young and thereby often super users of the internet. Further, the backpacker lifestyle, arisen from the hippie movement and materialised through the spread of youth hostels and the popularity of guidebooks like 'Lonely Planet', has been an important part of the international travel scene for decades. Indeed, typical 'backpacker values' such as sleeping as cheaply as possible, using lot of time for travelling, and now and then a wish to go beyond the paved road are prevalent among many members.

Another notable discourse is that of global awareness and environmental concern. Many members state that they are aware of taking care of the environment when travelling, for example by using eco-friendly travel agencies while in the rain forest or other places of wilderness.

There are also many general statements in the members' slogans. For example:

> Your planet needs you ... time to act! – Muya, Belgium.
> Many cultures ... one world. – Veronica, Texas.
> Travelling seriously damages your prejudices! – Bernd, Germany.

Members therefore present their travelogues, photographs, tips and advice within a certain aesthetic and emotional context. Aesthetic because images, lyrics, slogans and general remarks on the beauty of the world are often a main focus in the personal presentation. Emotional because people really do say something about the way they live, feel and travel. People strive to give an impression of who they are, or at least, who they want to be. In sum, Virtual Tourist users demonstrate a strong element of performance in sociologist Erwing Goffman's (1991) sense of the word. The personal profiles are 'front stages' for performances as a traveller. They can perform their ideal role of being a traveller without having to reveal the possible worries that might appear backstage: diseases, airport queues, home-sickness and huge expenses.

However, Virtual Tourist is not only about performance but also community. Core members emphasise that networking and making contact with new people is an important part of participating. At first, people might exchange information and ideas on travelling but many members go beyond those mere exchanges and form friendships, virtual as well as in the real world. Of course, in such circumstances it becomes difficult to uphold roles that are contrary to the actual person. Even though some might play roles, the general impression is that people are much more honest on Virtual Tourist than in many other online communities, first and foremost because dating and flirting is officially prohibited. Again, it is a community dedicated to a certain topic, travelling, and the clear guidelines contribute to the mostly smooth running of the discussions. However, one should also recognise the complex systems of hierarchies and status where one gains status in the community by being informative and helpful towards fellow members. Kollock (2000) emphasises that such virtual 'economies' contribute at least as much as official 'policing' to the well-being of online communities.

Besides the destination information and travel tips within the profiles, Virtual Tourist has three huge discussion boards. The VT Travel Forum is the largest. It is dedicated to asking questions, having discussions and sharing travel-related information on destinations all over the world. The discussions are organised according to various continents, countries and cities, and it is emphasised that members have to post to the right part of the forum: questions or comments on Norway in the Norway forum etc. Solely in the month of May 2007 there were thousands of posts and replies on all different destinations in the world. A special discipline among the members is to provide information on 'dangers and annoyances' from the risk of getting mugged in a foreign metropolis to the irritating appearance of beggars and touts on the road to major destinations. Thus again, many members feel obliged and committed towards each other.

Besides the possibilities of contacts through exchanging information, commenting upon each others' travel tips and exchanging private e-mails, Virtual Tourist has a formal system for networking, the 'Friends List'. It is not mainly aimed at finding new travel buddies like for example on the British, Travelling Companions web-site (2008). Rather, it is a feature where each member can add up to 255 other members to their friends list, thereby getting notified once they are online. The 'Friends List' is based on mutual recognition. Both members have to acknowledge the connection in order to establish the 'friendship'.

Contrary, Google Earth is not a member-based community and people do not have personal profiles. The overwhelming majority of users are just surfing around the virtual globe. However, some users participate and contribute to the application as well as the community surrounding it. Thereby, Google Earth is also fostering global social interaction where users interact, discuss and compare experiences, of physical travel as well as of Google Earth itself.

The users can share information in two ways, by virtual pins and by discussion boards. On Virtual Tourist all users are provided with a virtual 'world map' where they mark the countries they have actually visited. Thereby, the users appear as 'real' persons, living in time and space. By comparison, users of Google Earth can attach information to virtual 'pins' placed on certain locations, for example Mount Everest. Upon clicking such a 'pin', the attached information is revealed in a small text box. It might be a description of the place, an anecdote, a photograph or a link to further information. This information is stored in the virtual representation of the world and is available to all users if selecting it. All this information together forms the so-called 'Google Earth Community'.

Secondly, the information might be linked to discussions in the forum, Keyhole BBS. Here, thousands of Google Earth Community Members discuss places, travel, and a variety of other topics, including their experiences of Google Earth. Some of the discussions are related to physical destinations whereas others are related only to the information provided, shared, and developed within Google Earth.

By placing the pins, the users are 'writing the globe' and inscribing their presence. In the physical world certain youngsters try to do the same when applying graffiti to the cities' walls. In Google Earth, it is perfectly legal and you have the whole world as your playground. By writing the globe, the users position themselves spatially, in the world and within the community.

Google Earth has an important social dimension, too. Besides being a tool for looking up destinations and seeking information, it is also an online community where users interact by exchanging markers, information, and opinions. As a community, Google Earth shows some of the same tendencies as other online communities. Users are generally friendly and helpful towards each other and eagerly discuss real world destinations as well as improving and enhancing the application itself. They can present and exchange their real world experiences and by the virtual information of fellow users create new imaginations and aspirations and, ultimately, visit new physical places. Google Earth is a social guidebook, travel magazine, TV programme and tourist brochure at the same time.

Authentic Experiences? Online and Offline Worlds

Even though everybody is aware it is a simulation, Google Earth strives for an exact representation of the real thing. Where traditional maps represents the world, Google Earth aims to simulate the world, creating experiences close to 'being there'. Like films and computer games it aims for transparency and immediacy, creating a feeling among the users of experiencing reality. As Jay David Bolter and Richard Grusin put it, such media try to deny the fact of mediation (2000: 53). If succeeding, they evoke an immediate (and therefore authentic) emotional response. Google Earth might have a stronger emotional impact than other three-dimensional online communities incorporating spatial and corporeal elements, for example World of Warcraft and Second Life. There is no game play in Google Earth; it is rather a world in which to navigate, act, and perform – just as in the virtual world of Second Life. It does not simulate another, artificial world, but the very physical world in which we are all living. Movements in Google Earth might be replicated in real places and vice versa. Physical and emotional experiences around the world are referred to by the use of personal markers, stories and information. Users are able to reproduce earlier trips by drawing routes or record a flight across the Grand Canyon or a trek up Everest. All the time, the users can shift seamlessly between the 'God's eye view' of the whole globe and the details normally only available through physical presence.

Further, they use online media as a gateway to augment and strengthen experiences and relationships in the 'real world'. For example, the networking of Virtual Tourist is not limited to the Virtual World as physical gatherings among members often take place all over the world. According to core members of the community, several weddings have taken place where the initial contact between the lovers was established on Virtual Tourist. This is quite paradoxical because, as mentioned, explicit dating and flirting is not allowed.

By nature, online travel communities might be stronger linked to the 'physical world' than most online communities as their main purpose is to discuss, promote or present travel to physical locations. Thereby, geographic places are constantly referred to. Members use the information obtained online as an inspiration of actually going places. Users might find travel companions, nice hotels or travel bargains. As Jansson (2002) puts it there is a strong link between virtual, imagined and real travel activities. On Virtual Tourist such dualisms are twisted in new ways. People who have never met physically form friendships across distances and country borders and they engage in networks based on shared experiences and identities. The most striking feature is the VT meetings where members who might have never met arrange to show up at a certain location and have a gathering or a party. Although such meetings are purely arranged by voluntary members, they are explicitly promoted on the Virtual Tourist sites.

Google Earth and Virtual Tourist might invoke a certain existential authenticity among the users, a lived feeling of authenticity. But they do that by different means. Google Earth is a kind of virtual embodiment where as Virtual Tourist is much more centred on social interactions which might sometimes protrude to real-life interactions.

Conclusion

Virtual Tourist and Google Earth demonstrate how online tourism changes well-known concepts of place, space and authenticity. They combine self-presentation, information sharing and community building, all linked together through a strong emphasis on spatial representation of the actual world. From a cartographic perspective they revolutionise the possibilities of ordinary maps and globes. From an informational perspective, it foregrounds bright new ways of organising and distributing information. Online tourism technologies have the strengths of film and TV of invoking emotions among the users. Further, it might facilitate the bodily sensations of virtual reality devices, providing the users with an almost corporeal experience of navigation and acquisition of information.

It no longer makes sense to distinguish between physical and virtual space, to view the 'cyberspace' as something 'out there'. On a metaphysical level, of course, a phenomenon like Google Earth might exist only on servers and through hasty glimpses of electrons in the global informational infrastructure. But from the users' perspective through daily practices, online tourism facilitates a changing spatial experience: by enhanced geographical and corporeal sensations of the globe; by accessing vast amounts of information in new ways; and by exchanging knowledge and information with other users and possibly forming new relations and friendships.

Further, online tourist technologies are used to facilitate and enhance the experiences of physical travel. On the one hand, users bring in the physical world by discussing and referring to physical places. On the other hand, the internet users are likely to extend their 'virtual' presence to the 'real' world, going to new places and gathering physically with their new online acquaintances. As such online tourism provides the users with an augmented and enhanced space for social actions and experiences on a global scale.

Altogether, online tourism facilitates an increased range of personal and social actions. Users experience an increase of social space in addition to existing social and physical experiences obtained through social relations, mass media and corporeal experiences. In short, it contributes to an augmentation of informational, emotional and social space by strengthening the interplay between physical, mediated and imaginary experiences.

EMBODYING SPATIAL MYTHOLOGIES

Chapter 16

Journeys, Religion and Authenticity Revisited

TORUNN SELBERG

Introduction

A book entitled *Sjelen som turist* ('The Soul as Tourist'), with the subtitle *'About religion, therapy and magic'* was published some years ago, presenting the Norwegian writer, Bjørg Vindsetmo's, critique of the present-day's alternative religiosity or spirituality. We all share a yearning for a richer and deeper life, the writer states, but in her opinion, sincere *seeking* is increasingly being replaced by a form of mental *tourism* (Vindsetmo, 1995).

In their introduction to the book *Religiøse reiser* (Religious travels) the two scholars of religion Ingvild Gilhus and Siv Ellen Kraft assert that religious people have always travelled (Gilhus & Kraft, 2007: 13). The title of Vindsetmo's book is also a reference to religious travel, albeit referred to as 'tourism', a form of travel bringing up certain connotations. 'Tourism is a mystifying subject', writes Edward M. Bruner 'because being a tourist is deprecated by almost everyone. Even tourists themselves belittle tourism as it connotes something commercial, tacky and super-ficial' (2005: 7) In this perspective, the title 'The soul as tourist' suggests more genuine forms of both religion and travel, and the book writes itself into a meta-narrative about the genuine and spurious.

'New' is not a hallmark of religion, even though all religions have been new at one stage. 'New' is a designation which generates different associations depending on the field in which it is used (Gilhus, 1999). Coupled with religion, 'new' gives rise to a certain level of distaste, and an impression of a dubious religion which is not rooted and formed by an indigenous and continuous tradition. In this context, categories such as 'new' and 'tourist' are inter-connected and connote something spurious; the expression 'spiritual tourism' is part of a critical discourse on both New Age and tourism.

In this chapter I will discuss the sacred geography of alternative spirituality and the ways in which sacred geography colours current tourist-geography.[1] I will use *place-narratives* collected from both tourism and New Age contexts. Such narratives have many functions; my basic stance is that one of their aspects can be seen as part of a dialogue about the genuine and spurious, and is all about *authentication*. I see the narratives as part of a dialogic narration that is a polyphonic discourse based on tellings, retellings or references to important cultural narratives (Bruner, 2005: 182). The place-narrative category is used in a broad sense, incorporating collected material from holiday catalogues, the membership magazine of a spiritual book-club, the advertising material of tourist destinations, sites and places, articles from weekly magazines; in brief, examples of popular culture.

Place Narratives

Place narratives are included in a narrative geography in which various types of geographical information are put together to form a narrative that conveys a certain message (Wittermann, 1999: 239). Such narratives are constantly being produced thereby reshaping and re-evaluating ideas about the place. *'Sites themselves are not passive'*, writes Bruner,'they are given meaning and are constituted by the narratives that envelope them' (2005: 12).

However, place narratives are never constructed from nothing. They are linked to the landscape, to past events, be they of mythical or historical nature, and to real people. In a place-narrative, aspects of the place are selected and organised, thus helping to assign meaning to the place, and to distinguish it from other sites. Narratives reinforce and select both the past and the materiality of a place. When a place is being described as a tourist destination, certain aspects and dimensions that tourists want to experience will be emphasised, depending on who is being addressed.

Bruner tells us that the interpretations of a site are not monolithic. Different people associate different stories with a site, and place-narratives are constantly being produced and re-produced: The advertising material of the Norwegian City of Trondheim can serve as an example: 'What is it that gives Trondheim identity and distinctiveness? Is it the city of technology, of students, of Kings, of football or of Vikings? Yes please, all of the above, the locals answer. The City of Pilgrims has gradually become a label with which many identify. The city needed a narrative about itself, says pilgrim vicar Rolf Synnes of Nidaros Cathedral' (Trondheim, 2008).

Trondheim demonstrates that a place chooses its place-narrative from its different materialities, identities and pasts. In my opinion, the chosen narrative is the one which has a dialogue with current narratives beyond the borders of the city. In the first decennium of 2000 pilgrim narratives and medieval times have appeal in tourist geography. In this way a city like Trondheim is being re-sacralised. Its traditions associated with pilgrimage and the sacred places of medieval times are being actualised in new narratives that are also being ritualised in festivals (see Selberg, 2005, 2006). Every July, for example, Trondheim celebrates the annual Olav Festival, an event that focuses on the narrative about the city's past as a place of pilgrimage. The Festival presents itself in this way:

> Olav Haraldsøn fell in the battle of Stiklestad in 1030 in his attempt to christianise and unite the country. His body was rescued from the battlefield and buried near the Nidelva river. A church, the Olavskirken, was built on the riverbank. Shortly after, people witnessed signs and miracles near Olav's grave. He came to be considered a saint and became an object of worship, with pilgrims coming from all over Europe to attend the Olav's Mass in the Cathedral of Nidaros.[2] The Olav Festival continues a tradition which in modern times started in 1962 through the establishment of what at the time was called The Olav Days. There is an extensive programme in the Cathedral throughout the festival period and pilgrims from far and near choose to make one of Northern Europe's few international pilgrimages. (Olavsfestdagene, 2008)

Trondheim is an example of how narratives about events of the past are being actualised, thereby assigning meaning to the place by constructing continuity to the past. The example also demonstrates that a past with religious references is popular in our time. Places are being re-sacralised through various processes in which place narratives play an important role. The place of medieval pilgrimage is being actualised as a tourist destination in late modernity.

New Age and Sacred Geography

Religions have their sacred places, and narratives about such places are established in a canon of Holy Scriptures. Within New Age, which is a more fleeting, almost 'oral' religion without canonised scriptures, the holy geography is constantly being created in association with trends and thoughts that are present within this complex world of ideas. Places may be considered to be full of energies and powers, or they may be seen to have preserved unique wisdoms and knowledge. Alternatively, sacred places may be seen to harbour particular forces associated with 'prehistoric cultures', or where ancient rituals are still being performed: places where eternal wisdoms are being revealed. Pre-historic places like Delphi, the Egyptian pyramids, Machu Picchu in Peru – the holy place of the Incas – Indian areas in USA and the island of Bali in Indonesia are all key areas within this geography (Dallen & Conover, 2006: 44). In this context the sacred is situated in the Other, which significantly differs from Western civilisation, or with the Others, which in a New Age context are often considered to be superior, more genuine, more in keeping with the original than people of the modern Western world. New agers are seeking sources and original truths in the 'other', in the same way as Dean MacCannell (1999: 3) claimed that tourists were seeking the authentic in other places and other times, tourists were trying to find again meaning and totality in life. Tourism thus can be seen as a kind of modern pilgrimage (Wollan, 1999: 288).

One of many Norwegian book-clubs is 'Energica': the club presents itself as 'your source for increasing your knowledge about and for the body, mind and spirit' and for 'health, mysticism and spiritual development.' Like other book-clubs, Energica sells more than books: music, jewellery and other merchandise, and specifically – journeys: journeys you make by reading a book or listening to music, or by travelling for real. I have chosen the place narratives presented in their membership magazine as a basis for discussing how New Age sacred places are being presented, talked and argued about, and what message they convey about New Age.

The book *Entering the circle* written by Russian psychiatrist Olga Kharitidi was on the club's reading list for 1997. The book was presented under the headline 'Trans-Siberian journey of transformation', and the magazine tells us that:

> Have you ever dreamed about a journey on the Trans-Siberian Railway? The book of the month gives you an opportunity to take a Trans-Siberian journey of transformation to the legendary Altaj mountains. Expect a unique encounter with ancient mystical traditions and forceful shamanistic rituals, an encounter with the origin of the great religions of our time – the spiritual high culture in the holy land of Belovodja' ... Did it ever exist, people ask. Was this the cradle of our culture? Many signs tell us that the world religions as we know them are only bleak shadows of a spiritual greatness that the world once saw. Is Belovodja the same holy land as Shambala, the country featured in the myths of India and Tibet? (Energica, 1997: 1)

In this remote area of the world the narrator is being initiated to shamanism and, according to the magazine 'she is allowed to see into other worlds. The great empire of Belovodja is being disclosed to her. For those who have seen Belovodja, the concepts of time and space take on a whole new meaning ...' (Energica, 1997: 1).

The description of the 'Trans-Siberian journey of transformation' is a journey to the place of origin for all religions. This country is described as being both real and unreal, it exists in the hereafter and in reality it exists in the legendary Altaj Mountains 'where native tribes' people ruled supreme until recently.' In an area where humans – described as tribes' people – have lived unaffected by modern civilisations, this holy empire will be revealed to the chosen. Like Atlantis or Avalon it is a realm beyond the real world. The empire is described as the place of origin for the great religions, and it is suggested that all religions have the same source. A characteristic feature of New Age is that the borders between different religions are made increasingly obscure; the idea being that the same wisdom lies behind many different religious ideas. British religious scholar Paul Heelas compares these insights to romanticism where: '... the quest was for the unitary which lay "within" or "behind" (relatively) insignificant differences. The quest was to articulate the whole, namely that which runs through the human, the natural and the divine' (Heelas, 1998: 3).

The place narrative about Belovodja refers to an area where tribes' people have been in control without influence from Western civilisation, and in this area one can in fact meet and experience the origin of religions. It is a revelation of something eternal, about a religion far older than Christianity. It is not about new religiosity – rather the opposite. It is about wisdom uninfluenced by Western civilisation. In this narrative, new religiosity is being authenticated by virtue of its association with ancient religions and wisdom. The sacred geography is being extended through this kind of travel journal, the countries that harbour such wisdoms exist both in the real and mythical worlds. This narrative demonstrates that the journey can be undertaken in different ways; the *book* invites the reader on a journey of transformation. On the one hand, a very popular tourist-journey is being advertised, while on the other hand, there is something more to it: 'a journey of transformation'.

It has been said that New Age is not a movement, but that movement in the form of restlessness, experimenting and testing is important within alternative spirituality (Gudmundsson, 2001). The journey as a metaphor is widespread within post-modern thinking and so also within New Age; there is a celebration of disorder and movement. Mike Featherstone writes that within postmodernism '... there is frequent use of metaphors of movement and marginality. There are references to travel, nomadism, migrancy, border-crossings, living on the borders' (Featherstone, 1995: 126). The texts in the Energica magazine are bursting with metaphors of travel and journeying, from journeys of transformation via inner travels to drum journeys. The editor writes: 'What mankind is about to do now, is to reject the old maps of the universe. The map and the landscape no longer match. We are looking for new maps by which to be guided'. Within alternative spirituality it is vital to collect information from a diversity of places and cultures through travel, books and other media. In New Age, the idea about the 'other' takes the form of a critique against the seemingly superior Western culture (Gylland, 2006: 7), and the narrative about Belovodja carries the message that real wisdom is hidden in places untouched by Western civilisation. The journey there is also a journey in time. The expedition to the Altaj Mountains in Siberia is a journey to the time before Western civilisation and religious decline. We are told that there are still places on earth where traditions of wisdom have been hidden from and forgotten by modern people, but protected by the 'others'. Values such as origin and authenticity are attributed to such places, and within New Age significant energies and powers are also attributed to them.

The book *Entering the Circle* is accompanied by music, a CD that carries the same title. It is part of the club's CD series called Magical Music, and endeavours to take the listeners on magical journeys. We are told that the music 'throws us into a state of trance', and that 'we are being prepared for something unique'. Kaichi, the shaman, has stepped down 'from his secret shelter high in the mountains' to sing in the village. This is being described as a recording of an 'authentic happening' and gives listeners an opportunity to discover their 'inner shamanistic world where revelations and transformations' await them. Through this music, listeners will experience 'an authentic encounter with a shaman' that will lead to an inner journey. In the same issue, further magical music is on offer; music that promises journeys to 'the undisturbed and majestic Alhambra Palace', where the composer has interpreted 'the Spanish-Arabian medieval mysticism'. On the CD entitled ICON, shamans and monks meet 'in a ritual beyond any specific creed' and the music of 'Celtic Twilight' allows us to almost listen to the ancient Celtic culture (Energica, 1997: 1).

However, Energica also offers real journeys. In March and April 2008 members were invited to the empire of the Incas, to a passage through Peru and Bolivia 'with focus on spirit and energy'. Regressions and shaman initiations would allegedly take them back in time to the old Inca Empire on a journey of both body and soul. Among many experiences on offer were the hidden wisdom of the Incas, sacred places of initiation, a secret city of pilgrimage, group regression back to earlier Inca lives and shaman initiations. Words and concepts such as 'hidden wisdom', 'initiation', 'medieval mysticism', 'shamans', 'rituals' and 'earlier lives' form a message about a past and a spirituality that go beyond the present times, and it is possible to experience these pasts on a real journey to the Other. This helps establish continuity and indicates that New Age does not represent a new religion, but something unique and consequently authentic. Words and concepts such as 'secret', 'sacred places' and 'hidden' also recall MacCannells distinction between 'false fronts and intimate realities' (1999: 97), the presentation indicates that to the people joining this journey something – perhaps authentic – will be exposed that is not for everybody.

Travelling in the sacred geography can be achieved by reading books or listening to music, and indeed by undertaking real journeys – to normal tourist destinations, but with additional experiences and dimensions thrown in. These are trips to places described in words such as 'wisdom', 'mysticism', 'secrets' and 'revelations'. In many ways, the destinations and the wisdoms are located beyond time; eternal truths are being preserved in these places and can be revealed to those who are able to see, or by the help of people with particular abilities. The idea is that the wisdom has survived despite Western and Christian civilisation, and that it perhaps remains hidden, or can be found in areas untouched by modernity and modernisation. In this way the places represent something far more authentic than what can be found within Christianity. New solutions to mysteries, and answers to important questions are being sought in places where *we* have not yet looked but where *others* have already found the answers. This is about travel on different levels, and whether the seeking is described as tourism or exploration will depend on the point of view.

Tourist Geography

When a modern travel magazine – *Vagabond* (2000: 4) – publishes an article called 'The journey inwards', a title clearly associated with ideas from new spirituality, we see that present-day tourism is coloured by New Age ideas. The introduction reads: 'More and more people travel to explore their inner spiritual geography. Total denouncers of the Western consumer society and stressed career hunters: They travel to learn more about themselves and to understand others and the world a little better.' This is about journeys to rediscover lost values. The tourist industry also provides examples of how tourism and new spirituality are included in the same story. This also demonstrates how New Age has now become part of mainstream culture (see, for example, Alver *et al.*, 1999; Sutcliffe & Bowman, 2000).

The Norwegian city of Trondheim has chosen – as we have seen – to name itself the City of Pilgrims. This is because this particular description of Trondheim creates a narrative which appeals to more people than those who will in fact go on a pilgrimage, and perhaps also because pilgrims themselves – or the practice of pilgrimage – also seems to be an attraction. The region of Lofoten in Northern Norway presents itself as 'The magical archipelago of Lofoten' (Lofoten-Startside, 2008) the region of Finnskogen on the border between Norway and Sweden is described as a landscape filled with 'magic and mystique'; and the region of Telemark is described as a place where 'myths, mystique, fairy tales and legends are still alive' (Sogelandet, 2008). These are examples of how Norwegian communities try to market themselves as tourist destinations by making use of qualities associated with things spiritual. The same applies for the marketing of tourist destinations outside Norway. For instance, the Norwegian newspaper VG (140108) encourages us to 'discover the magic in the fairy tale city of San Fransisco', and the Greek island of Santorini is placed within the world of myths when we are told that: 'Standing high up in the dazzling white city of Fira while watching the sun set behind the neighbouring island of Thirassia, you cannot but wonder what hides down there in the depth of the old volcano crater; perhaps this was the site of legendary Atlantis'.

Atlantis has been the subject of countless speculations, for example as the home of advanced civilisations, and it has a special place in alternative spirituality. The narrative about this mythical paradise-like kingdom has been assigned to many different localities. The Norwegian area of Lofoten markets itself with grand nature, but also as a place of magic and myth (www.visitlofoten.no), with a history disappearing in the deep. The 'visitlofoten' web site alleges that 'what we in earlier times called "Nordlandene" may be the legendary land of "Hyperborea"':

> In Greek mystery-religion it is said that long, long ago there was a land to the far, far north – north of the Northern Wind, a kind of Paradise, a land of purity and god-fearing. The people who lived there were called the Hyperboreas; they had a highly developed

culture and a mystery religion. They were an inspired people, free of illness and old age. (www.visitlofoten.no)

Versions of well known narratives about Atlantis are being attributed to different localities, like the Greek islands and the northernmost parts of Norway. Mythical pasts become part of place narratives as they are attractive to the religious tourist as well as the traditional holiday-maker. Many references to myths and spirituality overlap another aspect of place descriptions in both sacred and tourist geographies: local history and events of the past. Narratives about present-day tourist destinations refer to the past in many ways. Within new spirituality discourse the wisdoms of the past surpass present-day knowledge, and to the tourist, the past is a source of experiences. Being a tourist is very much about visiting what was 'before', and the word 'before' casts its magic on the modern mind, writes historian of ideas Karin Johannisson (2001: 142). The romantic wanderer would experience history by visiting places charged with associations of the past (Eriksen, 1999). Any holiday catalogue will tell us that history forms an important reason for travelling even today. Significance is often attached to descriptions of various tourist destinations by virtue of their references to the past: 'No other country has a living history like Greece', says a travelling catalogue (Tema, 2005):

> In Olympia you can still 'hear' the cheers of the first Olympic Games. In Delphi it feels as if the crowds round the temple of the oracle have only just left. A journey to Greece means to re-discover one's roots while being introduced to one of the most charming countries in the Mediterranean where ever-lasting memorials are found in the midst of dramatic and beautiful landscapes.

We are told that in Greece we will be united with history, even on a personal level, as we will re-discover our roots. Greece is described as our ancestral land. As if by magic, the past is still present; it can be sensed when we are there; we will hear the cheering crowds in Olympia and feel the atmosphere around the oracle in Delphi. Travelling to the Greek past is therefore also an inner journey; Greece 'is more than a holiday destination in the sun. It is a journey to the best in you'. This is because:

> In Greece a dual method of time reckoning still exists, providing a source of great comfort to the stresses of present-day living. On the one hand there is modern time as measured by newspapers and watches ... on the other hand there is the time eternal, which goes back hundred and thousand of years. (Ving, *Small World*, n.d.)

In these descriptions past, myth and spirituality overlap and the past takes on religious dimensions. Venturing out into the world is also a journey to the past, thus providing a source of genuine experiences. A variety of pasts to which we attach extensive continuities and long-standing traditions, exist in the world. 'One of the paradoxes of modernity is that it has a dual relationship with history', writes Norwegian folklorist Anne Eriksen (1996: 43). 'History makes the past a foreign country, while at the same time providing us with the reasons and explanations for our own existence. The past is worthy of protection, yet is inaccessible. It is distant and lost while nevertheless being full of important values. The past constitutes another more significant universe'. This, in Eriksen's opinion, is the reason why the past has attracted so many values and functions which used to be associated with religion and mythology. One of the values we attribute to the past is authenticity, and by travelling to the past in foreign countries we experience coherence in a de-traditionalised and de-mythologised world (Bendix, 1997: 8).

It is not only in sacred geography that descriptions of destinations and places provide religious connotations. Tourism is also – perhaps increasingly – about secular travel to places that are presented by reference to magical and sacralised dimensions, and destinations are often presented in a language loaded with religious connotations:

> 'The morning of the world' was the name explorers gave Bali. 'The last paradise of the tropics' the travel reporters wrote. 'A gift from the Gods' the inhabitants themselves say. We are eager to hear your own comment. Everything you have heard about Bali is true. It is a magical island that will make a lasting impression on you. The whole island is like a frail shimmer of sound; like a large botanical garden through and through. Here is harmony between people, nature and religion unlike anywhere else. Everything and everybody appear to be helping each other to make life beautiful ... Look across the softly terraced rice fields and the lush tropical valleys. Listen to the lizards, the monkeys, the birds and the waterfalls. Enjoy the spectacular display of colours as the villagers start their seemingly ever-ongoing ceremonies around the island. (Ving, 94/95)

It is easy to recognise a vision of Paradise, and the holiday catalogue that presents this vision of Bali tells us that the lost Paradise – the object of all nostalgic longing – is actually a specific place on the other side of the world, characterised by great abundance, and 'harmony between people, nature and religion unlike anywhere else'. Modern people can in fact travel there.

Places Happen

Ideas about places are produced and re-produced, and places are constantly the subjects of re-evaluation. The place-narratives separate the world of tourism from everyday life; certain areas and places are elevated and segregated from the commonplace and profane. This is often achieved by making places unique, even holy (Selänniemi, 1999). It appears that current tourist geography is becoming steadily more magical and mythical.

New religiosity and tourism are both concepts, which in certain contexts are linked to the forged and spurious. The narratives presented here can be seen as comments on a meta-narrative about the fake and genuine. In my opinion, these narratives can be seen as efforts to authenticate tourist destinations as well as new religiosity. What, then, is the source of their authenticity?

The past is a key source; in new religiosity the values attributed to the past surpass those attributed to the present, because Western civilisation has broken down what is considered to be genuine and vigorous; the past is sought in areas of the world, which are considered to be untouched by modernity. Association with the past is considered an important value. The past also makes a place attractive to tourists. Visiting that which relates to 'before' is a modern aspiration motivated by a longing for a time when everything was coherent, providing the past with a potentially sacred dimension (Bendix, 1997). At the same time, it appears that religion and spirituality make places more attractive, albeit in different ways. There is an overlap and convergence of religious and tourist representations of space. The religious dimensions seem to be pleasing in tourist geography writes Thomas Bremer (2006: 33) '... the authentically sacred character of a religious place makes it an appealing attraction for traditional tourists'. This happens in various ways; religious sites are attractions in themselves, or places may be presented in religious language, providing reference to emotional impact and a source of peace, harmony etc.

The sacred and tourist geographies are both in a steadily process of change, and narratives are part of such a process by creating and re-creating places. However, the narratives are not created *ex nihilo* – they relate to the past and materiality of the place. Key aspects of its past and materiality are being shifted; new aspects are put to the front while others are put to the back. Place narratives also relate to other stories. When Trondheim now chooses – from many alternatives – to refer to itself as a city for pilgrims – thereby emphasising the medieval pilgrimages of the past – the city interacts with narratives in the greater world. It has been suggested that a pilgrim's renaissance is growing (Kraft, 2007). Also in the Protestant country Norway, medieval pilgrim routes are being restored. In spite of a break of several hundred years, referring to continuity and tradition is the argument for the revival. Creating continuity is a way of legitimising new religious ideas and praxis. When places and cities highlight spiritual aspects of their mythical and material past, they also relate to a steadily growing set of narratives and ideas.

We may ask if the religious aspect of journeys and tourism provide a level of authenticity which the modern tourist appears to have lost (cf. MacCannell, 1999), something that may explain 'tourists' desire for destinations "off the beaten path" [...] that bolsters one's own esteem as a traveller by ironically disparaging others as tourists' (Dallen, 2006: 32). Literary scholar Anka Ryall has analysed some of the many autobiographical accounts of walking the Camino to Santiago de Compostella. She claims that many of these writers dissociate themselves from 'common tourists' to Santiago, a dissociation that Ryall herself consider impossible. She writes: 'The imitation of medieval times that constitute the pilgrims' identity is being mobilised [...] to distinguish pilgrims from (other) tourists' (Ryall, 2007: 35). Analysing the book *Fra hjerte til hjerte* ('From Heart to Heart') by the Norwegian Princess Märtha and her husband Ari Behn about their wandering along the restored pilgrim's route to Trondheim to their own wedding in 2002, religious scholar Siv Ellen Kraft sees the modern pilgrimage in the context of New Age, where seeking and quest-culture are key features. Quest-culture is characteristic of the religiosity of our times, Kraft says: 'We see a shift from an accepting to a more questioning attitude, which overlap with important topics in popular culture' (Kraft, 2007: 48).

The title *The Soul as Tourist* places itself within a meta-narrative about the (post) modern human as a seeking individual. But the title refers to ideas about religious seeking in a way which generates negative associations and forms part of another meta-narrative about the genuine and spurious. The idea of authenticity and the contempt for the inauthentic form part of a long-established tradition in Western thought (Bendix, 1999) which is integral to tourism research as well as the tourists' understanding of their own role (Olsen, 2002). Narratives about the sacredness and spirituality of places – and their connections with the past – may help to demonstrate dissociation from this meta-narrative. A story cannot be viewed in isolation, but must be seen in a dialogic framework; all stories are told by voices in a dynamic chorus (see Bruner, 2005: 169–70). All these voices are part of a process in which places are being sacralised and re-sacralised, de-mythologised, re-mythologised and authenticated. Places are alive, they happen, and narratives are important parts of the process.

Notes

1. Relations between religion and tourism have lately been actualised within tourism, perhaps inspired by the increasing interest in pilgrimage. See for ex. A special issue of *Annals of Tourism Research* 1992:1, Badone & Roseman, 2004; Swatos & Tomasi, 2002; Dallen & Olsen, 2006; Gilhus & Kraft, 2007; Stausberg, 2008.
2. The old name for Trondheim.

Chapter 17

Walking Towards Oneself: The Authentification of Place and Self

JESPER ØSTERGAARD AND DORTHE REFSLUND CHRISTENSEN

Introduction

Most anthropological studies of pilgrimage give priority to place over individuals, in terms of analysing a place claimed to possess certain sacred or special qualities that motivate individuals to participate in pilgrimages to the site. We choose a different point of departure. In this article we argue theoretically that postmodern pilgrimage – that is pilgrimage made outside the interpretation of traditional religion – is about individuals engaging themselves in the qualifications and authentification of a certain place by engaging in mythologisation (legitimating storytelling), physical enrolment and personal investment in that place. They do so in order to meet the intentions they have framed as the focal point of the journey before its beginning, by mythologising and ritualising (transformative bodily practice) certain aspects of their lives and existences, and they reflect upon such matters while interacting with the physical landscape in which they walk. As such, pilgrimage is an illustrative example of emotional geography.

We will argue that, in terms of authenticity, postmodern pilgrimage transcends any sharp distinction among different/varying conceptualisations of authenticity (cf. Wang's three categories (Wang, 1999), below) since it has elements from all categories, and we further argue in favour of a fourth category: 'ritual authenticity', that is, an authenticity merging the authenticity claimed by the place and existential authenticity.

Pilgrimage to Santiago de Compostela: Traditional and Postmodern

Every year thousands of pilgrims walk one of the many pilgrim routes to Santiago de Compostela in far north-western Spain.[1] The pilgrimage tradition of Santiago has its mythological roots in the Christian narratives of the apostle James, his martyrdom and miracle working, and his tomb, contained in the cathedral of Santiago, making this the third most important goal for pilgrimages in medieval times, the two others being Jerusalem and Rome.

Pilgrims' journeys to Santiago have, obviously, undergone a process of development since the first pilgrims visited James' tomb around 850, both in regard to the motivations for, and the religious content of the pilgrimage. The pilgrim routes to Santiago are traditionally part of the Christian history of religion. According to sociologists Mellor and Shilling, Christianity of the Middle Ages was, among other things, dominated by bodily encounters with the sacred. After the rise of Protestantism in the 1500s, perceptions of the body as an agent for religious realisation were given up in favour of realisations based on the awareness of, and faith in, the Word of the Holy Scripture, and the dichotomy between 'mind and body' and 'sense and sensibility' became dominant (Mellor & Shilling, 1997). In this light, as Kraft & Gilhus point out, it makes no sense to travel to meet God, since He is much more easily found by staying at home and studying the Bible (Kraft & Gilhus, 2007: 16). The interesting thing, then, is that the bodily and sensory perceptions are revitalised in postmodernity, which has also become the age of revitalisation of pilgrimage.

Contemporary pilgrims to Santiago are drawn from many different European countries, Protestant as well as Catholic. For most pilgrims, religious confessions play a minor role, since the religious significance of the pilgrimage is considered to be a question of the transformative potentials to the individual of the route, more than a specific cosmological content. In other words, it takes physical investment. Routes taken vary, with the most popular being 'the French way' from Saint Jean Pied de Port in France, through the provinces of Navarre, La Rioja, Burgos, Palencia, Leon, Lugo and A Coruña to Santiago, 774 kilometres in all (Santiago Tourism, 2008)

The route itself is marked by signs made from scallop shells, being the traditional emblem referring to Saint James, and it goes through varied landscapes and areas with diverse historical and cultural histories. Most postmodern pilgrims give as the reason for undertaking the pilgrimage the opportunity for time and space for reflections and the need for a (marking of) change in life. On the journey the pilgrim may take part in local religious ceremonies in one of the many small churches, but individual rituals of contemplation are also widespread. Along the route small groups of pilgrims may emerge, depending on the speed of walking, but otherwise the social aspects of the pilgrimage take place at the pilgrims' hostels, refugios, where food and lodging and a space for discussing the significance of the pilgrimage are provided. The cathedral in Santiago the burial place of Saint James, is the goal of the pilgrimage, but also marks its physical endpoint.

How does postmodern pilgrimage differ from traditional pilgrimage? On several points, it seems. Firstly, traditional pilgrimage – not only to Santiago but to various pilgrimage sites around Europe – was basically about going to a specific site where, according to various mythologies, certain events had taken place within the Christian tradition; for instance, where holy men and women had experienced enlightenment, miraculous cures or the like, or where holy people were buried. Often tradition had it that things like miraculous healings etc. could occur at these sites. Basically, people walked to meet God or what was thought to be manifestations of His power. In contrast, postmodern pilgrims use an existing religious site, the routes to that site and the practices (walking); but the substance of the journey differs from one pilgrim to another. If one examines some of today's typical pilgrim accounts, pilgrimage is about seeking aspects of your self and your own life, thereby enrolling pilgrimage in the post-modern self-religion (Heelas 1996), the subjective turn (Heelas, 2005) and shrinking transcendence of postmodern spirituality (Luckmann, 1990). One might argue that pilgrimage today is an outstanding example of how contemporary culture is an event culture (Lash & Lury, 2007), where self-development is performed as a rite of passage with very clear-cut boundaries to *before* and *after*. Each specific pilgrimage is an individual performance of a particular set of *befores* and *afters*.

Secondly, where pilgrimages of the Middle Ages were also about Christian rearmament against the invasive Muslim Moors, postmodern pilgrimage might very well be considered a counter culture to the shallowness of late capitalist consumerism, and is part of the individual strategies promoting intensity, authenticity, intimacy, relationality and spirituality – all part of cultural practices such as performances of the Self and other cultural strategies of experience economy.[2]

Thirdly, focusing specifically on pilgrimage to Santiago, it is worth noting that in the traditional edition the landscape, the localities, the entire physical environment, all were connected to the meaning and content of the journey *per se*. The landscape was seen as a scene of mythological events, and the churches and chapels along the route were constant reminders of that connection. In contrast, the interrelation between place and content seems more profound or structural in postmodern pilgrim-age. It is individually negotiated between each pilgrim and the place, and is part of the pilgrim's *framing* of the journey leading to a ritualised authentification of the landscape (see below). Pilgrims today use a landscape and its traditional use as a pilgrim route, but without obligation to certain contents. Or the pilgrim simply suspends his or her disbelief in order to be able to use a medieval practice.[3] What connects the medieval and the postmodern pilgrim is the practice: walking to gain some kind of new knowledge. But where the medieval pilgrim walked towards God, the postmodern pilgrim walks towards him or herself.

During the last decade a great deal of literature – from self-biographical books to articles on web pages – on pilgrimage, especially to Santiago, has emerged. This literature is often personal testimonies from pilgrims describing the changing impact the pilgrimage as an old spiritual practice had on their personal life, but without taking the traditional pilgrimage's religious substance into greater consideration.

Some pilgrims organise themselves into loosely structured groups, called confraternities, often centred around a web page. One of these is the Confraternity of Saint James (see www.csj.org.uk). On this web page pilgrims will write articles in which they describe different aspects of their pilgrimage. We have quoted this web page on several occasions in this article as a basis for discussion.

Authenticity

Postmodern pilgrimage, then, is very much about the production and authentification of spaces – at least this is our basic argument: We want to qualify theoretically the idea that postmodern pilgrimage is about individuals engaging themselves in mythologising and ritualising practices of a liminal nature in order to re-conceptualise themselves and their lives.

We use the term *mythologisation* according to Russell T. McCutcheon (McCutcheon, 2000). In this line of theorising, mythologisation (as a process) as opposed to myth as a story with a fixed and specific content, is a uniquely legitimating way of telling about something, and thereby providing it with ultimate authority. A narrative strategy naturalising the issues dealt with.

The term ritualisation covers intentional actions where ordinary intentions are displaced in favour of intentions that give special privilege to the action in one way or another (Humphrey & Laidlaw, 1994). This implies that the same action can have varying meaning, interpretation, and intentionality, according to the framing projected to it.

The basic practice of physically enrolling yourself in the physical landscape: investing your body and thereby gaining new knowledge, is closely connected to the question of authenticity. Being on the walk has two very important aspects: the pilgrim invests him- or herself physically by walking the route and thereby projects his or her framed intentions and expectations into the physical environment. At the same time, the aura and tradition thought to be reflected in the physical environment are internalised by each pilgrim. On the journey the pilgrim engages in all kinds of existential reflections within the problem areas he or she has defined to begin with; mythologisations and ritualisations are done along the way. At the end, the ritual outcome of the journey, of course, reflects the basic framings (see Figure 17.1).

The initial intentions of the pilgrim frame the whole pilgrimage leading to a mythologisation and ritualisation of the journey. The liminal space then created opens for a relation between 'self' and 'place', where the body and movement of the self are put in relation to the goal and route of the place, and where the personal investment of self and intentions become related to the semantic environment's power and meaning. Ideally, an interchange occurs where the initial intentions of the self are projected on the place (the route) leading to an authentification of the landscape and where the created meaning of the landscape is internalised

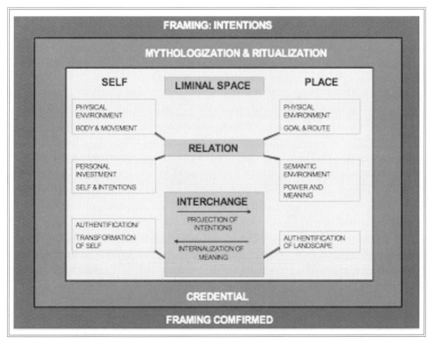

Figure 17.1 Framing the pilgrimage

by the pilgrim leading to an authentification and transformation of the self.

The construction of a liminal space with relation and interchange is the aim of mythologisation and ritualisation and its success is materialised by the credential given to the pilgrim at the end of the journey, confirming the overall framing, made by the pilgrim.

Ning Wang (Wang, 1999), aiming to produce some clarification of the meaning of authenticity in tourism experiences, has argued in favour of three different conceptualisations of authenticity, *objective* authenticity, *constructive* authenticity and *existential* authenticity. In Wang's understanding the two former are object-related, while the third is inter-relational or based on the experience of the traveller (in Wang's terms, activity-related). Wang understands all tourism experience to represent existential authenticity, and furthermore, he argues that this 'special state of Being in which one is true to oneself, and acts as a counterdose to the loss of "true self" in public roles and public spheres in Modern Western society' (Wang, 1999: 358) is a liminal state.

We agree that postmodern tourists are seeking their own *backstage*, to speak in Goffmanian terms, but moreover the pilgrim seeks existential turning points, new beginnings in life, closures, by creating a ritualised crossroads, a point of no return. In other words, we would like to add some refinements or further distinctions to those of Wang. It might be fruitful to introduce anthropologist Victor W.Turner's delicate distinctions here. Turner developed anthropologist Arnold van Gennep's ideas on *rites of passage* in regard to the ritual's most crucial category, *the liminal phase*, referred to by Turner as *liminality* (e.g. Turner 1974c, 1977). After many years of field work among the Ndembus in Africa, he returned to Europe and USA and became engaged in studies in modern Western culture, particularly pilgrimage and theatrical performances. Influenced by this new empirical field, he refined his theoretical ideas on the liminal, that is, the core of the ritual where the ritual change can and does take place, by introducing the term *liminoid*: that which resembles the liminal without having the same transformative powers. Following this distinction implies that tourism is a *liminoid everyday life ritualisation* where breathing spaces, refuges, are staged and performed, and after the holiday life goes on as always. In contrast to this, pilgrimage is a *liminalising rite of passage*, a journey taken, a mythologisation produced in order to move life forward, to create a space for new realisation; and in this process, the physical goal (Santiago) and the route taken are important agents and part of the mythologisations and ritualisations produced by each pilgrim along the way. Where the holiday is a break, the pilgrim's life is changed forever, that is, he or she was not just having *'an authentically good time'* (Brown, 1996, quoted in Wang, 1999: 352).

The Goals of Pilgrimage as Objective Authenticity

Most anthropological work on pilgrimage focuses on pilgrimage as a journey directed toward a certain place (Turner, 1974a, 1974b 1974c; Turner & Turner, 1978; Morinis, 1992; Coleman & Eade, 2004). One of the themes in these studies of pilgrimage has been the *'spiritual magnetism of the pilgrimage site'* (Preston, 1992). In this line of work, only the goal (e.g. a tomb, cathedral or the like) matters, and the route leading there adds to the magnetism of the place only in terms of how many people from how large an area a place inspires to move towards the goal. We suggest on the other hand that goal and route are two quite distinct elements of pilgrimage. The goal is important for the pilgrim, secular or religious, since it is situated within a tradition believed to have authentic power. In the pilgrimage in northern Spain, Santiago serves as the direction of the walk. The pilgrimage is one-directional, and a walk in the other direction is not considered to be a pilgrimage (The Confraternity of St James, 2008a) As such, the goal has power of legitimation; it is a unique goal since it is a manifestation of tradition, and even though you do not believe in it or share the religious connotations of its tradition, you are more than willing to suspend your disbelief in order to be able to share the practices. That means that even though you do not *decode* the goal of the pilgrimage according to the traditional Christian *encodings,* the fact that someone before you *has* in fact encoded it for purposes of pilgrimage is of fundamental value.

The goal has objective authenticity, since it is claimed by pilgrims to be the right location to go to. Here we do implicitly argue against Wang's category of objective authenticity as being limited to the object. We argue that all authenticity is authenticity for someone, and therefore always relational.

The Pilgrimage Route as Constructive Authenticity

We would argue, however, that 'the place' of the pilgrimage to Santiago is not so much the goal, Santiago itself, as the route, here referred to by its name, the *Camino.* It is on the route that space is made place (Buhl Pedersen, 2005; Lefebvre, 1991). By this we refer to a process through which an abstract, not-specified space is transformed into a place full of meanings and possible platforms for producing narratives and individual practices. It is on the route that authenticity is created, and it is on the route that self is transformed. In speaking of 'space' and 'place', we want to strongly emphasise the Camino, since it is on the route these practices are actually performed. It is on the route the pilgrim produces the mythologisations and gains the *knowledge* about him- or herself necessary in order to obtain the acquired transformation.

What we argue is that whereas the goal of pilgrimage is one place, and is considered by pilgrims to encompass objective authenticity, it is on the various pilgrimage routes to the one goal that constructive authenticity is created. Certain well-trodden routes have a reputation for being well suited for certain changes. But even though the authenticity is connected to route, and therefore 'object-related', the authenticity is constructed because of the diversity and changeability of routes – routes come and go, and they change course over time. Using these routes, the pilgrims get something for free; the certainty of a well tried authentic place and route. But it is an authenticity projected onto the routes, and in this sense pilgrimage also resembles some of Wang's concept of 'constructive authenticity'.

The route needs certain features to be usable for pilgrims. First of all it needs to lead to the goal and other pilgrims need to have walked the route before you. Then it also needs to be suited to a certain kind of walking. The anthropologist Tim Ingold describes how walking is not just a movement *on the ground*, but very much a movement *in the environment* (Ingold, 2000, 2003, 2004). It may therefore be difficult, if not impossible, to distinguish between body and route in walking. A tree branch might prove good as a handle when climbing and thereby limit the load on your muscles, or a stone might work as an extension of your legs. Therefore, the better route is the one you can, physically, mentally and performa- tively connect to and interact with. Such a route is not plastered with flat asphalt, since such a road is built to provide 'interaction-less' travelling. On the Camino, where the personal investment of self and intentions are important, the route needs to answer these concerns. The self is played out in the bodily investment of the long and strenuous walk, whereas the intentions are framed by the meaningful movements on the Camino.

Furthermore, many routes are marked with signs, and there are hostels along the route– like the Camino's scallop shells and refugios. Pilgrimage is not a practice of finding-your-way, but of *finding-your-self*. Therefore, for the Camino to be meaningful, it needs a certain amount of difficulty, but difficulties that provide a base for personal investment, not of finding the way.

The route has two different aspects. First, the route is a path in the landscape where topographic features are different degrees of physical obstacles and tools for the person moving through it. Second, the route is a path of knowledge for the pilgrim. When the walker frames his or her intentions and embodies these in a way of walking, attention to the route is also changed, and the route becomes a path of meaningful signs. The route is then not a series of obstacles, but a series of potentially meaningful 'moments' for the pilgrim.

Turner is close to these points when he defines the function of pilgrimage: 'Pilgrimage provides a carefully structured, highly valued route to a liminal world where the ideal is felt to be real, where the tainted social persona may be cleansed and renewed' (Turner & Turner, 1978: 30). Taking the idea of the liminal as an aspect of pilgrimage is a valuable contribution, but liminality is relational: an aspect of the pilgrim's intentional interaction with the physical environment. Only the walkers with the intention of doing the walk with a purpose may achieve that. Intentionality of a person creates a 'space of time' (i.e. a framed life situation) that in pilgrimage is transferred to 'space of land' (i.e. a framed route), within which changes may take place.

Walking as Existential Authenticity

A third aspect to pilgrimage besides the goal and the route is the walking itself, a technique borrowed from medieval pilgrimage, but reinterpreted as conveying meaning, and itself a source of activity-related authenticity for the pilgrim.

The aim of pilgrimage for the pilgrim is the creation of a space in which changes can be initiated. That space has its beginning and end according to the framing made by the pilgrim. The space created by framing is to be filled out by the pilgrim's body, invested in physical activity; therefore, the pilgrim needs to walk, to crawl, to prostrate or in other ways invest health and strength in order to achieve a non-reducible bodily state of certainty (Kraft & Gilhus, 2007: 49; referring to Solheim, 1998). In this sense, modern pilgrimage reintroduces the body to ritual activity – the self-movement of the body is a movement of the self. On a pilgrimage the body and the self of the pilgrim are convergent, and the intended improvements and changes for the pilgrim's self are connected to activities of the body: food, sex and general sustenance: accordingly a healthier life, a new partner or reconfirmation of old relationships and work-related life. Therefore, the movement to the pilgrimage site is an essential part of pilgrimage and a source of authenticity for the pilgrim. In movements the pilgrim invests his or her own body, since the pilgrim needs to walk or in other ways move his-or herself:

The 'traditional ways' are those that involve making the journey by one's own motive power, implying an investment of physical effort or sacrifice, an element of physical vulnerability, and a frame of mind that is open to encounter. (The Confraternity of St James, 2008b)

In his essay 'Technologies of the Body' (Mauss, 1935), Marcel Mauss has shown how all kinds of bodily/physical actions are socially learned technologies of the body. By comparing different bodily practices, from swimming to giving birth, he shows how the actions differ in various social settings, and how much emphasis is put on teaching children – and adults – the right way to do things (one only need consider how the proper way to eat is highly socially and culturally determined to see Mauss's point). Therefore, there is no natural way of walking, and to go on a pilgrimage is a technology to move the body. Not that there is a natural way of doing pilgrimage; but we will argue that by altering the mode by which one walks, it becomes a technology to move oneself; therefore walking the pilgrimage route becomes a walk towards oneself. The pilgrimage offers different techniques for altering the pilgrims' movement since, 'to be a pilgrim is to pray with your feet' (The Confraternity of St James, 2008c). One needs to be in as much contact with the ground as possible, and one way to do this is to carry a rucksack, which makes you heavier and thus the feet more connected to the ground and the walk slower. Another way is to use a walking stick. Both of these two, although minor alterations, serve to alter walking so as to make it slightly slower, which again allows one to frame the physical demands on movement and to use that framing in an internal and emotional fashion: towards one's self.

The altered way of walking is initiated by the intentions of the walker: intention-less walking is plain walking; intentional walking is an altered mode of walking with a more or less specific purpose. In this sense, an altered mode of walking may be described as embodied intentionality. The embodied intentionality is important, since it adds to the construction of space charged with special force, since 'mobile performances can help to construct – however temporarily – apparently sacredly charged places' (Coleman & Eade, 2004: 3).

Through movements, the pilgrim alters his or her perception of the environment; the environment does not just comprise physical obstacles for physiological movement, the environment becomes an authentic landscape loaded with semantic features. This is what we mean when we speak about the 'authentification of landscape', a process by which the liminality of the pilgrimage route is created again and again for each pilgrim walking the route. Therefore the authenticity of pilgrimage is played out in the interaction between a route and place believed to be embedded with certain values and transformative powers, and the intentionality of the pilgrim to encounter and use those transformative powers. By letting the pilgrim's body manifest the intentions and relating the body to the route, the liminal space is created. In this liminal space the self and identity of the pilgrim and the mythology and spatiality of the route merge in movements wherein the changes wished for by the pilgrim acquire a manifest form. In this sense the authenticity of pilgrimage is also connected to the activity when on pilgrimage, and therefore a category of Wang's concept of 'existential authenticity'.

The Creation of Ritualised Authenticity

Through the investment of the body, the embodied intentionality and the opening towards semantic dimensions of the routes through authentic behaviour, a close relationship between person and landscape is created, the main theme for embodied geography.

This interaction is not only physical, but through the intention of the pilgrim and through the altered way of walking it is also an interaction with the mythological background of the pilgrimage route, whereby the claimed legitimacy and authenticity of the route and the active mythologications and ritualisations produced by the pilgrim merge and create a liminal space within which self improvement can emanate, be it religious or secular.

This close interaction between the embodied intentionality of the pilgrim and the mythologised landscape creates the ritualised authenticity in which the self of the pilgrim is transformed and the landscape is made authentic.

Furthermore, the close interaction between body and landscape makes it possible for the pilgrim to exploit the well-tried practices connected to the route. By re-enacting the behaviour of the millions of pilgrims who have gone before, the strength, power and spirituality of the route is internalised and thereby becomes a pole of symbols, meanings and practices to be taken in, in the pilgrim's effort to re-tell or re-form his or her own life, thereby strengthening the force of pilgrimage's changing potential.[4]

We have argued that the 'meaning' of the pilgrimage is basically provided by the route, but the route only provides the proper frame, namely: '*This is a life transforming experience*', but by the intentional, altered walking, the 'meaning' is carried from home with the pilgrim, but lived out during the ritual performance. The intentionality from home is being ritualised, and the authentic self can be played out. As long as one has a purpose for walking on the pilgrimage route, one has the right to be there, even though all pilgrims may come for their own unique purposes, but without the framed intentions one is judged as a tourist and not welcomed on the pilgrimage route.

As a 'proof' for the right intention, the pilgrims receive at the end of the journey a credential, called 'Compostela':

> The *credencial*, a distant successor to the safe-conducts issued to medieval pilgrims, is a document printed and issued by the cathedral authorities in Santiago, and made available to *bona fide* pilgrims at points along the route – e.g. at Roncesvalles, and at some churches and *refugios* – and through the Spanish associations. It presupposes that the bearer is making the pilgrimage for spiritual reasons. This does not necessarily mean Roman Catholic. Pilgrims will not be asked about their denomination, or even whether they are Christian, although of course historically the pilgrimage itself has meant Christian pilgrimage. Today and in practice, however, the *credencial* covers anyone making the pilgrimage in a frame of mind that is open and searching. (The Confraternity of St James, 2008d)

To obtain this certificate, pilgrims need to undertake the journey for 'religious and spiritual reasons'; the term *spiritual* covering a range of phenomena and, among them, self-improvement. Before the journey starts, the pilgrim obtains a credential from the local parish or one of the confraternities. This token of the intention to set out on the journey with a specific purpose allows the pilgrim to stay in the network of hostels situated along the route. In this way the credentials are signs of the merging together of intention and route: of Self and Place.

The pilgrim's investment of the body and self in walking the original intentions for going on the pilgrimage are projected onto the route, whereby the content and expectations of the pilgrim's framing and intentions not only rest in the body but also on the physical landscape as a part of the extended body. The intentions are given space, and to physically walk through that space is to move mentally (or self-reflectively) through one's own life.

Notes

1. In 1989 a little fewer than 6000 pilgrims made the route, while in 2006 the number had increased to more than 100,000. Source: www.csj.org.uk/present.htm#Some%20statistics

2. Although it is important to stress that pilgrimage, like any other experientially oriented, cultural activity, *is* indeed itself a part of consumption.

3. *Suspension of disbelief*, concepts used by Dayan and Katz to account for the fact that people can engage themselves in (media) events that they do not necessarily believe in but nevertheless want to be a part of (Dayan & Katz, 1992).

4. Anka Ryall has referred to this as 'the poetics of repetition'(Ryall, 2007: 23–38).

Chapter 18
Thrillscapes: Wilderness Mediated as Playground

SZILVIA GYIMÓTHY

Introduction

This chapter studies the commercial construction of wilderness as playground, based on the case of Voss, a small West Norwegian township in Hordaland, Norway. In just 10 years, Voss has entered popular media to become a synonym with active leisure and extreme sports, harvesting several innovation awards. Local tourism marketers have abandoned stereotypical romantic and rural idyll clichés and repositioned Voss as an adventure destination. In the pursuit of *thrillscapes* (i.e. adventurous servicescapes), the chapter explores the mediation of thrill, joy and excitement in touristic media releases and in sportsmen–spectator interactions. It is argued that the experience economy verbalises and transfers intense sensory impressions into commercial products, which, taken together define play and thrill as an emerging metonymy for the entire region. Finally, the chapter concludes with a discussion of legitimacy and credibility of mediated emotions in place marketing narratives.

In 2002, the Danish Home Guard launched a recruitment campaign film, where the main appeal was exemplified by adventurous outdoor activities. The trailer featured young fans of extreme sports pursuing (in vain) geographic and climatic challenges in the Danish countryside. Finding a verdant cornfield instead of steep rock walls or gurgling whitewater, one of the characters sighs in despair: 'Men hvad gør man når man er i Danmark?' ('But what can one do in Denmark?'), and is answered by the voiceover claiming that the Home Guard might just be the place for disillusioned adventure aspirants. In a similar vein, the dullness of Danish topography is gently scrutinised by Roger Pihl in his *Guide til Danmarks Bjerge* (Guide to the Danish Mountains) (2005), insinuating that this landscape is only suited for mountaineers with a good portion of irony.

Both the Home Guard campaign film and Pihl's guidebook take their departure in a culturally defined segregation between wilderness and 'tamed' or cultural landscapes. Adventure sports cannot be exercised anywhere, but in the right spatial context: unviable, wild and risky places, far away from predictable civilised areas. And while wilderness is considered a cultural invention, so is our perception of outdoor leisure activities constrained by culturally pertinent narratives. This implies that the understanding of appropriate activities in the natural environment is changing over time. In European folklore wilderness is depicted as a frightening place, housing hideous creatures, outlaws and bandits. The most commonly known fairytales include scary episodes in impenetrable mountain passes or dark forests, warning ordinary people against wandering off the beaten track. It was not until the Enlightenment that romantic poems and paintings refigured wilderness as a landscape of sublime beauty to be gazed upon (see for instance Green, 1990), embedding excitement and transcendence in the experience of wilderness. Later on, the passive contemplation and artistic portrayal of wild nature was brought together with more physically oriented recreation activities (Michael, 2000). Walking and mountaineering became an elitist pastime reserved for upper class sportsmen, inspired by scientific discoveries and expeditions of the 19th century. With the mass travel boom in the mid-20th century, outdoor recreation has become a common pastime. Hence the idea of wilderness as an appropriate setting for adventure sports was born. Not only is it seen as a picturesque or breathtaking landscape, but also as an outdoor fitness arena and a space where strong masculine character and team moral is built (see for instance Frolich, 2005).

Recently, destination marketers began to exploit narratives and contemporary mythologies held about wilderness. This entails a physical and semiotic redesign of the environment with a commercial objective. In a study of whitewater rafting, Erik Arnould and his colleagues reveal four themes in the commercial mediation of the Colorado river, such as 'transcendental force', 'moulder of American character', 'restorative healing power' and 'last refuge' calling for stewardship (Arnould *et al.*, 1998). These authors argue that a new function is becoming attached to the spatial notion of wilderness. It is no longer only a *landscape* to be gazed upon (Green, 1990), a *taskscape* to be engaged with (Michael, 2000) but also a *servicescape* facilitating commercial interactions of outdoor leisure (Arnould *et al.*, 1997). Being such servicescapes, wilderness environments are turned into competitive places, dressed with slogans referring to contemporary cultural themes. Queenstown becomes 'The Adventure Capital of New Zealand', Voss (Norway) is marketed as the 'Extreme

Sports Mecca' and Tignes (France) is promoted as a 'Freestyle Playground' in order to appeal a growing and affluent market segment, namely adventure sport tourists (see for instance Puchan, 2004). The new feature in these representations is the absence of genuineness claims embedded in a local context. The commercial justification is not derived from historic or cultural authenticity, but from particular moods and feelings, like the thrill associated with the adventure activity itself. This practice may indicate an emerging new spatial ordering logic in tourism, where emotions replace or entwine with the omnipresent authenticity discourse of mass tourism.

The Extreme Sport Capital of Norway

The municipality of Voss (14,000 inhabitants) is located in the backcountry, 90 kilometres east of Bergen, surrounded by deep valleys, highlands and mountains rising to 1600 metres above sea level. Voss is considered to have close to 200 years of experience as a tourism destination, claiming to offer:

> [...] a marvellous cultural and scenic mixture: urban modernity and rural tradition ... There are few places you can get so many experiences springing from nature and culture as here in Voss. For nearly two hundred years we have taken pleasure in welcoming tourists who seek experiences that are out of the ordinary. Voss is situated between Norway's most famous fjords, the majestic and breathtaking Hardanger and Sognefjord, and is a natural starting point for exploring Fjord Norway. (Visit Voss, 2008)

Today Voss is the main hub in the 'Norway in a Nutshell' tour package, and as such hosts many international tourists visiting Hardanger and Sogn (including cruise ship passengers). It has a strong market position as both a summer and a winter destination, with nature based and extreme sports as part of its image. The area surrounding Voss provides excellent conditions for skiing as well as white water rafting, rock climbing and mountain hiking.

The strongest card in the adventure profile is the Extreme Sports Week (*Ekstremsportsveko*), the world's largest and most comprehensive adventure sport event held in June. Since its establishment in 1997 as a non-profit foundation by four local sports clubs in Voss, this event has developed from being a small, informal meeting for extreme sportsmen into a commercially viable festival product, attracting several thousand visitors (active sportsmen, spectators and volunteers). The festival concept is unique, uniting elements of spectator sports and professional championships in 16 extreme disciplines (BASE-jumping, Big Air, climbing, MTB/ BMX, hanggliding, paragliding, kayaking, rafting, skydiving, riverboarding, longboarding, kiting, multisport, mountain running and swooping). Officially acclaimed competitions (both Norwegian and European Cup in some disciplines) and national television broadcasting may indicate that these (traditionally underground activities, some even prohibited) are now formally legitimised through the festival.

However, the festival is not exclusively designed for extreme sportsmen: 'Ekstremveko is about music, playfulness and the amazing nature of Western Norway' claims the festival foundation (Ekstremsportveko, 2008). The hybrid festival concept combines spectator-friendly extreme sport shows, competitions and underground music concerts in order to appeal to a wider urban youth culture. Apart from watching competition venues, a number of 'thrill merchandise' products are available for passive spectators. They can buy various memorabilia (t-shirts, jumpers, posters), magazines and books on extreme sports (such as the jubilee edition *Ekstremt Naturleg*) and a DVD-compilation of 'Today's Video' episodes (an edited version of actual highlights, put on show every night in the festival tent to summarise, enhance and promote adventure experiences to laymen). Bolder adventure aspirants are offered an all-inclusive 'Try-it!'-package, which gives a sample of 10 different disciplines facilitated by professional instructors.

The following sections present an analysis of interviews (with festival organisers, athletes and guests) and of audiovisual media products. The sections explore both the phenomenological and semiotic construction of thrillscapes, approaching it as material/kinaesthetic and as interpretive practice. As such, the complex and heterogeneous relations between environment, mind and body will be unveiled from a transdisciplinary perspective – beyond established boundaries of phenomenology, human geography and psychophysiology.

Verbalising Extreme Sport Experiences

In 2002, the Voss region was promoted as 'The Parachute Valley' (Cater & Mykletun, 2003), and since then, Voss has marketed itself as a sort of *axis mundi* for extreme sportsmen:

> Voss is known as the Extreme Sports Mecca of Northern Europe. Few places offer so many different activities in one place – a wide variety from family friendly excursions and to more challenging adventures. (Ekstremvoss, 2008)

Nothing is too wild for the adventure pilgrims who converge on Voss, Norway, for summer thrills. The truly intrepid should inquire about the local delicacy, *smalahove*, a sheep's head served eyes and all. Clearly, the berserker spirit is alive and well. (Wieners, 2004)

It is not a coincidence that marketers use connotations of extraordinary religious experiences (Mecca, spirituality, pilgrimage) in order to create the image of an adventurous servicescape. Individuals often recall deep euphoric states when verbalising experiences arising during the performance of extreme sports, such as 'runner's high' (Ackerman, 1999). Skydivers in Voss use the term 'hoppeglede' [joy of jumping], referring to an intense feeling of pleasure during free fall in the air. A BASE-jumper novice recounting the first dive from the cliffs of *Kjerag*, reported of an overwhelming experience:

I landed in the centre of the landing ground. The Americans stood there waiting for me. I was shivering so much that I could hardly stand on my feet. My arms and my knees were shaking because of the adrenalin rush. My eyes were wide open and round, and I started swearing in Norwegian using every single ugly word I knew. The Americans were taping it all on video, close up, they probably thought I was expressing something of how marvellous it was. But you have to get it out, some way or the other. (Hallin & Mykletun, 2006)

The link between adventure sports and thrill is often highlighted as a reward of feeling happy (you get high if you push yourself to the limits) and can be physiologically explained as a result of increased adrenaline, endorphin and dopamine production. Peak emotions related to adventure pursuits even appear in iconic adverts and promotion texts of sport equipment producers, asserting a scientific seriousness of their products. A Norwegian outdoor garments manufacturer, Helly Hansen uses, for instance, the following campaign text in one of its catalogues:

It is called exhilaration. Billions of electro-chemical impulses are fired along pathways called neurons. This stimulates large areas of the brain, producing an ecstatic, almost spiritual high. ... Blood flow to the brain increases dramatically and a chemical messenger called nor-epinephrine is released by the neurons. This heightens the senses and makes us feel totally alive. (Helly Hansen catalogue, 2001)

'Feeling totally alive' is referred as *arousal* by psychologists. Arousal covers a wide emotional spectrum spanning from positive feelings, like pleasure, happiness, fun and ecstasy to more negative emotions like stress or fear. One can get addicted to chasing an 'adrenaline rush' by confronting mental or physical challenges – without losing control. Existential psychologists describe this extraordinary state as *peak experience* (Maslow, 1970) or the feeling of *flow*, achieved by keeping an optimal level of stimulus between boredom and stress (Csíkszentmihályi, 1988) or as a skill to balance between chaos and control, also called *edgework* (Lyng, 2004). A common denominator for all these concepts is a transcendental mental state; because of a deep concentration on the activity, the individual becomes distanced from the everyday world and its limitations and even from his/her everyday ego. Adventure is about immersion, participation and spiritual depth (Ackerman, 1999; Lewis, 2000), and the sentiments of transcendence are apparent in the words of the whitewater kayak champion Mike Abbot:

> Paddling is a sport when you get fully absorbed, both mentally and physically. Sometimes when paddling hard whitewater I become unaware what is happening around me, just completely absorbed in the moment. There is something about the water that fascinates me both the predictability and unpredictability of it, moving on and sometimes in it. (Olsen, 2007: 111)

The body is our fundamental communication device and interface towards the world; we register (and act upon) our environment through our senses (Hubbard, 2005). According to emotional geographers (Bondi *et al.*, 2005; Lupton, 1998) this embodied ontology of human experience entails that 'emotions are effects of transactions between people, places and things' (Parkinson, 1998: 616). Abbot's portrayal above recalls the notion of affect as an unstructured sensation instantly arising during paddling. This is a nonconscious experience of intensity (Lipman, 2006), which is difficult to depict in language ('there is *something* about the water ...'), hence it is qualitatively different to long-term attitudes and rational beliefs about extreme sports. While existential psychologists are concerned about giving an explanation *why* someone would engage in life threatening outdoor activities, it is also important to describe *how* these peak emotions arise during the intercorporeal exchange between the sportsman's body and the environment. As adventurers perceive their environment in motion, it is through kinaesthesis rather than visuality alone that they sense the world around them (Lewis, 2000). Kinaesthesis as an embodied state of awareness[1] can be clearly identified in the excerpts of rafting champion Silje Skorve and paraglider Øyvind Kindem:

> Extreme sports are about moving around in nature. You must understand and read the element and learn how to move in the water. [...] You can always test new things, use the stream to get along more smoothly. (Olsen, 2007: 102)
>
> Everything is great from a silky smooth flight to a rough ride that makes you sick and frightened. The experience of nature you get when you are hanging from a paraglider over the plateaus and mountain tops is inexpressible. (2007: 57)

The embodied character of the adventure results in the blurring of the distinction between bodily interiors and exteriors. Several respondents recalled a feeling of being reunited (being one) with nature while climbing or paddling. It is noteworthy though that nature is seldom experienced and sensed unmediated during these activities (Michael, 2000). Sportive technologies and equipment extend one's bodily boundaries and manipulate (enhance or restrict) the kinaesthetic sense of perception in movement, during, say, a smooth ride. The dynamic body image (Warnier, 2001) entails that technical objects (oars, skis, paraglider canopies and climbing harnesses) become incorporated in the aura of bodily consciousness. This is illustrated by the experiences of winter trekkers on Svalbard:

> I feel like I can do any slope with skis on, no matter how steep it is. [...] Also, I got used to wearing a gun on my back while skiing. Really ... it got to the point where I would feel naked without it. (Interview, in Gyimóthy & Mykletun, 2004: 868)

The sensory-motoric skills of adapting body consciousness and equipment to move safely and gracefully is a result of a reciprocal act, a dialogue with the given material context. Through engagement with nature, the climber's body becomes gradually trimmed and shaped providing a better configuration for climbing: 'The practice of touching the rock inscribes itself upon the [climber's] body' (Lewis, 2000: 75). At the same time, movement in nature also alters the way we regard and read the surroundings: the climber is looking for foot and hand grips in cracks; fissures of a rock wall, whirlpools and waterfalls become important crux when kayakers define the difficulty category of a mountain river; and off-piste skiers look for fallen trees and clifftops to 'make their own line'. Extreme sportsmen inscribe themselves into the environment; they transform nature into a sportive playground. Sites appropriate for extreme sports may be thus also considered as socially constructed 'thrillscapes', the emotional terrain of peak experiences. However, thrillscapes and the sensory experiences described above are not restricted for adventurers only. It is a 'public' domain, which is made available to a wider audience by mediating processes.

The Mediation of Thrillscapes

Thrillscapes are not necessarily easily reached or instantaneously perceivable spaces for everyone. Fans and spectators are sometimes unable to watch extreme competitions close up because of inaccessible venues or distances. Skydivers and big wall climbers are only seen as small dots against a blue/grey background. However, as a result of helmet camera recordings, even laymen can re-experience these activities at arm's length when watching 'Today's Video'. It is the most important media product of the festival, functioning both as a material souvenir as well as a platform gathering sportsmen and their fans. As mentioned earlier, 'Today's Video' is an edited version of real-time competition highlights, mixed with upbeat musical subtitles (techno, dance, rap, funk, rage rock), matching the rhythm of pulse during adrenaline rushes. Extreme sensory impressions of borderlining are reflected in the texts: 'you make me crazy', 'I can't go fast enough', 'out of control' or 'I lost myself', which accelerates and intensifies the mediated experience. Backley (2004) refers to the passive and visual experiences of extreme sports as *drive-in adventure*, and interviewees among spectators have confirmed that just watching these sequences was enough to prompt physiological responses similar to those of sportsmen's:

> The best is Today's Video, especially skydiving … I love watching skydiving … I just get this sinking feeling in my stomach, and I'm ready to try any of these things. ('Sissel', 45, local shop assistant)

Apart from peak experiences, playfulness is also an important element in the construction of thrillscape. The organisers of the Extreme Sport Week explicitly state the ludic objective of the festival, emphasising the importance of 'play[ing] with the four elements: Water, Air, Earth and Fire' (Ekstremsportsveko, 2008). This was also achieved by physically altering the environment to resemble a spectator arena, for instance by (temporarily) placing visual gimmicks and props in the wilderness. During the limited period of the festival, blank rock faces, forest edges and even cows were converted into organic advertising surfaces promoting BULA leisure garments (Figure 18.1). As E.M. Forster foresaw in *Howard's End* (1931: 243, quoted in Urry, 2005): 'Trees and meadows and mountains will only be a spectacle.'

Figure 18.1 Organic advertising surfaces in Voss

However, this spectacle no longer focuses on the untamed and uninhabited features of wilderness, but rather on a landscape cultivated by the experience economy. In this commodification process, narratives pertinent to Hordaland's nature or regional cultural heritage were replaced by (or at least merged) with non-native leisure features. The video footage of Extreme Sports week depicts how inaccessible clifftops at *Nebbet* or *Lønehorgi* are turned into concert scenes or open-air cafés (Figure 18.2), serving the ritual last meal for helicyclists[2] before they set off their breathtaking dirt-downhill. Even the inspiration for the menu and drinks served comes from a distant context:

> Russian fighter pilots drank tea made from lemon balm before they'd go for a mission. The bikers and the paragliders that take off from Lønehorgi do the same. The tea is supposed to have a relaxing and focusing effect, says the chief of the regiment fighter pilots in Siberia. (Pilot Knut Finne, quoted in Olsen, 2007: 65)

Lemon balm tea has never been a part of the culinary tradition of the Voss region. However, the construction of the thrillscape entails that the local cultural and historic profile becomes secondary to connotations

Figure 18.2 Temporary helicyclist café on Lonehorgi

evoked by extreme sport activities. Extremsportsveko is beset with references to adventure, also as provocation, borderlining and fun, pointing at contemporary popular cultural texts circulating among young people. For instance, the winning amateur video in 2006 was inspired by Bollywood musicals, portraying a kayaker's dilemma of choosing between his girlfriend and his hobby. Furthermore, BASE jumpers every year 'kill' an oversized mascot of Kenny known from *South Park* cartoons[3] or Today's Video features the unofficial multisport discipline, 'Chinese Bush Downhill',[4] emulating the dramaturgic style of *Jackass* films.

At first sight, it would seem that such infantile and boorish gags would only attract a (perpetual) male adolescent audience, also referred to as 'dudes' or 'mook' (Rushkoff, 2006). However, a semiotic analysis of Today's Video and the publicity stunts reveals a dual ideology. Beyond the hedonism of playful and negativist activities, a classic formation philosophy can be seized, sending a message of responsibility and discipline. The video also features a sober driving campaign, solidarity promotions by Amnesty International as well as instructive examples of 'proper adventure', suggesting that feeling well is closely related to physically active and healthy lifestyle. These ideas are demonstrated by sportive role models with celebrity status, who all have in common to *'have a passion for their sports, and have their heart in the right place'* (Olsen, 2007: 52).[5] The festival is built around a 'no-frills', 'no trace', 'small is beautiful'-philosophy. This implies that only locally produced food is sold for festival visitors, and sponsors are advised not to distribute giveaways during the concerts. The implicit moral agenda embedded in global popular cultural references (MTV, Bollywood, *Jackass*, *South Park*) gives an impression of Extremsportsveko being different from main-stream commercial products. Thus, it also appeals to a wider group of young urban consumers (aptly termed as 'Letande Ludvigs' ['Searching Ludwigs']), who aspire to build an identity through unique, 'cool' and 'right' experiences. Little do they know that by their sheer presence, they contribute to Voss becoming a commercially viable thrillscape.

Emotion as New Spatial Ordering Logic

The positioning of Voss as an extreme sport Mecca recalls the notion of 'metropolitanising nature' around Paris described by Nicholas Green (1990), or the mediated aesthetisation process by which Romantic poets and painters visiting Lake District or Skagen introduced these regions into European literature and art. Voss is put onto the map in a similar manner, with the only difference that it is the popular cultural artists (musicians, video editors and tourism marketers) who redefine and enshrine the region as an extreme playground. The focus is moved away from idyllic clichés of empty and abandoned landscapes to a vibrating, youthful and cosmopolitan environment, populated with athletes, performance artists, press photographers and partying youngsters. The thrillscape of Voss is socially constructed and merged by primetime live reports on NRK, photograph series in the Fri Flyt magazine, or even Norwegian stamp series.[6] What makes Voss particularly appealing is the simultaneous use and skilful mixing of global popular cultural codes with classic wilderness narratives and Nordic outdoor leisure ideals. It simultaneously embraces aspects that are contrived and pure, romantic and banal, hedonic and ascetic, commercialised and uncommodified.

Thrill as a special atmosphere attached to Voss (in pure and mediated forms) becomes a commercial metonymy for the region, rendering the notion of unspoilt wilderness obsolete. By performing or just watching adventure activities, individuals are confronted with intense sensory impressions, which may enable them to attain existential highs. The commercial interest in emotions triggered by adventure is refreshing, because it entails that authenticity as a place-specific narrative (embedded in local cultural heritage) becomes secondary to authenticity as embedded in the physical activity. This will open up novel approaches in place marketing allowing connections between places far away, based on common denominators embedded in popular culture, rather than on geographic vicinity or shared history. For instance, the reinvention of Voss as a cool playground demolishes the established segregation between wilderness and urban spaces typically determining the form of leisure activity. Just as much as wilderness can be exploited as a cosmopolitan festival venue, everyday urban topographies (bus sheds, fences and stairs) can be turned into exotic and wild thrillscapes. This is further exemplified by recent youth culture hypes of moving acrobatically in three-dimensional public space (e.g. street-surfing and parcours). These activities are represented by narratives that focus on instantaneous emotions and kinaesthetic sensing rather than on culturally constructed beliefs. This implies that marketers of Voss, Queensland, Tignes and other regions are not restricted to a handful of trite narratives of wilderness, but may bring into play a broader range of symbols, stories and media in order to convey the particular mood of playfulness and excitement.

Notes

1. 'Kinaesthesis is the sense that informs you of what your body does in space through the perception or sensation of movement in the joints, tendons and muscles' (Lewis, 2000: 69).
2. Mountainbikers transported to a mountain top with a helicopter.
3. The character Kenny gets killed in each episode of the cartoon series, followed by an exclamation: 'Oh my God, they've killed Kenny.' This one-liner has become a trite expression for the MTV generation.
4. Snowboarding on stone, grass and old snow combined with nudist bathing.
5. Best-known role models are freestyle-skier (and local entrepreneur) Kari Traa or the hangglider (and Amnesty activist) Jon Gjerde, both native Voss-inhabitants and both with an international sports career.
6. In 2006 the *Norwegian Post* launched the stamp series 'Aktiv Fritid', featuring Voss by two skydivers.

References

Aarhus Kommune, Sport & Fritid (2006) Globe1. Multiaktivitetscenter i Urbanområdet. Memorandum.

Ackerman, D. (1999) *Deep Play*. New York: Vintage Books.

Adorno, T. (1973 [1964]) *The Jargon of Authenticity*. London: Routledge.

Agergaard, S. (2006) From engine shed to sports centre. *Stadion. Zeitschrift für Geschichte des Sports* 32, 173–190.

Agergaard, S. (2007) En topografisk tilgang til studier af integration i idræts- og fritidsrum, *Nordnytt* 99, 117–129.

Agergaard, S. (2008) Unges idrætsdeltagelse og integration i idrætsforeninger i Århus Vest. Online document: www.idan.dk/vidensbank/forskningoganalyser/ stamkort.aspx? publikation ID = 9883af93-ed74-464f-8085-9af000f1116e. Published 7.8.08.

Alver Bente G., Gilhus I.S., Mikaelsson, L. and Selberg, T. (1999) *Myte, magi og mirakel i møte med det moderne*. Oslo: Pax.

Ambrius, J. (2004) Wallanders Ystad. Platser i böcker och filmer om Kurt Wallander. *Sportförlaget & Ystad Allehanda*.

Amin, A. and Thrift, N. (2002) *Cities: Re-Imagining the Urban*. Cambridge: Polity Press.

Amin, A. and Thrift, N. (2007) Cultural-economy and cities. *Progress in Human Geography* 31 (2), 143–161.

Andersen, F. (1998) En følsom rejsende. Retorisk realisme og orientalistisk slør hos Carsten Jensen. *Kritik* 132, 1–10.

Andersen, F.T. (ed.) (2002) *Et besøg hos Lars Vilks på Kullen*. København: Det Kongelige Danske Kunstakademi, Billedkunstskolerne.

Anderson, N.D. (1992) *Ferris Wheels. An Illustrated History*. Bowling Green: Bowling Green State University Popular Press.

Anderson, S. (2002) Civilizing children. Children's sport and civil society in Copenhagen, Denmark. PhD thesis, Department of Anthropology, University of Copenhagen.

Andersson Cederholm, E. (2007) Att 'bara væra' – ægthed, relationer og intimitet i oplevelsesindustrien. In J. Baerenholdt & J. Sundbo (eds) *Oplevelsesøkonomi. Produktion, forbrug, kultur*. Forlaget Fredriksberg: Samfundslitteratur.

Andreasen, U. (2005, October 29) Berlin er en chance for dansk kulturliv. *Berlingske Tidende* (available at www.berlingske.dk/article/20051029/dineord/ 110290779). Last accessed 9.12.08.

Anholt, S. (2003) Nation Branding: A Continuing Theme. *Journal of Brand Management* 10, 59–60.

Anholt, S. (2006) Why brand? Some practical considerations for nation branding. *Place Branding* 2, 97–107.

Arke, Pia (2003) *Scoresbysundhistorier [Scoresbysund Stories]*. Copenhagen: Borgen.

Arnould, E., Price, L. and Tierney, P. (1998) Communicative staging of the wilderness servicescape. *The Service Industries Journal* 18(3), 90–115.

Arvidsson, A. (2005) Brands. A critical perspective. *Journal of Consumer Culture* 5, 235–258.

Arvidsson, A. (2006) *Brands: Meaning and Value in Media Culture.* London: Routledge.

Augé, M. (1995) *Non-Places: Introduction to an Anthropology of Supermodernity.* London: Verso.

Bachelard, G. (1957) *La poétique de l'espace.* Paris: Presses Universitaires de France. (English: *Poetics of Space,* 1958.)

Backley, R. (2004) Skilled commercial adventure: The edge of tourism. In T.V. Singh (ed.) *New Horizons in Tourism: Strange Experiences and Stranger Practices* (pp. 37–48). Wallingford: CABI.

Badone, E. and Roseman S.R. (eds) (2004) *Intersecting Journeys. The Anthropology of Pilgrimage and Tourism.* Urbana and Chicago: University of Illinois Press.

Baerenholdt, J. and Sundbo, J. (eds) (2007) *Oplevelsesøkonomi. Produktion, forbrug, kultur.* Fredriksberg: Forlaget Samfundslitteratur.

Baerenholdt, J.O., Framke, W., Larsen, J. and Haldrup, L.M. (eds) (2004) *Performing Tourist Places.* London: Routledge.

Barthes, R. (1980) *La chambre claire. Note sur la photographie.* Paris: Gallimard Seuil. (English: *Camera Lucida: Reflections on Photography,* 1982.)

Barton, A. (1998) *Northern Arcadia.* Carbondale: Southern Illinois Press.

Bataille, G. (1949) *La part maudite, La Notion de dépense.* Paris: Minuit (English: *The Accursed Share,* 1991.)

Batchen, G. (2001) Vernacular Photographies. In Batchen (2001) *Each Wild Idea: Writing, Photography, History.* Massachusetts: MIT Press.

Batchen, G. (2004) Ere the substance that fade. Photography and hair jewellery. In E. Edwards and J. Hart (eds) (2004) *Photographs. Objects. Histories. On the Materiality of Images.* London/New York: Routledge.

Baudrillard, J. (1976) *L'échange symbolique et la mort.* Paris: Gallimard. (English: *Symbolic Exchange and Death,* 1996.).

Baudrillard, J. (1981) *Simulacres et Simulation.* Paris: Galilée. (English: *Simulacra and Simulation,* 1994.)

Bauman, Z. (1998) The stranger revisited – and revisiting. In N. Albertsen and B. Diken (eds) *Indvandrere, forskning og planlægning* (pp. 22–33). Aarhus: Arkitektskolen.

Bedbury, S. (2002) *A Brand New World.* New York: Penguin Books.

Beeton, S. (2005) *Film-Induced Tourism.* Clevedon: Channel View Publications.

Bendix, R. (1989) Tourism and cultural displays. Inventing traditions from whom? *Journal of American Folklore* 102, 131–146.

Bendix, R. (1997) *In Search of Authenticity. The Foundation of Folklore Studies.* Madison: The University of Wisconsin Press.

Benjamin, W. (1974) Das Kunstwerk im Zeitalter seiner technischen Repro-duzierbarkeit (English: The Work of Art in the Age of Mechanical Reproduction 1960) (Erste Fassung). In R. Tiedemann and H. Schwepen-Haüsser (eds) *Gesammelte Schriften,* Frankfurt am Main: Suhrkamp Verlag 1, 1471–508.

Berács, J. (2006) How has place branding developed during the year that *Place Branding* has been in publication? *Journal of Place Branding* 2, 6–17.

Berlin (2007) *Kreativ- /Kulturwirtschaft in Berlin*. (Available at www.berlin.de/sen/waf/register/kulturwirtschaft.html). Last accessed 3.1.08.

Berlin Partner (2007) *Branding exercise for Berlin*. (Available at www.berlin-partner.de/index.php?id = 642&L = 1). Last accessed 20.11.07.

Berlin Partner (2008) *Location marketing*. (Available at www.berlin-partner.de/hauptstadt/?L = 1). Last accessed 3.1.08.

Boltanski, L. (1999) *Distant suffering. Morality, Media and Politics*. Cambridge: Cambridge University Press.

Bolter, J.D. and Grusin, R. (2000) *Remediation. Understanding New Media*. Cambridge, MA: MIT Press.

Bolter, J.D., Fetveit, A., Jensen, K.B., Manovich, L. and Stald, Gitte (2007) Online debate on digital aesthetics and communication. In A. Fetveit and G. Stald (eds) *Northern Lights* (Vol. 5, pp. 141–158). London: Intellect Books.

Bondi, L., Davidson, J. and Smith, M. (2005) Introduction: Geography's 'Emotional Turn'. In J. Davidson, L. Bondi and M. Smith (eds) *Emotional Geographies* (pp. 1–18). Burlington, VT: Ashgate.

Bonnell, V.E. and Hunt L. (1999) Introduction. In V.E. Bonnell and L. Hunt (eds) *Beyond the Cultural Turn. New Directions in the Study of Society and Culture*. Berkeley: University of California Press.

Boorstin, D. (1961/1992) *The Image: A Guide to Pseudo-Events in America*. New York: Vintage Books.

Borer, I. (2006) The location of culture: The urban culturalist perspective. *City & Community* 5(2), 173–197.

Bourdieu P. (1996b) Et steds betydning. In P. Bourdieu (ed.) *Symbolsk Makt* (pp. 149–158). Oslo: Pax Forlag.

Bourdieu, P. (1977) *Outline of a Theory of Practice*. Cambridge: Cambridge University Press.

Bourdieu, P. (1979) *La Distinction*. Paris: Minuit. (English: *Distinction: A Social Critique of the Judgement of Taste*, 1984.)

Bourdieu, P. (1996a) Det kabylske huset – eller verden snudd på hodet. In P. Bourdieu (ed.) *Symbolsk Makt* (pp. 7–26). Oslo: Pax Forlag.

Boltanski, L., Bourdieu, P., Castel, R., Chamboredon, J.C. and Schnapper, D. (1965/1990) *Photography. A Middle-Brow Art*. San Francisco: Stanford University Press.

Bourriaud, N. (1998) *Relational Aesthetics*. London: La Presse du Reel.

Bowman, M. (2007) Å følge strømmen. Moderne pilegrimsferd i Glastonbury. In Ingvild S. Gilhus and Siv Ellen Kraft *Religiøse reiser. Mellom gamle spor og nye mål* (pp. 51–62). Oslo: Universitetsforlaget.

Boym, S. (2001) *The Future of Nostalgia*. New York: Basic Books.

Break the Da Vinci Code. Visit Rosslyn Chapel on Service 15 A (2006). Bus Timetable from Lothian Buses, Edinburgh.

Brecht, B. (1938) *Gesammelte Werke*. London: Malik-Verlag.

Bremer, T.S. (2006) Sacred spaces and tourist places. In T.J. Dallen and D.H. Olsen (2006) *Tourism, Religion and Spiritual Journeys* (pp. 25–35). London: Routledge.

Brown, D. (1996) Genuine fakes. In Tom Selwyn (ed.) *The Tourist Image. Myths and Myth Making in Tourism* (pp. 33–47). Chichester: John Wiley & Sons.

Brown, D. (2003) *The Da Vinci Code*. London: Corgi Books.

Brown, S. and Patterson, A. (eds) (2000) *Imagining Marketing: Art, Aesthetics and the Avant-Garde*. London: Routledge.

Brun, F. (1799, 1791) Reise nach den Kullen in Schonen 1786. In *Prosaische Schriften* II (pp. 179–200). Zürich: Orell & Füssli.

Bruner, E.M. (1994) Abraham Lincoln as authentic reproduction: A critique of postmodernism. *American Anthropologist* 96, 397–415.

Bruner, E.M. (2005) *Culture on Tour. Ethnographies of Travel.* Chicago: Chicago University Press.

Brønn, S.P. and Wiig, R. (eds) (2002) *Corporate Communication. A Strategic Approach to Building Reputation.* Oslo: Gyldendal Akademisk.

Buhl Søren, P. (2005) *Making Space: An Outline of Placebranding*, CBS, PhD dissertation. Series 4.

Burke, E. (1756, 1998) *A Philosophical Inquiry into the Origin of Our Ideas of the Sublime and the Beautiful.* Oxford: Penguin Classics.

Busby, G. and George, J. (2004) The Tailor of Gloucester: Potter meets Pooter – literary tourism in a Cathedral City. Paper at the conference on Tourism and Literature: Travel, Imagination and Myth, Centre for Tourism and Cultural Change, Leeds Metropolitan University.

Busby, G. & Klug, J. (2001) Movie-induced tourism: The challenge of measurement and other issues. *Journal of Vacation Marketing* 7(4), 316–332.

Buskoven, C., Brügmann, S.P. and Andersen, H. (2002) *Muligheter og utfordringer ved merkevarebygging av Norge i et kulturelt perspektiv.* Oslo: Siviloppgave, BI Norges Markedshøyskole.

Butler, J. (1993) *Bodies that Matter. On the Discursive Limits of 'Sex'.* New York and London: Routledge.

Böhme, G. (1997) *Atmosphäre. Essays zur neuen Ästhetik.* Frankfurt a.M.: Suhrkamp.

Caldwell, N. and Freire, J.R. (2004) The differences between branding a country, a region and a city: Applying the brand bow model. *Brand Management* 12.

Callon, M. (1998) Introduction: the embeddedness of economic markets in economics. In M. Callon (ed.) *The Laws of the Markets.*

Carson, D. (2000) Environmental Storytelling: Creating Immersive 3D Worlds Using Lessons Learned From the Theme Park Industry. Online document: www.gamasutra.com/features/20000301/carson_pfv.htm. Last accessed 9.11.09.

Casey, E. (1997) *The Fate of Place. A Philosophical History.* Berkeley, Los Angeles, London: University of California Press.

Casey, E.S. (2001) Body, self, and landscape. A geophilosophical inquiry into the place-world. In P.C. Adams, S. Hoelscher and K.E. Till (eds) *Textures of Place: Exploring Humanist Geographies* (pp. 403–425). Minneapolis: University of Minnesota Press.

Castells, M. (1991) *The Informational City.* Oxford: Blackwell.

Castells, M. (1997) *The Power of Identity: The Information Age – Economy, Society and Culture*, Vol. 1 and 2. Oxford: Blackwell.

Castells, M. (2000) *The Information Age: Economy, Society and Culture.* Oxford: Blackwell.

Cater, C.I. and Mykletun, R.J. (2003) Selling the extreme: Marketing adventure destinations in New Zealand and Norway. Paper presented at Taking Tourism to its Limits, Waikato University, 9–12 December 2003.

Chambers, E. (2000) *Native Tours: The Anthropology of Travel and Tourism.* Long Grove, IL: Waveland Press.

Clough, P.T. (ed.) with Halley, J. (2007) *The Affective Turn, Theorizing the Social.* Durham and London: Duke University Press.

Cochrane, A. and Jonas, A. (1999) Reimagining Berlin: World city, national capital or ordinary place? *European Urban and Regional Studies* 6, 145–164.

Cohen, E. (1988) Authenticity and commoditization in tourism. *Annals of Tourism Research* 15(3), 371–385.

Cohen, E. (1979) A phenomenology of the tourist experience. *Sociology* 13, 179–201.

Cohen, E. (1996) A phenomenology of tourist experiences. In Y. Apostolopoulos, S. Leivadi and A. Yiannakis (eds) *The Sociology of Tourism. Theoretical and Empirical Investigations* (pp. 90–111). London/New York: Routledge.

Cohen, E. (2007) Authenticity in tourism studies: Après la lutte. *Tourism Recreation Research* 32(2), 75–82.

Cohen, E. (2008) The changing faces of contemporary tourism. *Society* 45(4), 330–333.

Cohen-Hattab, K. and Kerber, J. (2004) Literature, cultural identity and the limits of authenticity: A composite approach. *International Journal of Tourism Research* 6(2), 57–73.

Cole, S. (2007) Beyond authenticity and commodification. *Annals of Tourism Research* 34(4), 943–960.

Coleman, S. and Eade, J. (eds) (2004) *Reframing Pilgrimage: Cultures in Motion.* London and New York: Routledge.

Conran, M. (2006) Commentary: Beyond authenticity. Exploring intimacy in the touristic encounter in Thailand. *Tourism Geographies* 8(3), 274–285.

Couldry, N. and McCarthy, A. (eds) (2004) *Mediaspace: Place, Scale and Culture in a Media Age.* London, New York: Routledge.

Couldry, N. (2005) On the actual street. In D. Crouch, R. Jackson and F. Thompson (eds) *The Media and the Tourist Imagination* (pp. 60–75). London, New York: Routledge.

Cox, S. (2004) *Cracking the Da Vinci Code.* London: Michael O'Mara Books.

Crang, M. and Travlou, P.S. (2001) The city and topologies of memory. *Environment and Planning D: Society and Space* 19(2), 161–177.

Couldry, N. (2003) *Media Rituals – A Critical Approach.* London: Routledge.

Crang, M., Crang, P. and May, J. (1999) *Virtual Geographies. Bodies, Space and Relations.* London and New York: Routledge.

Crang, M. and Thrift, T. (eds) (2000) *Thinking Space.* London: Routledge.

Cresswell, T. (2004) *Place. A Short Introduction.* London: Blackwell.

Crossland, D. (2006) Is Germany ready for a gay Chancellor? *Spiegel Online* (available at www.spiegel.de/international/0,1518,437943,00.html). Last accessed 24.09.06.

Crossley, N. (1997) Corporeality and communicative action: Embodiment and the renewal of critical theory. *Body and Society* 3(1).

Crouch, D. and Lübbren, N. (eds) (2003) *Visual Culture and Tourism.* Oxford, New York: Berg.

Crouch, D. (1999) Intimacy and expansion of space. In D. Crouch (ed.) *Leisure/ Tourism Geographies. Practices and Geographical Knowledge.* London and New York: Routledge.

Crouch, D. (1999) Introduction: encounters in leisure/tourism. In D. Crouch (ed.) *Leisure/Tourism Geographies. Practices and Geographical Knowledge.* London: Routledge.

Crouch, D. (2001) Spatialities and the feeling of doing. *Social and Cultural Geography* 2(1), 61–75.

Crouch, D., Aronsson, L. and Wahlström, L. (2001) Tourist encounters. *Tourist Studies* 1(3), 253–270.

Crouch, D., Jackson, R. and Thompson, F. (eds) (2005) *The Media and Tourist Imagination. Converging Cultures.* London and New York: Routledge.

Csikszentmihalyi, M. (1988) The Flow experience and its significance for human psychology. In M. Csikszentmihalyi and I.S. Csikszentmihalyi (eds) *Optimal Experience. Psychological Studies of Flow in Consciousness* (pp. 15–35). New York: Cambridge University Press.

Culler, J. (1981) Semiotics of tourism. *American Journal of Semiotics* 1, 127–40.

Dallen, T.J. and Conover, P.J. (2006) Nature religion, self-spirituality and New Age tourism. In T.J. Dallen and D.H. Olsen (2006) *Tourism, Religion and Spiritual Journeys* (pp. 139–155). London: Routledge

Dallen, T.J. and Olsen, D.H. (2006) *Tourism, Religion and Spiritual Journeys.* London: Routledge

Davidson, J., Bondi, L. and Smith, M. (2005) *Emotional Geographies.* Great Britain: Ashgate.

Davin, S. (2005) Tourists and television viewers: Some similarities. In D. Crouch, R. Jackson and F. Thompson (eds) *The Media and the Tourist Imagination* (pp. 170–182). London and New York: Routledge.

Dayan, D. and Katz, E. (1992) *Media Events. The Live Broadcasting of History.* Cambridge, MA & London: Harvard University Press.

De Certeau, M. (1984) *The Practice of Everyday Life.* Berkeley: University of California Press.

De Paoli, D. (2003) Den estetiske organisasjonen. In A. Danielsen, D. De Paoli, A-B. Gran and J. Langdalen (eds) *Kunsten å hellige middelet – nye forbindelser mellom kunst og næringsliv.* Kristiansand: HøyskoleForlaget.

Dean, M. (1994) *Critical and Effective Histories: Foucault's Methods and Historical Sociology.* London: Routledge.

Deleuze, G. and Guattari, F. (1980) *Mille Plateaux.* Paris: Minuit. (English: *A Thousands Plateaux: Capitalism and Schizophrenia,* 1987.)

Diken, B. (1998) *Strangers, Ambivalence and Social Theory.* Aldershot: Ashgate.

Dreitzel, H-P. (1983) Der Körper als Medium der Kommunikation. In Arthur E. Imhof (ed.) *Der Mensch und sein Körper.* Munich: Beck.

Du Gay, P. and Pryke, M. (eds) (2002) *Cultural Economy, Cultural Analysis and Commercial Life.* London, New Delhi: Sage.

Eco, U. (1986) Travels in hyperreality. In U. Eco *Travels in Hyperreality Essays* (pp. 1–58). New York: Harcourt Brace Jovanovich.

Economic Review Committee – Services Subcommittee Workgroup on Creative Industries (2002) *Creative Industries Development Strategy: Propelling Singapore's Creative Economy.* Singapore: ERC.

Edensor, T. (2001) Performing tourism, staging tourism. (Re)producing tourist space and practice. *Tourist Studies* 1(1), 59–81.

Edwards, E. and Hart, J. (eds) (2004) *Photographs. Objects. Histories. On the Materiality of Images.* London: Routledge.

Edwards, E. (2006) Photographs and the sound of history. *Visual Anthropology Review* 21(1 + 2). California: University of California Press.

Egeland, H. and Johannisson, J. (eds) (2003) Kultur, Plats, Identitet. Det lokalas betydelse i en globaliserad värld. *Sister, Skrifter* 9. Riga: Bokförlaget Nya Doxa.

Ek, R. and Hultman, J. (2007) Produktgörandet av platser – En introduktion. In R. Ek and J. Hultman (eds) *Plats som produkt. Kommersialisering och paketering.* Lund: Studentlitteratur.

Ek, R. (2003) *Öresundsregion – bli till!* Lund: Lunds Universitet.

Ekstremvoss (2008) Available at www.ekstremvoss.no. Last accessed 05.05.08.

Ektremsportveko (2008) Available at www.ekstremsportveko.com. Last accessed 05.05.08.

Eliasson, P. (1999) *Platsens Blick.* Umeå: Umeå Universität.

Elling, A. *et al.* (2001) The social integrative meaning of sport: A critical and comparative analysis of policy and practice in the Netherlands. *Sociology of Sport Journal* 18(4), 414–434.

Energica Book Club (1997) Reading List.

Engdahl, H. (2002) Philomena's tongue: introductory remarks on witness literature. In H. Engdahl (ed.) *Witness Literature. Proceedings of the Nobel Centennial Symposium* (pp. 1–14). Singapore: World Scientific.

Enzensberger, H.M. (1996) A theory of tourism. *New German Critique* 68, 117–135.

Epinion (2005) Evaluering af Urbanprogrammet. Available at www. aarhuskommune.dk/files/aak/aak/content/filer/urban/2005_Evaluering_ af_Urbanprogrammet_20-10-05.pdf. Last accessed 25.06.07.

Eriksen, A. (1996) Vi må kjenne våre røtter. Historien og modernitetens mytologi. Pg32 In L. Mikaelsson (ed.) *Myte i møte med det moderne* (p. 32) = KULTs skriftserie 63.

Eriksen, A. (1999) *Historie, minne og myte.* Oslo: Pax.

Eriksen, J.M. (2006) *Timernes Bro – rejser i Vietnam, Cambodja, Thailand og Malaysia.* København: Lindhart & Ringhof.

Etling, W. (2002) Round and round and round we spin. *Santa Barbara News Press.*

Evans, G. (2001) *Cultural Planning. An urban renaissance.* London and New York: Routledge.

Falkenheimer, J. and Jansson, A. (2006) Towards a geography of communication. In J. Falkenheimer and A. Jansson (eds) *Geographies of Communication. The Spatial Turn in Media Studies* (pp. 9–25). Göteborg: Nordicom.

Falkenheimer, J. and Jansson, A. (eds) (2006) *Geographies of Communication: The Spatial Turn in Media Studies.* Göteborg: Nordicom.

Fawcett, C. and Cormack, P. (2001) Guarding authenticity at literary tourism sites. *Annals of Tourism Research* 28(3), 686–704.

Featherstone, M. (1991) *Consumer Culture and Post-modernism.* London: Sage Publications.

Featherstone, M. (1995) *Undoing Culture: Globalization, Postmodernism and Identity.* London: Sage Publications.

Feifer, M. (1985) *Going Places.* London: Macmillan.

Firmino, R.J. (2003) Not just portals: Virtual cities as complex sociotechnical phenomena. *Journal of Urban Technology* 10, 41–62.

Florida, R. (2003) *The Rise of the Creative Class* (new edition). New York: Basic Books.

Fornäs, J. (2000) The crucial in between: The centrality of mediation in cultural studies. *European Journal of Cultural Studies* 3(1), 45–65.

Foster, H. (1996) *The Return of the Real. The Avant-Garde at the End of the Century*. Cambridge: MIT Press.

Foucault, M. (1971/2001) *Talens Forfatning*. København: Hans Reitzels Forlag.

Foucault, M. (1972) *The Archaeology of Knowledge*. London: Routledge.

Foucault, M. (1976/98) *The History of Sexuality*. London: Penguin Books.

Foucault, M. (1980) Power and Strategies. In C. Gordon (ed.) *Power/Knowledge. Selected Interviews and Other Writings 1972–1977* (pp. 135–145). New York: Pantheon Books.

Franklin, A. and Crang, M. (2001) The trouble with tourism and travel theory? *Tourist Studies* 1(1), 5–22.

Frey, N.L. (1998) *Pilgrim Stories: On and Off the Road to Santiago. Journeys Along an Ancient Way in Modern Spain*. London: University of California Press.

Frolich, S. (2005) That playfulness of white masculinity: mediating masculinities and adventure at mountain film festivals. *Tourist Studies* 5(2), 175–193.

Frost, W. (2006) Braveheart-ed Ned Kelly: Historic films, heritage tourism and destination image. *Tourism Management* 27(2).

Frow, J. (1991) Tourism and the semiotics of nostalgia. *October* 57, 123–151.

Frykman, J. and Gilje, N. (2003) Being there. In Jonas Frykman and Nils Gilje (eds) *Being There*. Lund: Nordic Academic Press.

Frykman, J. and Löfgren, O. (2004) *Hur känns kultur? Kulturella perspektiv, Svensk etnologisk tidskrift, 4*.

FutureBrand (2007) *Country Brand Index 2006*. New York: Future Brand.

Gade, R. and Jerslev, A. (eds) (2005) *Performative Realism: Interdisciplinary Studies in Art and Media*. København: Museum Tusculanum Press.

Gellner, E. (1997) *Nationalism*. London: Phoenix.

Giddens, A. (1979) *Central Problems of Social Theory: Action, Structure and Contradiction in Social Analysis*. London: The Macmillan Press.

Giddens, A. (1984) *The Constitution of Society. Outline of the Theory of Structuration*. Cambridge: Polity Press.

Giddens, A. (1991) *Modernity and Self-Identity. Self and Society in the Late Modern Age*. Cambridge: Polity Press.

Gilhus, I.S. and Kraft, S.E. (eds) (2007) *Religiøse Reiser. Mellom gamle spor og nye mål*. Oslo: Universitetsforlaget.

Gilhus, I.S. (1999) Nye religioner i hellenistisk-romersk tid og i dag. Kritiske spørsmål til komparasjonenes mulighet. In: P. Bilde and M. Rothstein (eds) *Nye religioner i hellenistisk-romersk tid og i dag* (pp. 24–38). Aarhus University Press.

Gilhus, I.S. and Kraft, S.E. (2007) Innledning. In Ingvild Sælid Gilhus and Siv Ellen Kraft (eds) *Religiøse reiser. Mellom gamle spor og nye mål* (pp. 11–22). Oslo: Universitetsforlaget.

Goffman, E. (1959) *The Presentation of Self in Everyday Life*. London: Penguin.

Goffman, E. (1991) *Relations in Public*. New York: Harper & Row.

Goh, C.L. (2006, September 2) Wanted: A single brand for Singapore. *The Straits Times*.

Google Earth. Downloadable at http://earth.google.com.

Gorning, M. and Häussermann, H. (1998) Städte und regionen im Süd-Nord und West-Ost-Gefälle. In H. Wollmann and R. Roth (eds) *Kommunalpolitik. Politisches Handeln in Städten und Gemeinden* (pp. 338–360). Bonn: Bundeszentrale für politische Bildung.

Graham, S. and Nigel, T. (2007) Out of order: Understanding maintenance and repair. *Theory, Culture and Society* 24(3), 1–25.

Gran, A.B. (2002) The fall of theatricality in the age of modernity'. *SubStance* 98/99, 31(2 & 3).

Gran, A.B. (2004) *Vår teatrale tid – om iscenesatte identiteter, ekte merkevarer og varige mén.* Oslo: Dinamo Forlag.

Gran, A.B. (2006) Forestillinger om æstetisering af økonomien. In U. Bisgaard and C. Friberg (eds) *Det æstetiskes aktualitet.* København: Multivers Academic.

Gran, A.B. and De Paoli, D. (2005) *Kunst og kapital. Nye forbindelser mellom kunst, estetikk og næringsliv.* Oslo: Pax Forlag.

Grayson, K. and Martinec, R. (2004) Consumer perceptions of iconicity and indexicality and their influence on assessments of authentic market offerings. *Journal of Consumer Research* 31, 296–312.

Grazer, B. and Calley, J. (Producers), and Howard, R. (Director) (2006) *The Da Vinci Code.* (Motion Picture). Columbia Pictures.

Green, N. (1990) *The Spectacle of Nature.* Manchester: Manchester University Press.

Gren, M. and Hallin, P.-O. (2003) *Kulturgeografi – en ämnesteoretisk introduktion.* Malmö: Liber.

Grodal, T. (2003) Historier for øjne, ører og muskler. Computerspil set under en mediehistorisk og evolutionær synsvinkel [Stories for eyes, ears and muscles. Computer games in a media historical and evolutionary perspective]. *Mediekultur* 36, 36–52.

Gudmundsson, M. (2001) *Tarot. New age i bild och berättelse.* Lund, Carlssons

Guillet De Monthoux, P. (1998) Estetik som organisationsteori. In B. Czarniawska (ed.) *Organisationsteori på svenska.* Malmö: Liber ekonomi.

Gyimóthy, S. and Mykletun, R.J. (2004) Play in adventure tourism: The case of Arctic trekking. *Annals of Tourism Research* 31(4), 855–878.

Gylland, G. (2006) *Tilbake til fortiden. Etableringen av Egypt som et hellig sted innen New Age.* Masteroppgave i religionsvitenskap. Norges teknisk-naturvitenskapelige universitet.

Hall, S. (1999) Encoding, decoding. In Simon During *Cultural Studies Reader* (pp. 507–517). London: Routledge.

Hallin, C. and Mykletun, R.J. (2006) Space and place for BASE: On the evolution of a BASE-jumping attraction image. *Scandinavian Journal of Hospitality and Tourism* 6(2), 95–117.

Hammer, O. (1997) *På spaning efter helheten. New age, en ny folktro?* Stockholm: Wahlström och Widstrand.

Hannigan, J. (2003) Symposium on branding, the entertainment economy and urban place building. *International Journal of Urban and Regional Research* 27, 352–360.

Hansen, R. and Wilbert, C. (2006) Setting the crime scene. Aspects of performance in Jack the Ripper guided tourist walks. *Merge* 1.

Hardt, M. (2007) Foreword: What affects are good for. In P.T. Clough (with J. Halley) *The Affective Turn* (pp. ix–xiii). Durham and London: Duke University Press.

Hartmann, R. (2000) *Deutsche Reisende in der Spätaufklärung unterwegs in Skandinavien.* Frankfurt a.M.: Peter Lang.

Harvey, D. (1993) From space to place and back again: Reflections on the conditions of postmodernity. In J. Bird (ed.) *Mapping the Futures. Local Cultures, Global Change.* London and New York: Routledge.

Hastrup, K. (2005) Social anthropology. Towards a pragmatic enlightenment? *Social Anthropology* 13(2).

Hatch, M.J. and Schultz, M. (2000) Scaling the Tower of Babel: Relational differences between identity, image, and culture in organizations. In M. Schultz, M.J. Hatch and M. Holten Larsen (eds) *The Expressive Organization. Linking Identity, Reputation, and the Corporate Brand*. New York: Oxford University Press.

Heelas, P. (1996) *The New Age Movement: The Celebration of the Self and the Sacralization of Modernity*. Oxford: Blackwell.

Heelas, P. (1998) Introduction: On differentiation and dedifferentiation. In P. Heelas (ed.) *Religion, modernity and postmodernity* (pp. 1–18). London: Blackwell.

Heelas, P. (2005) *The Spiritual Revolution: Why Religion is Giving way to Sprituality*. Malden, MA: Blackwell.

Helly Hansen Catalogue (2001) *HH Active Wear Catalogue*, Summer.

Heidegger, M. ([1951] 1971) Building, dwelling, thinking. In *Poetry, Language, Thought* (pp. 141–160). New York: Harper & Row.

Herbert, D. (1996) Heritage as literary place. In D.T. Herbert (ed.) *Heritage, Tourism and Society*. London: Bell and Hyman.

Herbert, D. (2001) Literary places, tourism and the heritage experince. *Annals of Tourism Reasearch* 28(2), 312–333.

History of Rosslyn Chapel (n.d.). Retrieved 27.03.08 from https://www.rosslynchapel.com/history/history-pt1.htm.

Hobsbawm, E. and Ranger, T. (1983) *The Invention of Tradition*. Cambridge: Cambridge University Press.

Hoem, E. (2007) Staden vi kjem frå, staden vi er på, staden vi skal til. In Knut Sprauten (ed.) *Sted, tilhørighet og historisk forskning. Lokalhistoriens form og funksjon i det 21. århundrede*. Oslo: Norsk lokalhistorisk Institutt.

Hoj, J. (2006) Between two cultures. *Velkommen. Danish Days in Solvang*, 42–43.

Holmes, Oliver Wendell (1859/1980) The stereoscope and the stereograph. In Alan Trachtenberg (ed.) *Classic Essays on Photography*. Connecticut: Leete's Island Press.

Hubbard, P. (2005) The geographies of going out: emotion and embodiment in the evening economy. In Davidson, Bondi and Smith (eds) *Emotional Geographies* (pp. 117–134). Aldershot: Ashgate.

Humphrey, C. and Laidlaw, J. (1994) *The Archetypical Actions of Ritual. A Theory of Ritual Illustrated by the Jain Rite of Worship*. Oxford: Clarendon Press.

Hydén, L-C. (1998) Body and soul. Soma and Psyche as cultural and narrative resources. In J. Frykman, N. Seremetakis and S. Ewert (eds) *Identities in Pain*. Lund: Nordic Academic Press.

Häussermann, H. and Colomb, C. (2003) The New Berlin: Marketing the city of dreams. In L.M. Hoffman, S.S. Fainstein and D.R. Judd (eds) *Cities and Visitors. Regulating People, Markets and City Space* (pp. 200–218). Oxford: Blackwell.

Ind, Nicholas. (2001) *Living the Brand*. Kogan Page: London.

Indregard, M. (2006) Skulpturlandskap Nordland – stedsspesifikk kunst?: en analyse av utvalgte skulpturer. Dissertation in Art History, University of Oslo.

Ingold, T. (2000) *The Perception of the Environment: Essays in Livelihood, Dwelling and Skill*. London and New York: Routledge.

Ingold, T. (2003) Three in one: How an ecological approach can obviate the distinctions between body, mind and culture'. In A. Roepstorff, N. Bubandt and K. Kull (eds) *Imagining Nature: Practices of Cosmology and Identity*. Aarhus: Aarhus University Press.

Ingold, T. (2004) Culture on the ground: The world perceived through the feet. *Journal of Material Culture* 9, 315–340.

Iversen, N.M. (1999) *Effekter av nasjonale image – på vurdering av nasjonale merkeallianser. Teoridrøfting og forskningsspørsmål*. Bergen: Stiftelsen for samfunns- og næringslivsforskning.

Jacobsen, B. and Pedersen, R. (2005) *På Apostlenes Heste. En pilgrimsvandring fra Djursland til Santiago de Compostela*. København: Books on Demand GmbH.

Jansson, A. and Falkheimer, J. (2006) Towards a geography of communication. In J. Falkheimer and A. Jansson (eds) *Geographies of Communication. The Spatial Turn in Media Studies* (pp. 9–25). Göteborg: Nordicom.

Jansson, A. (2002) Spatial phantasmagoria: The mediatization of tourism experience. *European Journal of Communication* 17(4), 429–443.

Jansson, A. (2006) Textural analysis: Materialising media space. In J. Falkenheimer and A. Jansson (eds) *Geographies of Communication: The Spatial Turn in Media Studies*. Göteborg: Nordicom.

Jansson, A. (2006) Specialized spaces. Touristic communication in the age of hyper-space-biased media. *Arbejdspapirer fra Center for Kulturforskning*, 137–38.

Jansson, A. (2007) A sense of tourism: New media and the dialectic of encapsulation/decapsulation. *Tourist Studies* 7(1), 5–24.

Jay, M. (2006) Taking on the stigma of inauthenticity. Adorno's critique of genuineness. *New German Critique* 97(1), 15–30.

Jennings, D. (1947) Little Denmark. *The Saturday Evening Post* (pp. 28–29, 60, 63, 65, 68).

Jensen, C. (2003) *Jorden rundt: Jeg har set verden begynde & Jeg har hørt et stjerneskud*. København: Rosinante.

Jensen, G. (2002) *Solvang Tivoli Wheel Initiative Measure*. Solvang.

Jensen, K.D. (2002) *Røde kager & grøn te. Japanske meditationer*. København: Gyldendal.

Johannisson, K. (2001) *Nostalgia. En känslas historia*. Stockholm: Bonniers.

Jones, A. (1998) *Body Art/Performing the Subject*. London and Minneapolis: University of Minnesota Press.

Jost, E.E.T. (2005) *Landschaftsblick und Landschaftsbild*. Berlin: Rombach Litterae.

Just, Gitte (2007) *Nordeuropæiske Badehoteller*. København: Jepsen & Co.

Kaijser, L. (2002) And the rest . . . is history! In A. Eriksen, J. Garnert and T. Selberg (eds) *Historien in på livet. Diskussioner om kulturarv och minnespolitik*. Lund: Nordic Academic Press.

Kant, I. (1968 [1790]) *Kritik der Urteilskraft*. Frankfurt am Main: Suhrkamp. (English: *The Critique of Judgement*, 1952.)

Kapferer, J.N. (2002) Corporate brand and organizational identity. In B. Moingeon and G. Soenen (eds) *Corporate and Organizational Identities. Integrating Strategy, Marketing, Communication and Organizational erspectives*. USA and Canada: Routledge.

Kavaratzis, M. and Ashworth, G.J. (2005) City branding: An effective assertion of identity or a transitory marketing trick? *tijdschrift voor Economische en Scoial Geografie* 96, 506–514.

Kayser Nielsen, N. (2005) *Steder i Europa. Omstridte byer, grænser og regioner*. Aarhus: Aarhus Universitetsforlag.

Kayser Nielsen, N. (1997) *Krop og kulturanalyser. Den levede og den konstruerede krop.* Odense: Odense Universitetsforlag.

Keane, W. (2003) Semiotics and the social analysis of material things. *Language and Communication* 23, 425.

Kim, H. and Richardson, S.L. (2003) Motion picture impacts on destination images. *Annals of Tourism Research* 30(1), 216–237.

King, A.D. (1996) *Re-presenting the City.* London: Macmillan.

Kleivan, B. (2004) Det eksotiske nord. Fotografier fra Grønland 1854–1940. In M. Sandbye (ed.) *Dansk Fotografihistorie.* Copenhagen: Gyldendal.

Klitgaard Povlsen, K. (2005) Kulturrevolution og Kulturkamp 1789. In S. Sørensen and K. Klitgaard Povlsen (eds) *Kunstkritik og Kulturkamp* (pp. 16–32). Aarhus: Klim.

Klitgaard Povlsen, K. (2007a) Travelling mythologies of the North around 1760. In K. Klitgaard Povlsen (ed.) *Northbound* (pp. 129–150). Aarhus: Aarhus University Press.

Klitgaard Povlsen, K. (2007b) Persistent patterns: The genre of travel literature. In K. Klitgaard Povlsen (ed.) *Northbound* (pp. 325–340). Aarhus: Aarhus University Press.

Knudsen, B. Timm (2005) It's live. Performativity and role playing. In R. Gade and A. Jerslev (eds) *Performative realism.* Copenhagen: Museum Tusculanum Press.

Knudsen, B.T. (2006) Emotional geography: Authenticity, embodiment and cultural heritage. *Ethnologia Europaea/Journal of European Ethnology* 36(2), 5–25.

Knudsen, B.T. and Thomsen, B.M. (eds) (2002) *Virkelighedshunger, Nyrealismen i visuel optik.* København: Tiderne Skifter.

Kollock, P. (2000) The economies of online cooperation: Gifts and public goods in cyberspace. In M. Smith and P. Kollock *Communities in Cyberspace* (pp. 220–242). London: Routledge.

Kornberger, M. and Clegg, S.R. (2006) *Space, Management and Organization Theory.* Malmö: Liber & Copenhagen Business School Press.

Koschorke, A. (1990) *Die Geschichte des Horizonts.* Frankfurt a.M.: Suhrkamp.

Kotler, P. and Keller, K. (2006) *Marketing Management.* New Jersey: Upper Saddle River.

Kotler, P. and Lee, N. (2005) *Corporate Social Responsibility: Doing the Most Good for Your Company and Your Cause.* Hoboken, NJ: John Wiley and Sons.

Kotler, P., Asplund, C., Rein, I. and Haider, D.H. (1999) *Marketing Places: Europe.* New York: Financial Times/Prentice Hall.

Kraft, S.E. (2007) En senmoderne pilegrimsreise. Prinsesse Märtha Louise og Ari Behns Fra hjerte til hjerte. In I.S. Gilhus and S.E. Kraft (eds) *Religiøse reiser. Mellom gamle spor og nye mål* (pp. 39–50). Oslo: Universitetsforlaget.

Krolikowski, C.A. and Chappel, S.J. (2004) In the footsteps of Günter Grass: literary landscapes in the city of Gdansk. Paper at the conference on Tourism and Literature: Travel, Imagination and Myth, Centre for Tourism and Cultural Change, Leeds Metropolitan University.

Krätke, S. (2004) City of Talents? Berlin's regional economy, socio-spatial fabric and 'worst practice' urban governance. *International Journal of Urban and Regional Research* 28, 511–529.

Kunde, J. (2000) *Corporate Religion.* Larvik: Hegnar Media.

Lagerkvist, A. (2004) We see America: Mediatized and mobile gazes in Swedish postwar travelogues. *International Journal of Cultural Studies* 7(3), 321–342.

Lagerkvist, A. (2006) Terra (In)cognita. Mediated America as thirdspace experience. In J. Falkheimer and A. Jansson (eds) _Geographies of Communication. The Spatial Turn in Media Studies_ (pp. 261–278). Göteborg: Nordicom.

Lakoff, G. and Johnson, M. (1980) _Metaphors we Live By_. Chicago: University of Chicago Press.

Land of Ideas (2006) Claudia Schiffer promotes 'Germany – Land of Ideas'. Available at www.land-of-ideas.org/CDA/investment_promotion_cs,6359,0,img-2,en.html. Last accessed 27.04.07.

Lange, B., Kalandides, A., Stöber, B. and Mieg, H.A. (2008) Berlin's creative industries: Governing creativity? _Industry & Innovation_ 15, 531–548.

Langford, M. (2001) _Suspended conversations. The Afterlife of Memory in Photographic Album_. Montreal: McGill-Queen's University Press.

Larsen, H.P. (2006) Solvang, CA: 'The Danish Capital of America': A little bit of Denmark, Disney, or Something Else? PhD thesis, University of California, Berkeley.

Lash, S. and Lury C. (2007) _Global Culture Industry: The Mediation of Things_. Cambridge: Polity Press.

Lash, S. (2002) _Critique of Information_. London: Sage Publications.

Lash, S. and Friedman, J. (1992) _Modernity and Identity_. Oxford: Blackwell.

Lash, S. and Lury, C. (2007) _Global Culture Industry: The Mediation of Things_. Cambridge: Polity Press.

Leder, D. (1990) _The Absent Body_. Chicago and London: The University of Chicago Press.

Lee, B. and LiPuma, E. (2002) Cultures of circulation: The imaginations of modernity. _Public Culture_ 14(2), 191–214.

Lefebvre, H. (1974/1991) _The Production of Space_. Oxford: Blackwell.

Lewis, N. (2000) The climbing body, nature and the experience of modernity. _Body & Society_ 6(3/4), 58–80.

Lennon, J. and Foley, M. (1996) JFK and dark tourism: A fascination with assassination. _International Journal of Heritage Studies_ 2(4), 198–211.

Linde-Laursen, A. (1997) Främmande böjningsformer av det Danske. In G. Alsmark (ed.) _Skjorta eller Själ? Kulturella Identiteter i Tid och Rum_ (pp. 174–198). Lund: Studentlitteratur.

Linde-Laursen, A. (1998) Solvang: A historical anthropological illustration of an ethnicized space. _Wolkenkuckucksheim International Zeitschrift für Theorie und Wissenschaft der Architectur_.

Lindholm, C. (2008) _Culture and Authenticity_. USA, UK, Australia: Blackwell.

Linaa, J. and Waade. A.M. (2009) _Medier og Turisme_. Aarhus: Academica.

Lipman, C. (2006) The emotional self. Review essay. _Cultural Geographies_ 13, 617–624.

Lipovetsky, G. (2006) _Le Bonheur paradoxal, Essai sur la société d'hyperconsommation_. Paris: Gallimard.

Lofoten-Startside (2008) Available at www.lofoten-startside.no/lofothist.htm.

Luckmann, T. (1990) Shrinking transcendence, expanding religion. _Sociological Analysis_ 50(2), 127–138.

Lund-Hansen, A., Andersen, H.T. and Clark, E. (2001) Creative Copenhagen: Globalization, urban governance and social change. _European Planning Studies_ 9, 851–869.

Lupton, D. (1998) _The Emotional Self_. London: Sage.

Lury, C. (2003) *Consumer Culture.* Cambridge: Polity Press.

Lury, C. (2004) *Brands: The Logos of the Global Economy.* Oxford and New York: Routledge.

Lübbren, N. (2001) *Rural Artists' Colonies in Europe.* Manchester: Manchester University Press.

Lynch, K. (1960) *The Image of the City.* Cambridge, MA: The MIT Press.

Lyng, S. (2004) *Edgework: The Sociology of Risk-Taking.* London: Routledge.

Lyngnes, S. (2007) *Kultur og turistattraksjoner. Jakten på det norske. Jakten på opplevelser.* Oslo: Universitetsforlaget.

Löfgren, O. (1999) *On Holiday. A History of Vacationing.* Berkeley: University of California Press.

Löfgren, O. (2003) The new economy: A cultural history. *Global Networks* 3(3), 239–254.

Löfgren, O. and Willim, R. (eds) (2005) *Magic, Culture and the New Economy.* Oxford, New York: Berg.

MacCannell, D. (1973) Staged authenticity: Arrangements of social space in tourist settings. *American Journal of Sociology* 79(3), 589–603.

MacCannell, D. (1999 [1976]) *The Tourist: A New Theory of the Leisure Class.* Berkeley, Los Angeles, London: University of California Press.

MacCannell, D. (2001) Tourist agency. *Tourist Studies* 1, 23–37.

MacCannell, D. (2008) Why it never really was about authenticity. *Society* 45(4), 334–337.

Mahoney, M. (2002, September 12) Dear parishioner/friend of the Mission (Letter). Solvang.

Manovich, L. (1999) *The Language of New Media.* Cambridge, MA: The MIT Press.

Maslow, A. (1970) *Motivation and Personality.* New York: Harper and Row.

Massey, D. (1998) A global sense of place. In T. Barnes and D. Gregory (eds) *Reading Human Geography* (pp. 315–323). London: Arnod.

Mathiasen, L. (2002) It is a Ferris wheel. *Santa Barbara News-Press*: A5.

Mauss, M. (2006 [1935]) *Techniques, Technology and Civilization.* New York and Oxford: Durkheim Press; Berghahn Books.

Mauss, M. (1997 [1923–24]) *The Gift: The Form and Reason for Exchange in Archaic Societies.* London: Routledge.

May, J. and Thrift, N. (eds) (2001) *TimeSpace: Geographies of Temporality.* London: Routledge.

McCutcheon, R. (2000) Myth. In Braun and McCutcheon (eds) *Guide to the Study of Religion* (pp. 190–208). Cassel.

Melberg, Arne (2005) *Resa och Skriva. En guide till den moderna reselitteraturen.* Göteborg: Daidalos.

Mellor, P.A. and Shilling, C. (1997) *Re-forming the Body. Religion, Community and Modernity.* London: Sage Publications.

Merleau-Ponty, M. (1962) *Phenomenology of Perception.* London: Routledge.

Meurling, B. (2006) Hemmavid i tid och rum. Musealisering av två konstnärshem. *Kulturella Perspektiv. Svensk etnologisk tidskrift* 1.

Meyrowitz, J. (1985) *No Sense of Place: The Impact of Electronic Media on Social Behaviour.* New York: Oxford University Press.

Michael, M. (2000) These boots are made for walking ...: Mundane technologies, the body and human-environment relations. *Body & Society* 6 (3/4), 107–125.

Miller, V. (2006) The unmappable: Vagueness and spatial experience. *Space and Culture* 9(4), 453–467.

Ministry of Information and the Arts (MITA) (2005) *Renaissance City Report: Culture and the Arts in Renaissance Singapore.* Singapore: MITA.

Mitchell, W.J.T. (1990) Was ist ein Bild? In Volker Bohn (ed.) *Bildlichkeit* (pp. 17–68). Frankfurt a.M.: Suhrkamp.

Mitchell, W.J.T. (1994) *Picture Theory. Essays on Verbal and Visual Representation.* Chicago: University of Chicago Press.

Moingeon, B. and Soenen, G. (eds) (2002) *Corporate and Organizational Identities. Integrating Strategy, Marketing, Communication and Organizational Perspectives.* London: Routledge.

Moor, E. (2003) Branded spaces. *Journal of Consumer Culture* 3, 39–60.

Mordue, T. (2001) Performing and directing resident/tourist cultures in *Heartbeat* country. *Tourist Studies* 1(3), 233–252.

Morinis, A. (1992) Introduction: The territory of the anthropology of pilgrimage. In A. Morinis (ed.) *Sacred Journeys: The Anthropology of Pilgrimage.* Westport Connecticut and London: Greenwood Press.

Mossberg, L. (2007) *Å skape opplevelse. Fra OK til WOW.* Bergen: Fagbokforlaget.

Murray, J.H. (1997) *Hamlet on the Holodeck. The Future of Narrative in Cyberspace.* Cambridge, MA: The MIT Press.

Mäkinen, T. (1988) *Kotimaan matkanähtävyydet ja Suomen matkailun pääkohteet kuntien mukaan.* Borgå *et al.*: Söderströms.

Møllefryd, A.W. (1978) *Mölle-Kullen genom Tiderna.* Helsingborg: Viken.

Möller, H. (2002) When we don't speak, we become unbearable, and when we do, we make fools of ourselves. In H. Engdahl (ed.) *Witness Literature. Proceedings of the Nobel Centennial Symposium,* 15–32. Singapore: World Scientific.

Naper, H.G. (2002) *Når steder blir til produkter: en studie av merkevaren Nydalen.* Oslo: Hovedoppgave i samfunnsgeografi, Universitetet i Oslo.

Newby, P.T. (1994) Tourism: Support or threat to heritage? In *Building a New Heritage: Tourism, Culture and Identity in the New Europe* (pp. 206–228). London: Routledge.

Nonnecke, B. and Preece, J. (2000) Lurker demographics: Counting the silent. *Proceedings of CHI 2000.* The Hague: ACM.

O'Dell, T. (2001) Are you experienced? *Kulturella Perspektiv* 3.

O'Dell, T. (2002) Upplevelsens lockelser, tingens dynamik. In T. O'Dell (ed.) *Upplevelsens materialitet.* Lund: Studentlitteratur.

O'Dell, T. and Billing, P. (eds) (2005) *Experience-scapes: Tourism, Culture and Economy.* Copenhagen: CBS Press.

O'Donohoe, S. (1997) Raiding the postmodern pantry. Advertising intertextuality and the young adult audience. *European Journal of Marketing* 32(3/4), 234–253.

Oe, K. (2002) Elaborations of testimony. In H. Engdahl (ed.) *Witness Literature. Proceedings of the Nobel Centennial Symposium* (pp. 99–112). Singapore: World Scientific.

Olavsfetdagene (2008) Available at www.olavsfestdagene.no.

Olins, W. (2000) How brands are taking over the Corporation. In M. Schultz, M.J. Hatch and M. Holten Larsen (eds) *The Expressive Organization. Linking Identity, Reputation, and the Corporate Brand.* New York: Oxford University Press.

Olsen, K. (2002) Authenticity as a concept in tourism research. The social organization of the experience of authenticity. *Tourist Studies* 2, 159–182.

Olsen, R.D. (2007) *Extremt Naturleg: Ekstremsportsveko.* Leikanger: Skald.

Ooi, C-S. (2004a) Poetics and politics of destination branding: Denmark. *Scandinavian Journal of Hospitality and Tourism, 4,* 107–128.

Ooi, C-S. (2004b) Brand Singapore: The hub of New Asia. In N. Morgan, A. Pritchard and R. Pride (eds) *Destination Branding: Creating the Unique Destination Proposition* (pp. 242–262). London: Elsevier Butterworth Heinemann.

Ooi, C-S. (2005) State-civil society relations and tourism: Singaporeanizing tourists, touristifying Singapore. *SOJOURN: Journal of Scoial Issues in Southeast Asia* 20, 249–272.

Ooi, C-S. (2007) The creative industries and tourism in Singapore. In G. Richards and J. Wilson (eds) *Tourism, Creativity and Development* (pp. 240–251). London: Routledge.

Ottesen, M.H. (1998) Giddens og integrationsbegrebet. In L. Zeuner (ed.) *Sociologisk teori om social integration* (pp. 87–104). København: Socialforsknings-instituttet.

Oxford Dictionary of English Etymology (1996) Oxford: Oxford University Press.

Paine, L.S. (2003) *Value Shift. Why Companies Must Merge Social and Financial Imperatives to Achieve Superior Performance.* New York: McGraw-Hill.

Palin, T. (1999) Picturing a nation. In Tuomas M.S. Lehtonen (ed.) *Europe's Northern Frontier. Perspectives on Finland's Western Identity* (pp. 208–235). Borgå: WSOY.

Parkinson, B. (1998) What we think about when we think about emotions. *Cognition and Emotion* 12, 615–624.

Parks, L. (2004) Kinetic Screens. Epistemologies of Movement at the Interface. In N. Couldry and A. McCarthy (eds) *MediaSpace: Place, Scale and Culture in a Media Age* (pp. 37–57). London: Routledge.

Pearce, P. (2007) Persisting with authenticity: Gleaning contemporary insights for future tourism studies. *Tourism Recreation Research* 32(2), 86–89.

Peck, J. (2005) Struggling with the Creative Class. *International Journal of Urban and Regional Research* 29, 740–770.

Pedersen, S.B. (2005) *Making Space. An Outline of Place Branding.* Copenhagen Business School, Samfundslitteratur.

Perkins, H. and Thorns, D.C. (2001) Gazing or performing?: Reflections on Urry's *Tourist Gaze* in the context of contemporary experiences in the Antipodes. *International Sociology* 16(2), 185–204.

Pihl, R. (2005) *Guide til Danmarks Bjerge.* København: Introite Publishers.

Pine, B.J. and Gilmore, J.H. (1999) *The Experience Economy. Work Is Theatre and Every Business is a Stage.* Boston, MA: Harvard Business School Press.

Pine, B.J and Gilmore, J.H. (2007) *Authenticity: What Consumers Really Want.* Harvard Business School Press.

Pink, S. (2007) *Doing Visual Ethnography* (2nd edn). London: Sage Publications.

Pink, S. (ed.) (2007) *Visual Interventions. Applied Visual Anthropology.* Oxford: Berghahn Books.

Pinney, C. and Peterson, N. (eds) (2003) *Photography's Other Histories.* Duke University Press.

Pinney, C. (1997) *Camera Indica: The Social Life of Indian Photography.* London: Reaktion Books.

Pratt, M.L. (1992) *Imperial Eyes. Travel Writing and Transculturation*. London, New York: Routledge.

Praul, D. (1960) Denmark city's amusement park proposal unfolded at hearing. *Santa Ynez Valley News*.

Preece, J. (2000) *Online Communities: Designing Usability, Supporting Sociality*. Chichester: John Wiley & Sons.

Preston, J. (1992) Spiritual magnetism: An organizing principle for the study of pilgrimage. In A. Morinis (ed.) *Sacred Journeys: The Anthropology of Pilgrimage*. Westport Connecticut and London: Greenwood Press.

Price, T. and Miller, J. (1997) *Miracle Town: Creating America's Bavarian Village in Leavenworth, Washington*. Vancouver: Price & Rodgers.

Programbestyrelsen (2005) Programbestyrelsens strategi mod ghettoisering. Strategi 2005–2008. Last accessed 15.11.07 from www.nyidanmark.dk/bibliotek/publikationer/strategier_politikker/2005/programbestyrelse_strategi_0508/index.htm).

Puchan, H. (2005) Living 'extreme': Adventure sports, media and commercialisation. *Journal of Communication Management* 9(2), 171–178.

Rasmussen, H.H. (1998) Postkolonialistiske fortællinger – om Pia Arkes etnoæstetiske undersøgelser ved hjælp af fotografiet. *Passepartout* 11(6). Aarhus: Institut for Kunsthistorie.

Ray, L. and Sayer, A. (eds) (1999) *Culture and Economy after the Cultural Turn*. London, New Delhi: Sage Publications.

Ray, N.M., McCain, G., Davis, D. and Melin, T.L. (2006) Lewis and Clark and the corps of discovery: Re-enactment event tourism as authentic heritage travel. *Leisure Studies* 25 (4), 437–454.

Redfoot, D.L. (1984) Tourist authenticity, tourist angst, and modern reality. *Qualitative Sociology* 7, 291–309.

Regeringen (2004) Regeringens strategi mod ghettoisering. Last accessed 28.11.07 from http://www.nyidanmark.dk/bibliotek/publikationer/regeringsinitiativer/2004/regpub_ghettoisering/index.htm.

Reisinger, Y. and Steiner, C. (2005) Reconceptualizing object authenticity. *Annals of Tourism Research* 33(1), 65–86.

Reisinger, Y. and Steiner, Carol J. (2006) Reconceptualising interpretation: The role of tour guides in authentic tourism. *Current Issues in Tourism* 9(6), 481–498.

Reynolds, B. and Fitzpatrick, J. (1999) The transversality of Michel de Certeau: Foucault's panoptic discourse and the cartographic impulse. *Diacritics* 29(3), 63–80.

Richards, G. (1996) Production and consumption of European cultural tourism. *Annals of Tourism Research*, 23, 261–283.

Riley, R.W., Baker, D. and Van Doren, C.S. (1998) Movie induced tourism. *Annals of Tourism Research* 25(4), 919–935.

Robertson, R. (1995) Glocalization: Time-space and homogeneity-heterogeneity. In M. Featherstone, S. Lash and R. Robertson (eds) *Global Modernities* (pp. 25–44). London: Sage Publications.

Robinson, M. and Andersen, H.C. (ed.) (2003) *Literature and Tourism: Essays in the Reading and Writing of Tourism*. London: Thomson.

Rodanthi, T. (2004) Constructing the 'cinematic tourist': The 'sign industry' of The Lord of the Rings. *Tourist Studies* 4(1).

Rojek, C. (1993) *Ways of Escape: Modern Transformations in Leisure and Travel.* London: MacMillan.

Rojek, C. (1997) Indexing, dragging and the social construction of tourist sights. In C. Rojek and J. Urry: *Touring Cultures. Transformations of Travel and Theory* (pp. 52–74). London: Routledge.

Roland, T. (1998) Hvordan får vi styr på Gellerupparken. In A.S. Preis (ed.) *Kan vi leve sammen? Integration mellem politik og praksis* (pp. 70–95). København: Munksgaard.

Rorty, R. (1967) *The Linguistic Turn: Recent Essays in Philosophical Method.* Chicago: University of Chicago Press.

Ryall, A. (2007) Også Jeg. Gjentakelsens Poetikk i litterære pilegrimsreiser til Santiago de Compostela, 23–38. In Ingvild Sælid Gilhus and Siv Ellen Kraft (eds) *Religiøse Reiser. Mellom gamle spor og nye mål* (pp. 23–38). Oslo: Universitetsforlaget.

Sandvik, K. and Waade, A.M. (2007) Crime Scene as a Spatial Production On-screen, Online and Offline. Paper presented at Nordisk Medieforskerkonference, Helsinki, 16–19 August 2007.

Sandvik, K. and Waade, A.M. (2008) Crime Scenes as augmented reality On-screen Online and Offline. Online document: www.krimiforsk.aau.dk/awpaper/KSAWcrimesceneas.w5.pdf.

Santa Ynez Valley News (1947) An Open Letter to Solvang. Solvang 3.

Santa Ynez Valley News (1947) Visitors flock to valley following magazine article. Solvang 8.

Santiago Tourism (2008) Available at http://santiagoturismo.com/Camino/Caminos/index.asp?pagina = frances.

Saren, M. (2006) *Marketing Graffiti.* Amsterdam: BH.

Schmitt, B. and Simonsen, A. (1997) *Marketing Aesthetics. The Strategic Management of Brands, Identity and Image.* New York: Free Press.

Schultz, M., Hatch, M.J. and Holten Larsen, M. (eds) (2000) *The Expressive Organization. Linking Identity, Reputation, and the Corporate Brand.* New York: Oxford University Press.

Scotsman (2006) Rosslyn priest quits over Da Vinci Code hype. Retrieved June 20, 2006, from http://heritage.scotsman.com/topics.cfm?tid = 542&id = 792572006.

Seaton, A.V. (1996) Guided by the dark: From thanatopsis to thanatourism. *International Journal of Heritage Studies* 2(4), 234–244.

Selberg, T. (2005) The Actualization of the Sacred Place of Selja and the Legend of Saint Sunniva. *Arv. Scandinavian yearbook of folklore.*

Selberg, T. (2006) Festivals as celebrations of place in modern society: Two examples from Norway. *Folklore: The Journal of the Folklore Society* 117(3), 297–312.

Selberg, T. (2007) Mennesker og steder. Innledning. In Torunn Selberg and Nils Gilje (eds) *Kulturelle landskap. Sted, fortelling og materiel kultur.* Bergen: Fakbokforlaget.

Selwyn, T. (1996) *The Tourist Image. Myths and Myth Making in Tourism.* London: John Wiley and Sons.

Selänniemi, T. (1999) Sakrale steder og profane turister. In Jens kr. Steen Jacobsen and Arvid Viken (eds) *Turisme. Stedet i en bevegelig verden* (pp. 88–95). Oslo, Univeristetsforlaget.

Sheller, M. and Urry, J. (2004) *Tourism Mobilities: Places to stay, Places in Play.* London: Routledge.

Singapore Parliament Hansard (2004) *Singapore Parliament Hansard*, Vol. 77, Session 1. Singapore: Singapore Parliament.

Sjöholm, C. (2003) *Gå på bio. Rum för drömmar i folkhemmets Sverige.* Stehag/ Stockholm: Brutus Östlings bokförlag Symposion.

Sogelandet (2008) Available at www.sogelandet.no.

Soja, E. (1996) *Thirdspace.* Oxford: Basil Blackwell.

Soja, E. (1999) Thirdspace: Expanding the scope of the geographical imagination. In D. Massey, J. Allen and P. Sarre (eds) *Human Geography Today* (pp. 260–278). Cambridge: Polity Press.

Solheim, J. (1998) *Den Åpne Kroppen.* Oslo: Pax Forlag.

Southwell, J.M.J. (1947) To the Editor. *Santa Ynez Valley News.* Solvang 4.

Sproull, L. and Faraj, S. (1995) Atheism, Sex and Databases: The Net As a Social Technology. In B. Kahin and J. Keller (eds) *Public Access to the Internet* (pp. 62–81). Cambridge, MA: The MIT Press.

Squire, S. (1994) The cultural values of literary tourism. *Annals of Tourism Research* 21, 103–120.

Stanislavskij, K. (1994–1997) *The Collected Works of Konstantin Stanislavsky.* Rushden: Methuen Drama.

Stausberg, M. (2008) [Review of] Timothy J. Dallen and Daniel H. Olsen 2006: *Tourism, Religion and Spiritual Journeys. Religion* 2008, 96–98. London: Routledge.

Storey, J. (2003) Popular culture as the 'roots' and 'routes' of cultural identities in *Inventing Popular Culture. From Folklore to Globalization* (pp. 78–91). Blackwell.

Strati, A. (1999) *Organization and Aesthetics.* London: Sage Publications.

Strömberg, P. (2007) *Upplevelseindustrins turistmiljöer. Visuella berättarstrategier i svenska turistanläggningar 1985–2005.* Fronton Förlag.

Stöber, B. (2008) How the private create the public. In H. Krause Hansen and D. Salskov-Iversen (eds) *Critical Perspectives on Private Authority in Global Politics* (pp. 169–187). MacMillan.

Sutcliffe, S. and Bowman, M. (eds) (2000) *Beyond New Age. Exploring Alternative Sprituiality.* Edinburgh: Edinburgh University Press.

Suttles, G.D. (1984) The cumulative texture of local urban culture. *American Journal of Sociology* 90(2), 283–304.

Swatos, W.H. and Tomasi L. (eds) (2002) *From Medieval Pilgrimage to Religious Tourism. The Social and Cultural Economics of Piety.* London: Praeger.

Sydney-Smith, S. (2006) Changing places. Touring the British crime film. *Tourist Studies*, 6(1), 79–94.

Sørensen, K. (2004) Danske Kunstnere på Kullen. Kullabjerget.

Saarnio, M. (1994) Tango magic. In Finnair (ed.) *Blue Wings.* August-September 1994.

Taylor, John P. (2001) Authenticity and Sincerity in Tourism. *Annals of Tourism Research* 28(1), 7–26.

Teo, P. and Li, L.H. (2003) Global and local interactions in tourism. *Annals of Tourism Research*, 30, 287–306.

Teo, P. (2003) The limits of imagineering: A case study of Penang. *International Journal of Urban and Regional Research* 27, 545–563.

The Confraternity of St James (2008a) Available at www.csj.org.uk/i-faqs. htm#backwards.

The Confraternity of St James (2008b) Available at http://www.csj.org.uk/spirit.htm.

The Confraternity of St James (2008c) Available at http://www.csj.org.uk/bull-arts/h-hilton-art.htm.

The Confraternity of St James (2008d) Available at http://www.csj.org.uk/passport.htm).

The Da Vinci Code (n.d.) Last accessed 27.03.08 from http://en.wikipedia.org/wiki/The_da_vinci_code.

The Economist (2007, November 28) Where the grass is greener. *The Economist*.

The Straits Times (2007, April 20) Formula for future success: Singapore = East + West plus. *The Straits Times*.

Thompson, K (2007) *The Frodo Franchise: The Lord of the Rings and modern Hollywood*. Berkeley: University of California Press.

Thrift, N. (2004a) Intensities of feeling: Towards a spatial politics of affects. *Geografiska Annaler* 86 B(1), 57–78.

Thrift, N. (2004b) Driving in the city. In *Theory, Culture and Society* 21(4/5), 41–59.

Thrift, N. (2008) *Non-Representational Theory. Space, Politics, Affect*. London: Routledge.

Thyssen, O. (2003) *Æstetisk ledelse – om organisationer og brugskunst*. København: Gyldendal.

Tomlinson, J. (1999) *Globalization and Culture*. Cambridge: Polity Press.

Travelling Companions (2008) Available at www.travellingcompanions.co.uk.

Trilling, L. (1972) *Sincerity and Authenticity*. London: Oxford University Press.

Trondheim (2008) Available at www.trondheim.com/content.ap?thisId = 631740.

Tuan, Y. (1974) *Topophilia: A Study of Environmental Perception, Attitudes, and Values*. New York: Morningside/Columbia University Press.

Tuan, Y. (1977) *Space and Place: The Perspective of Experience*. Minneapolis: University of Minnesota Press.

Turkle, S. (1995) *Life on the Screen – Identity in the Age of the Internet*. New York: Simon and Schuster.

Turner, V. and Turner, E. (1978) *Image and Pilgrimage in Christian Culture: Anthropological Perspectives*. New York: Columbia University Press.

Turner, V. (1974a) Social Drama and Ritual Metaphors. In Victor Turner *Dramas, Fields, and Metaphors: Symbolic Action in Human Society*. Ithaca and London: Cornell University Press.

Turner, V. (1974b) Pilgrimage as Social Processes. In V. Turner *Dramas, Fields, and Metaphors: Symbolic Action in Human Society*. Ithaca and London: Cornell University Press.

Turner, V. (1974c) Liminal to liminoid, in play, flow, and ritual: An essay in comparative symbology. In *Rice University Studies* 60, 53–92.

Turner, V. (1974d) Pilgrimage and Communitas. In *Studia Missionalia* 23, 305–327.

Turner, V. (1977) Variations on a theme of liminality. in Moore and Meyerhoff *Secular Ritual* (pp. 36–52). Van Gorcum.

Tzanelli, R. (2004) Constructing the 'cinematic tourist'. The 'sign industry' of *The Lord of the Rings. Tourist Studies* 4(1), 21–42.

Urbain, J.D. (1993) *L'idiot du Voyage. Histoires de touristes*. Paris: Petite bibliotèque Payot.

Urbanprogram (2004) Bæredygtigt bysamfund gennem lokale partnerskaber. Last accessed 15.08.08 from http://www.aarhuskommune.dk/files/aak/aak/content/filer/urban/URBAN_II_program_rev_maj04_til_internet.pdf.

Urry, J. (1990, 2002) *The Tourist Gaze*. London, New Delhi: Sage Publications.

Urry, J. (1995) *Consuming Places*. Routledge: London.

Urry, J. (1999) Sensing leisure spaces. In D. Crouch (ed.) *Leisure/Tourism Geographies. Practices and Geographical Knowledge*. London and New York: Routledge.

Urry, J. (2005) The place of emotions within place. In J. Davidson, L. Bondi and M. Smith (eds) *Emotional Geographies* (pp. 77–86). Burlington, VT: Ashgate.

Van Riel, C.B.M. (2002) Defining Corporate Communication. In S.P. Brønn and R. Wiig (eds) *Corporate Communication. A Strategic Approach to Building Reputation*. Oslo: Gyldendal Akademisk.

Veijola, S. and Jokinen, E. (1994) The Body in Tourism. *Theory Culture Society* 11, 125–151.

Vindsetmo, B. (1995) *Sjelen som turist. Om religion, terapi og magi*. Oslo: Gyldendal.

Virtual Tourist (2008) Available at http://members.virtualtourist.com/vt/x/2/

Visit Scotland (2006) Promoting Scotland through *The Da Vinci Code*. Last accessed 30.05.06 from www.scotexchange.net/news_item.htm?newsID = 39425.

Visit Scotland (2007) Kelvingrove and Edinburgh Castle top Scottish visitor attractions. Last accessed 08.05.07 from www.visitscotland.org/news_item. htm?newsID = 45123.

Visit Voss (2008) Available at www.visitvoss.no.

Walther, B.K. (2005) Notes on the methodology of pervasive gaming. In F. Kishino *et al.* (eds) *Entertainment Computing, ICEC 2005, LNCS 3711* (pp. 488–495)). 7th International Conference, Sanda, Japan, September 19–21, 2005. Proceedings.

Wang, N. (1999) Rethinking authenticity in tourism experience. *Annals of Tourism Research* 26(2), 349–70.

Wang, N. (2000) *Tourism and Modernity*. Amsterdam: Pergamon.

Wang, Yu (2007) Customized authenticity begins at home. *Annals of Tourism Research* 34(3), 789–804.

Warnier, J. (2001) A praxeological approach to subjectivation in a material world. *Journal of Material Culture* 6, 5–24.

Watson, G.L. and Kopachevsky, J.P. (1994) Interpretations of tourism as commodity. *Annals of Tourism Research* 21, 643–660.

Wellman, B. and Gulia, M. (1998) Virtual communities as as communities: Net surfers don't ride alone. In M. Smith and P. Kollock (eds) *Communities in Cyberspace* (pp. 167–94). Berkeley: Routledge.

Westwood, J. (2003) *On Pilgrimage. Sacred Journeys around the World*. Mahwah, New Jersey: Hidden Spring.

Whyte, S.R. (1994) Diskurser om defekte kroppe. *Tidsskriftet Antropologi* 29, 57–68.

Whyte, S.R. (1998) Anthropology of consequence: Problem and practice in a complex world. Inaugural lecture, Department of Anthropology, University of Copenhagen.

Wieners, B. (2004) Go Berserker. Destinations: European Meccas. *Outside Magazine*, May.

Willim, R. (2005) It's in the mix. Configuring industrial cool. In O. Löfgren and R. Willim (eds) *Magic, Culture and The New Economy*. Oxford: Berg.

Wittermann, Å.P.T. (1999): Landskapets budskap. In Jens kr. Steen Jacobsen and A. Viken (eds) *Turisme. Stedet i en bevegelig verden* (pp. 239–252). Oslo, Univeristetsforlaget.

Wohl, R.R. and Strauss A.L. (1958) Symbolic representation and the urban milieu. *The American Journal of Sociology* 63(5), 523–32.

Wollan, G. (1999) Kulturarvsturisme og autentisitetens logikk. In Jens kr. Steen and Arvid Viken (eds) *Turisme. Stedet i en bevegelig verden* (pp. 285–296). Oslo, Univeristetsforlaget.

Waade, A.M. (2006) Armchair travelling with pilot guides. Cartography and sensuous strategies. In J. Falkheimer and A. Jansson (eds) *Geographies of Communication. The Spatial Turn in Media Studies* (pp. 155–168). Göteborg: Nordicom.

Yates, F.A. (1966) *The Art of Memory.* Chicago: The Chicago University Press.

Yin, R.K. (2002) *Case Study Research. Design and Methods* (3rd edn). Thousand Oaks: Sage Publications.

Yusuf, S. and Nabeshima, K. (2005) Creative industries in East Asia. *Cities* 22, 109–122.

Zavisca, J. (2003) Contesting capitalism at the post-Soviet Dacha: The meaning of food cultivation for urban Russians. *Slavic Review* 62(4), pp. 786–810.

Zizek, S. (2002) *Welcome to the Desert of the Real! Five essays on September 11 and Related Dates.* London: Verso.

Zizek, S., Butler, R. and Stephens, S. (eds) (2006) *Interrogating the Real.* London and New York: Continuum.

Zukin, S. (1995) *The Cultures of Cities.* Cambridge: Blackwell.

Index